A History of New Mexico

Susan A. Roberts, Ph.D.
Calvin A. Roberts, Ph.D.

Illustration: Betsy James

Cartography: William L. Nelson

University of New Mexico Press
Albuquerque

© 1986 by the University of New Mexico Press. All rights reserved.
Manufactured in the United States of America.
International Standard Book Number 0-8263-0796-5.
First edition.

A History of New Mexico

New Mexico

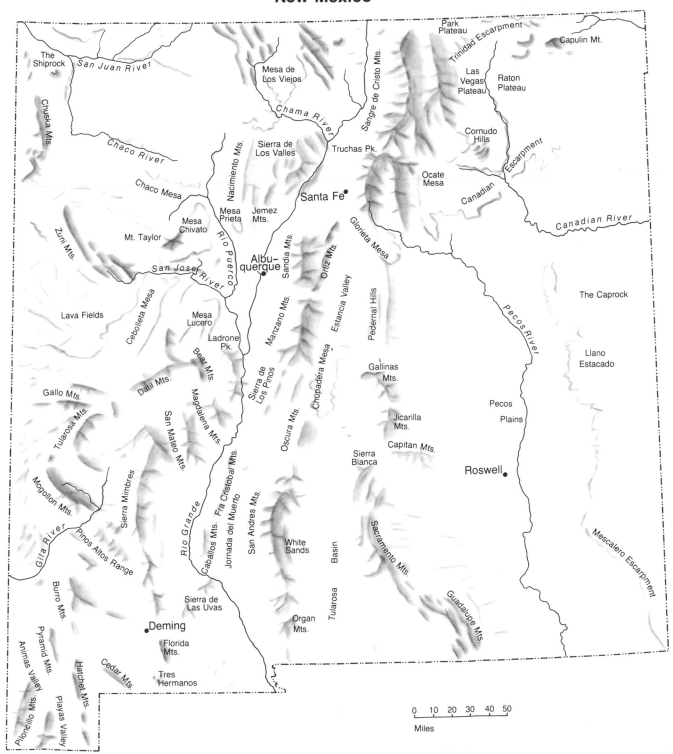

For David and Laura

Contents

Features

Time Lines

Chart

Maps

Time Line:
Early People in New Mexico

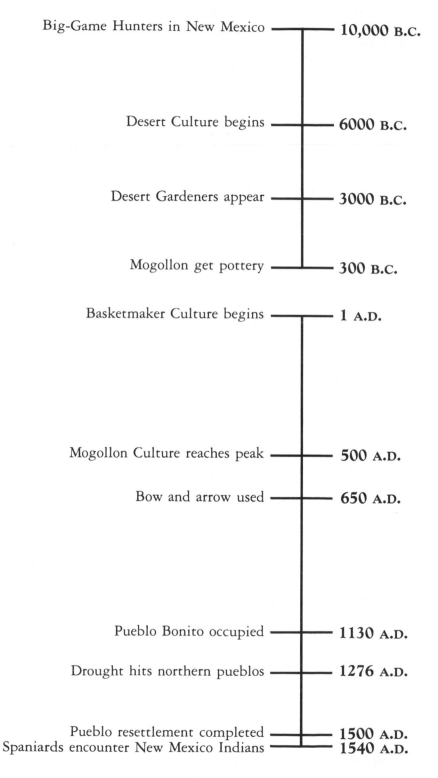

Big-Game Hunters in New Mexico	10,000 B.C.
Desert Culture begins	6000 B.C.
Desert Gardeners appear	3000 B.C.
Mogollon get pottery	300 B.C.
Basketmaker Culture begins	1 A.D.
Mogollon Culture reaches peak	500 A.D.
Bow and arrow used	650 A.D.
Pueblo Bonito occupied	1130 A.D.
Drought hits northern pueblos	1276 A.D.
Pueblo resettlement completed	1500 A.D.
Spaniards encounter New Mexico Indians	1540 A.D.

New Mexico Is Settled by Early People and Remains the Home of Indian Cultures

Most of you reading these words live in the state of New Mexico. Some of you were born here. Others of you moved here from some other place. As New Mexicans, you already know something about your state. You know most, of course, about the area in which you live. But New Mexico covers a large area and is a land where different peoples have developed different ways of living. In order to learn more about the land and its people, you will need to study the history of New Mexico. In chapter 1 you will read about the land itself and how the land has affected the ways in which people live. You will also read about the first people who lived in New Mexico. In chapter 2 you will learn about the Indians of New Mexico at the time the Spanish arrived.

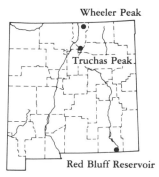

Wheeler Peak

Truchas Peak

Red Bluff Reservoir

Eyewitness to New Mexico's History
New Mexico's Landscape

From: Oliver La Farge, "New Mexico," in *The Spell of New Mexico,* ed. Tony Hillerman (University of New Mexico Press, 1976), p. 8.

The state partakes of the nature of all its species. It is large, the fifth largest in the Union, 121,666 square miles—but we don't think of ourselves as being so big, it's just that so many of the other states are smaller. . . . Its lowest portion, in the southeast, [Red Bluff Reservoir] dips below 3,000 feet. . . . In the north, its mountains climb high; two of its highest peaks, Truchas and Wheeler, reach above 13,000 feet. . . .

Between those extremes the variety is great. You can be camping up in the northern mountains, and in the morning break up your camp under blue spruce and fir, wrangling your horses out of the lush grass and the columbines in the meadow where you caught your breakfast trout. By noon you can take your break under cottonwoods in an irrigated section of orchards and corn and chili fields, and camp that night in desert where you are lucky, and distinctly relieved, when you find a water hole. You could, alternatively, stay in the mountains until the heavy winter snows close you in.

CHAPTER 1

New Mexico: The Land and Its Early Peoples

What you will learn in this chapter—

New Mexicans proudly call their state the Land of Enchantment. Enchantment means being under a magic spell or being completely charmed. New Mexicans use the word enchantment to explain the effect New Mexico has on the people who love it. The deep blue sky, the golden sunshine, the open spaces, and the ever-changing landscape have charms all their own. Enchanting as well are the different peoples who have helped make New Mexico a special place.

But New Mexico has not always been a land of enchantment to its people. Early people were more interested in survival than in scenery. They had to find ways to live on the land. They had to live with what the land had to offer. In this chapter you will learn more about the land of New Mexico. You will learn about the early people who settled in New Mexico. As you read, you will find answers to the following questions:

1. What is the land of New Mexico like?
2. Who were the first people to live in New Mexico?
3. Who were New Mexico's first villagers?

1. What is the land of New Mexico like?

New Mexico is part of the Southwest. New Mexico is located in the southwestern part of the United States. The Southwest is an area that includes New Mexico and Arizona. It also includes parts of Utah and Colorado on the north and parts of Nevada and California on the west. Because of its size and location, New Mexico has boundaries in common with five other states. To the east lie Texas and the western tip of Oklahoma. To the north is Colorado. To the west is Arizona. Utah is the fifth state that borders New Mexico. Utah's southeast corner touches New Mexico's northwest corner. Joined here as well in what is called the four corners area are Colorado and Arizona. There is no other place in the United States where four states come together in a single spot. New Mexico shares its southern border with Texas and Mexico.

The Location of New Mexico

You can see where New Mexico is located and who its neighbors are by looking at the map on this page. You can also see that except for its southwest corner the state is very nearly square. From north to south New Mexico measures 391 miles. From east to west the distance is 352 miles. Altogether, the state has an area of 121,666 square miles. If you have traveled through the state by car, bus, or train, you know something about the size of New Mexico. Cities, towns, and other points of interest are often far apart. In fact, New Mexico by area is the fifth largest state in the Union. Only Alaska, Texas, California, and Montana are bigger in area.

The land in New Mexico has different physical provinces. Again because of its size and location, New Mexico has certain *geographical conditions.* By geographical conditions we mean such things as the surface of the land, rainfall, altitude, and temperature. In general, four distinct provinces make up New Mexico's land surface. These four are plains, mountains, plateau, and basin and range. The *plains* province is an extension of the Great Plains, which form the western fringe of the North American lowland. Plains are vast areas that are flat and treeless. The plains in New Mexico cover the eastern third of the state. The *Llano Estacado,* or staked plains, some of the earth's flattest land, is located in this area. The Llano, as it is often called, lies between the Canadian and Pecos rivers and extends to the southeast corner of the state.

geographical conditions: such things as the surface of the land, rainfall, altitude, and temperature

plains: large areas that are flat and treeless; in New Mexico the eastern third of the state

4

The mountains province runs through north-central New Mexico. The mountains here are part of the Rocky Mountains. These high and rugged mountains extend to a point just south of Santa Fe. The state has other mountains, but they are not part of the mountains province. The *plateau* province is part of the Colorado Plateau. A plateau is an elevated area of mostly flat or level land. To the east of the Colorado Plateau lie the Rocky Mountains. To the west are the mountain ranges that run along the Pacific coast. The Colorado Plateau itself is an area where the Colorado River and its tributaries (streams that flow into the Colorado) have dug canyons. In some places where the water has dug through many layers of rock, the canyons are deep. In New Mexico the Colorado Plateau extends across the northwestern part of the state.

The fourth and final province—the basin and range province—is large. It extends across the southwestern, the central, and the south-central portions of the state. This province consists of mountain ranges that are separated from one another by broad, dry *basins* (drainage areas). Two such basins are the Estancia Basin and the Tularosa Basin. Two other basins are the Plains of San Agustin and the Rio Grande Valley. The mountain ranges in this province are many. The Sandia and Manzano mountains are east of Albuquerque. Between Alamogordo and Roswell is the Sacramento Range. To the west of Socorro are the San Mateo Mountains. Between Socorro and Las Cruces are the San Andres Mountains. And in southwestern New Mexico are the Mogollon Mountains. There are other mountains as well. Look at the map on page 7. There you can see the basin and range province of the state. You can also see the areas of the state covered by the Great Plains, the Rocky Mountains, and the Colorado Plateau.

New Mexico is a very dry land. The state's physical features do, of course, affect where and how people live. But other geographical conditions have an effect as well. In New Mexico, water is the key factor. Whether people can live in this or that part of New Mexico depends largely on whether there is a supply of water. The fact is that New Mexico, a large state, has little water. Its *surface water* area—about 250 square miles—is quite small. Surface water is water that is on top of the earth's surface. In addition, New Mexico's average precipitation rate is only 15 inches a year. The precipitation rate includes all forms of moisture from the sky. The term rainfall—often used in place of the term precipitation—is used here to include all types of moisture.

Not all parts of the state, however, receive the same amount of rainfall. The Sangre de Cristo Mountains in the northern part of the state receive more than 40 inches of moisture a year. So, too, mountains elsewhere in the state have a higher than average rainfall. The plateau area and the eastern one-third of the state (the Great Plains) are average in rainfall. They receive between 12

plateau: elevated area of mostly flat or level land; in New Mexico the Colorado Plateau, an area where the Colorado River and its tributaries have dug canyons

basins: drainage areas; in New Mexico, areas that separate mountain ranges from one another

surface water: water that is on top of the earth's surface; water that in New Mexico totals only about 250 square miles

The Sierra Blanca range near Alamogordo

and 17 inches of moisture a year. The amount of rainfall is in general below average in the southwestern, the central, and the south-central parts of the state. Here are the driest areas. Some of these low areas receive an average of fewer than 10 inches of rainfall yearly. These low areas include the broad, dry basins of the basin and range province of the state. Some of these low-lying areas are very nearly true deserts.

New Mexico's rainfall is useful. But it is not just the amount of rainfall that determines where and how people can live in New Mexico. When the rainfall occurs is very important. New Mexicans are fortunate that they receive about three-fourths of their rainfall between June and September. This is the growing season. The remainder of the moisture comes mostly during the winter. Snow falls in the mountains and higher elevations, while rain falls in the lower elevations. The snow in the mountains then melts in the spring and flows into the streams and rivers. The rivers, in turn, bring water to people. They allow them to live in parts of the state that might otherwise be too dry to support a group of people. Rivers have, of course, always been vital to people. New Mexico's rivers have been no exception.

The Physical Features of New Mexico

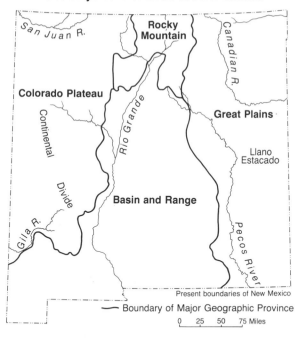

Present boundaries of New Mexico
— Boundary of Major Geographic Province
0   25   50   75 Miles

New Mexico has important rivers. The most important of New Mexico's rivers are the Rio Grande, the Pecos, the Canadian, the San Juan, and the Gila. The Rio Grande is the third longest river in the United States. It is also the state's main river. You can see on the map on this page that the Rio Grande flows through the center of New Mexico. It crosses the entire state from north to south. You can also see the location of the other major rivers as well as where the *continental divide* crosses the state. The continental divide is a fold in the earth's surface that separates the direction in which the rivers of North America flow. East of the divide rivers flow or drain into the Atlantic Ocean. The water from rivers west of the divide drains into the Pacific Ocean.

Whether east or west of the continental divide, New Mexico's rivers have supported life for hundreds of years. They have provided water for *irrigation,* the artificial watering of crops. People have lived and irrigated crops in the Rio Grande Valley for more than 400 years. Dams on the Pecos have in this century controlled flooding along that river. As a result of flood control, thousands of acres of land along this river are now used for farming. Much of this land is near the cities of Carlsbad and Roswell. The Conchas Dam on the Canadian has provided water for irrigating land near Tucumcari since 1940. And irrigation also takes place along the San Juan and the Gila but with less success.

continental divide: fold in the earth's surface that separates the direction in which the rivers in North America flow; crosses the state of New Mexico

irrigation: artificial watering of crops with either ground water or surface water

7

Taos Creek at Taos Pueblo, 1888

New Mexico's ground water is also important. The rivers have made it possible for people to live by irrigating crops in places otherwise too dry for farming. This has been most true—and for hundreds of years—of people living along the Rio Grande. Besides river water, there is one more important source of water in New Mexico. That source is *ground water*. Ground water is water under the ground that people pump to the surface. New Mexicans today use a lot of ground water. Indeed, they get more than half their water for irrigation from ground water sources. An underground lake beneath the city of Albuquerque supplies its people with water for drinking and for other needs. Ground water also meets the needs of people who live in many other New Mexico cities and towns.

ground water: water under the ground that is pumped to the earth's surface; in New Mexico it is important both for irrigation and for everyday living

Apache Pass near New Mexico–Arizona border, 1876

Still, water has always been a major concern. New Mexico's rainfall has at times been unreliable. The people have suffered from *droughts,* long periods without rainfall. In addition, scientists disagree among themselves on the question of how much ground water remains in various parts of the state. It could happen that people in some parts of the state will use up their water supply. Then they might have to move elsewhere.

New Mexico's altitude affects plant and animal life. Besides its land surface and its water supply, New Mexico's *altitude* has affected ways of living. The altitude, the elevation above sea level, differs from one region of the state to another. In general, the state slopes from north to south and from west to east. Standing as part of the Rockies, Wheeler Peak near Taos rises to

drought: long period without rainfall; periodic problem in New Mexico because of unreliable rainfall

altitude: elevation above (or below) sea level; altitude in New Mexico is important because of its effect on climate and plant life

9

ZONE	ALTITUDE (above sea level)	DESCRIPTION AND USE
Lower Sonoran	2,817–5,000 feet	Most important agricultural region. Located in river valleys in southern part of the state.
Upper Sonoran	5,000–7,000 feet	Covers three-quarters of the state. Ranching, dry land farming here.
Transition	7,000–9,000 feet	Major timber zone. Some range for stock.
Canadian	8,500–11,500 feet	Very important for water supplies from melting snow in spring.
Hudsonian	11,500–12,500 feet	Narrow zone at the timber line. Some summer grazing.
Arctic-Alpine	Above 12,500 feet	Smallest zone in New Mexico. Above the timber line at the tops of mountains.

an altitude of 13,160 feet. This is the highest elevation in the state. The lowest elevation is in the southern part of the state. Red Bluff on the Pecos south of Carlsbad has an altitude of only 2,817 feet. But for the most part, New Mexico has a high altitude. Eighty-five percent of the state has an altitude of greater than 4,000 feet.

And why is altitude important? Altitude is important because plant life changes with both altitude and *latitude*. Latitude is the number of degrees north or south of the equator. New Mexico's location north of the equator is fixed. But its high altitude has the effect of moving the state's climate farther north. Every 500 foot rise in altitude is the same as moving about 100 miles nearer the North Pole at sea level. Higher elevations are colder than lower elevations.

New Mexico has different life zones. New Mexico's differences in altitude have created six different *life zones*. By life zones we mean areas that have similar climates, plants, and animals. New Mexico's life zones become colder and wetter as they become higher in altitude. The plant life and the animal life become different as well. You can see many different kinds of cactus, lizards, and snakes in the lowest life zone. In two of the mountain life zones,

latitude: number of degrees north or south of the equator

life zone: area that has a similar climate, plants, and animals; in New Mexico changes in altitude have created six different life zones

COMMON VEGETATION	COMMON MAMMALS
mesquite, cactus, creosote, valley cottonwood, black grama grass	desert fox, rabbits, bats, kangaroo rats, squirrels
juniper, piñon, willow, blue grama grass, sagebrush	deer, coyotes, antelope, prairie dogs
Ponderosa pine, scrub oak	mountain lions, bears, mountain bobcats, deer, elk
aspen, Douglas fir, spruce	elk, deer, chipmunks, varieties of squirrels
Siberian juniper, Engelmann spruce, berries	Rocky Mountain woodchucks, cony, mountain sheep
Very hardy grasses and flowers	Some come in summer from lower zones

you can see lots of grass and big trees. You can also see animals and birds that make their homes in mountain forests. New Mexico's highest life zone rises above 12,500 feet. It supports very few plants or animals. The chart on pages 10 and 11 names the six life zones.

People do, of course, have some control over what grows in life zones. You know that irrigation allows people to grow crops where rainfall is scarce. In fact, New Mexico's main farming area is the area of the state's lowest-lying life zone. This area is dry, but there is water available for irrigation. The temperature here is mild. Indeed, a mild or moderate climate is typical of most of the state. This means that the climate is neither extremely hot nor extremely cold. At the same time temperatures over the course of a single day often vary by as much as 40 degrees Fahrenheit. New Mexico's dry air quickly gains heat during the day and quickly loses heat at night.

New Mexico has shortcomings. The geographical conditions present in New Mexico have clearly affected ways of living. Today the mountains provide scenery and recreation for the people of the state. They are a source of water in the spring when the snow melts and runs off into lower areas. The flat land—whether plains, plateau, or basin—supports most of the state's population. Land is available for farming in all of these areas. Farming, however, requires good soil and a good growing season. In many areas it requires water for irrigation.

But the fact remains that New Mexico has shortcomings. The land itself has, for the most part, discouraged settlement. The shortage of water, both rainfall and surface water, has been the biggest shortcoming. Not only is the state dry, but the rainfall has also been unreliable at times. In addition, the surface waters, namely the rivers, have not provided a source of transportation. While rivers were America's first highways, people traveling through New Mexico had to do so on foot. Later, explorers and settlers had only horses and oxen. These conditions tended to isolate or separate New Mexico from other centers of population. In the remainder of this book, you will read about people and their adjustments to conditions in New Mexico. You will learn how New Mexico became less isolated.

Section Review

1. (a) In what part of the United States is New Mexico located?
    (b) What states does New Mexico border on?
2. (a) What are the four provinces that make up New Mexico's land surface?
    (b) Where is each of these four areas located?
3. (a) What is New Mexico's average rainfall?
    (b) Which parts of the state are below average in rainfall?
4. (a) What are New Mexico's most important rivers?
    (b) Why are these rivers important?
    (c) What is ground water, and why is it important to New Mexicans?
5. (a) Why is altitude an important geographical condition in New Mexico?
    (b) How many life zones are there in New Mexico?
    (c) What happens to the climate as the life zones become higher in altitude?
6. What are the shortcomings of New Mexico's geographical conditions?

2. Who were the first people to live in New Mexico?

Early people come from Asia. At least as early as 12,000 years ago, the first Americans began to arrive on this continent. They came during the Ice Age. Most likely they moved from Siberia across a land link with Alaska. The last ice sheet of the Ice Age created this bridge of land. Sea level was lowered 300 feet due to water frozen in the ice sheet.

These early people may have come in pursuit of the animals that were their source of food. These animals were very large and are no longer in existence. Once in the Americas, these early people spread out. They followed the animals

they hunted. Some of them went where they could find wild fruits, nuts, and berries. They settled across North America. They moved down into and through Mexico. They moved into Central and South America and onto the Caribbean Islands. This movement of peoples into the Americas may have taken place over hundreds of years.

Some of these early people came to what is today New Mexico. We know about these early people because of the studies made by *archaeologists*. Archaeologists are men and women who study the *artifacts* and other things that ancient people left behind. Artifact is a term used to describe anything made by people. Archaeologists have found and dug up many of the campsites of these early people. They have found and studied such artifacts as weapons and tools. They have unearthed animal remains as well. They have used a number of methods of dating to determine when people lived at various places. (See Special Interest Feature.) With the evidence they have gathered, archaeologists can tell us how these early people lived in what is today New Mexico.

archaeologist: person who studies as a science the things that ancient people have left behind; tells us how early people in New Mexico lived

artifact: term used by archaeologists to describe anything made by people; important because of what it tells us about how early people lived

Scientific Methods of Dating

Scientists have developed a number of methods of dating. They use these methods to determine when people lived at various places. One of these methods is to examine tree rings in certain trees. Tree rings are thick in years that are wet during the growing season. They are thin in dry years. And trees weathered under the same conditions and in the same area tend to have the same pattern of thick and thin rings. Knowing this, scientists can start with living trees and work backward in time. In this way they have found that trees in the Southwest followed a tree-ring growth pattern that lasted more than 2,000 years.

By using tree-ring dating, scientists can tell when a dead tree was cut. To fix the date they carefully match the dead tree's ring pattern to the pattern of a living tree. If the tree was used in building a room, scientists can then tell when people built that room. Tree-ring dating also helped scientists determine that a drought hit New Mexico in 1276. They further know that the drought lasted 23 years.

A newer method of dating is radioactive, or carbon-14, dating. Carbon-14 is present in all plant and animal life. As carbon-14 decays, living organisms take in new carbon-14 atoms. But when plants and animals die, they can no longer replace the decaying carbon-14 atoms. So the carbon-14 begins to change form. It changes back into nitrogen. Half the carbon-14 changes to nitrogen within the first 5,600 years after a plant's or an animal's death. Half the remaining carbon-14 changes to nitrogen within the next 5,600 years. Carbon-14 continues to change in this way until it is virtually gone.

By using carbon-14 dating, scientists can date plants and animals that lived as long as 35,000 years ago. Here is how they do it. First, they know how much carbon-14 the plant or animal contained while living. Second, they measure the amount of carbon-14 that remains in the plant or animal they are examining. Third, they figure when the plant or animal died. Carbon-14 dating is thought to be accurate 95 percent of the time. Tree-ring dating and carbon-14 dating add to our knowledge about when early people were here.

Early people develop distinctive ways of living. Not all of New Mexico's early people lived in the same way. Rather, ways of living changed as people learned new skills and new ways of living. Because these ways of living were quite distinctive, they help us identify early people with different time periods. They help us fit early people into a *culture*. By culture we mean the living patterns, customs, and skills of a given people at a given time.

The first New Mexicans are big-game hunters. The very earliest people to live in New Mexico were hunters of big game. They lived here between 12,000 and 8,000 years ago. Keep in mind that New Mexico's climate at that time was not like its climate today. Back then New Mexico was covered with grasslands and forests where big game lived. The weather was wet and cool. Under these conditions the big-game hunters hunted and killed animals that are now extinct (no longer exist). Among them were the mammoth and mastadon, both extinct, and extinct forms of the sloth, bison, antelope, camel, and horse. Archaeologists have found material or physical remains of all these animals at *kill sites*. These were areas where the hunters killed game for food.

For killing game, hunters made spearpoints from stone such as quartzite, flint, obsidian, jasper, and chert. The big-game hunters of one group made their spearpoints in the same way. Their sons, in turn, made spearpoints like the ones their fathers had made. But spearpoints made by some other group of hunters living elsewhere were different. It is these differences in spearpoints that have enabled archaeologists to identify the groups of big-game hunters who lived in New Mexico. Archaeologists have named the spearpoints and the people who made them for the place where each distinctive spearpoint was first found.

Early people may have lived near Albuquerque. New Mexico's earliest people may have lived in the Sandia Mountains near present-day Albuquerque. In 1927 the discovery of a claw in a mountain cave provided the first evidence that big-game hunters may have lived there. Further exploration of the cave in the 1930s uncovered both artifacts and animal remains. Using this evidence, some archaeologists stated their belief that big-game hunters lived in the area and were likely New Mexico's earliest people. They named these people Sandia Man and said they lived perhaps as long as 20,000 years ago.

Other archaeologists have questioned the material found in Sandia Cave. They doubt that the evidence is authentic. They doubt the very existence of Sandia Man. Today, then, the question of whether there was a Sandia Man remains unanswered.

Early people live in eastern New Mexico. Whether or not Sandia Man existed, big-game hunters lived in what is today the far eastern side of the state. Archaeologists have named two groups of these early people Clovis Man and Folsom Man. Of the two, Clovis Man, identified by a spearpoint found in 1932 near present-day Clovis, is older. No one knows much about Clovis Man except that these people were big-game hunters. They tipped their

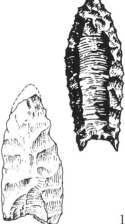

15

Desert Culture projectile points

spears with uniquely chipped and sharp stone spearpoints. They hunted and killed the giant mammoth, the musk-ox, the wide-horned bison that weighed more than 2,000 pounds, the sloth, and other animals long since extinct.

The first evidence that there was a Folsom Man surfaced in 1908. In that year George McJunkin, a black cowboy and former slave, discovered bison bones in an arroyo near present-day Folsom. McJunkin's discovery finally led archaeologists to dig up the first Folsom site beginning in 1926. There they found more bones of the extinct animals hunted by these early people. They found finely chipped spearpoints that were smaller and better made than the Clovis point. Archaeologists used these spearpoints to identify Folsom Man. They found other artifacts that helped them understand how Folsom Man lived.

Folsom Man was a big-game hunter much like Clovis Man. Folsom Man especially hunted the giant bison, an animal that probably provided food as well as materials for clothing and shelter. The hunters' homes were campsites along the trail of the bison. Scientists have used carbon-14 dating to determine when Clovis Man and Folsom Man lived. They have dated Clovis spearpoints at about 9200 B.C. Folsom spearpoints are younger by about a thousand years. In other words, both Clovis Man and Folsom Man lived about 10,000 years ago. Look at the map on page 19. There you can see the sites where archaeologists first found evidence of Clovis Man and Folsom Man. Other big-game hunters lived in New Mexico as well.

16

People of the Desert Culture live in New Mexico. Big-game hunters continued their way of life as long as big game was plentiful. But in time, the big game disappeared, most likely for various reasons. One reason was a change in the climate. The Ice Age came to an end, and the weather in New Mexico and elsewhere became drier and warmer. The grasslands dried up. As a result, big game suffered from lack of food and perhaps from disease as well. Another reason was that early people had probably overhunted the big game. With the big game gone from the Southwest, many of the big-game hunters moved elsewhere. They moved for the most part to an area of the United States known today as the Great Plains. There they found enough game to enable them to continue their basic living pattern as hunters.

With the big-game hunters gone, people moved into the Southwest from the west. They moved into the western part of present-day New Mexico. These people were desert dwellers. They developed ways of living that fit them into a culture known as the Desert Culture. As they developed their culture over the years, these desert dwellers went through two stages of development. The first-stage desert dwellers lived in the Southwest between 8,000 and 5,000 years ago. These people were hunter-gatherers. They hunted and trapped deer, antelope, and rodents. They fished. They gathered seeds, nuts, and berries.

The desert dwellers become gardeners. The second-stage desert dwellers lived in the Southwest between 5,000 and 2,500 years ago. These people became gardeners. They began to notice that seeds left behind in a certain place one year had by the next year grown into new plants. So the desert dwellers began leaving some seeds behind on purpose. The following year they returned to the place where they had left these seeds. In this way the people of the Desert Culture added gardening to their ways of living. They still moved around. They lived in such natural shelters as caves. At the same time they began to build some shelters of brush.

In time the people of the Desert Culture became known for two items. These items were the basket and the milling stone. The desert dwellers used baskets to gather and store food. They also cooked some foods in baskets by dropping heated stones into liquids. They used the milling stone to grind seeds into flour. Archaeologists have found thousands of artifacts left behind by the desert dwellers. They have found many, many baskets and milling stones. They have discovered that desert dwellers lived throughout the Southwest.

As with all the early peoples discussed so far, the desert dwellers had no permanent homes. They moved where their sources of food took them. In other words, their way of life was *nomadic*. They were wanderers. They had no permanent homes. Further changes in ways of living would have to take place before the land that is today New Mexico had its first true villagers.

Human footprints carved into rock at Mimbres petroglyph site near Cooks Peak (from *Indian Rock Art of the Southwest,* by Polly Schaafsma, UNM Press)

nomadic: word used to describe a way of life marked by having no permanent home, but rather moving from place to place

Section Review 1. (a) Where did the first people to live in the Americas come from, and how did they get here?

(b) What may have brought these people to America?

2. Describe the climate and the land of New Mexico about 10,000 years ago or more.

3. (a) Where and when did Clovis Man and Folsom Man live?

(b) What artifacts have archaeologists used to identify each of these very early peoples?

(c) Describe the way in which these first New Mexicans lived.

(d) Why did the big game and the big-game hunters disappear from New Mexico?

4. (a) Who moved into New Mexico once the big game and the big-game hunters were gone?

(b) How did the first group who belonged to the Desert Culture live?

(c) What new way of living was developed by the second group of desert dwellers?

(d) What two items were the mark of the Desert Culture, and how did the desert dwellers use these two items?

3. Who were New Mexico's first villagers?

Important cultures evolve from the desert dwellers. As time passed, the early people of the Southwest made changes in their ways of living. Not all the early people of the Southwest, however, changed their lives in the same ways or at the same time. Changes in life-styles depended in part on people learning new ways of doing things. Often these new ways were learned from other people. Over a long period of time, three new important cultures appeared. The Desert Culture provided the foundation for each of these three cultures. Indeed, some archaeologists believe that the Desert Culture provided the foundation for all the later southwestern cultures.

All three cultures developed somewhat distinctive ways of living. Of the three cultures, people from two of them lived in parts of present-day New Mexico as well as elsewhere. The third culture, the Hohokam, lived in Arizona. People from all three cultures had one thing in common. Their life-style was *sedentary*. In other words, these early people began to settle down. They began to build permanent homes.

The Mogollon live in west-central New Mexico. Of the two cultures who settled in New Mexico, the Mogollon were the first to develop advanced ways of living. The Mogollon derived their name from the mountains and the rim where their remains have been found. They lived in the mountains

sedentary: word used to describe a way of life in which a people settle down and build permanent homes

18

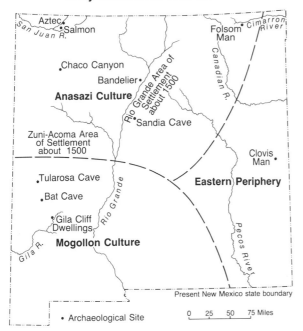

Early Cultures in New Mexico

Aztec
Salmon
San Juan R.
Folsom Man
Cimarron River
Chaco Canyon
Bandelier
Anasazi Culture
Canadian R.
Rio Grande Area of Settlement about 1500
Sandia Cave
Zuni-Acoma Area of Settlement about 1500
Clovis Man
Tularosa Cave
Rio Grande
Bat Cave
Eastern Periphery
Gila Cliff Dwellings
Pecos River
Mogollon Culture
Gila R.
Present New Mexico state boundary
• Archaeological Site
0   25   50   75 Miles

of west-central New Mexico and east-central Arizona. (See the map on this page.) And because they lived near the people of Mexico, they learned new ways of doing things. As early as 3000 B.C., the ancestors of the Mogollon had learned to grow a type of corn from their neighbors in Mexico. At about the same time and from the same source, they got squash. They added the red kidney bean to their diet about 1000 to 400 B.C. They began to use pottery in about 300 B.C. They got both the bean and pottery from Mexico. Now these mountain people were true farmers.

Because the Mogollon had by 300 B.C. become farmers, they built permanent homes. They dug round or oval pits 2 to 4 feet deep into the ground. They then covered these pits with timber and dirt roofs. These pit houses, built close together, formed villages. To feed themselves, the Mogollon farmed the mountain valleys. They grew corn, squash, beans, and perhaps cotton. They made a variety of stone tools. They made pottery, finer and finer pottery as time passed. For storage of food, the people used pits dug both inside and outside their houses. One larger pit house in most villages probably served as a religious center. Some burial remains suggest a Mogollon belief in life after death. In pit graves pots have been found alongside bodies. The dead were apparently to use these pots in their afterlives.

The Mogollon people never seemed to have had to worry about defenses.

19

At first they were far removed from other peoples. They had mountains on three sides of them and a desert on the fourth side. They built their villages on high ground, perhaps in part for defensive reasons. Yet from their homes in the mountains, the Mogollon people spread out. They moved into new mountain valleys. They moved particularly to the north and the west. And they came into contact with other groups of people. Through this contact the Mogollon shared their corn, squash, beans, and pottery with others. The Mogollon Culture most likely reached its peak about A.D. 500.

The Anasazi live in northern New Mexico. To the north were a group of people who developed more slowly than the Mogollon. These were the Anasazi. Anasazi is a Navajo word that means "the Ancient Ones." It can also be translated as "enemies of our ancestors." The earliest Anasazi were small-game hunters and food gatherers. They lived on the Colorado Plateau in what is today the four corners area. Here the states of New Mexico, Colorado, Utah, and Arizona come together. Because the Anasazi lived in the same general location for more than 1,500 years, archaeologists know a great deal about them. Anasazi Culture in different time periods reflected the ways in which the Anasazi changed their living patterns.

The Anasazi Culture from A.D. 1 to 500 was a culture of Basketmakers. These people were named Basketmakers because of their great skill in making baskets. They made such tightly woven baskets that they could use them for carrying water and cooking food. But they had no pottery at a time when the Mogollon Culture to the south was reaching its peak. The Basketmakers gathered seeds, nuts, and berries in their baskets. They hunted game with a weapon called the *atlatl*. Atlatl is the Aztec word for a spear-throwing device many early peoples used to hurl spears and darts. The atlatl had the effect of lengthening the throw of the person using it. By using the atlatl, hunters could send their darts and spears much greater distances. Burial sites have revealed that the Basketmakers also had domesticated (tame) dogs. Archaeologists have found the remains of two types of dogs in human burial sites. One was a collie-like dog. The other was a smaller black and white terrier-like dog.

The Anasazi become villagers. The Anasazi Culture from A.D. 500 to 700 was a Modified Basketmaker Culture. The Anasazi still hunted, depending on game animals for most of their meat. At the same time the Anasazi settled down. They built villages of pit houses. They grew corn, squash, and beans. Knowledge of these crops had come from the south. To process corn into meal for corn cakes, they used a flat stone called a *metate* and a grinding tool called a *mano*. The Anasazi also learned how to make pottery. They continued to make baskets, but pottery made it easier to cook and store foods. Using the fibers of yucca plants, they made sandals, rope, baskets, and other useful items.

atlatl: spear-throwing device used by early peoples to hurl spears and darts; effective in enabling hunters to send their darts and spears greater distances

metate: flat stone on which corn is ground into meal

mano: tool used to grind corn into meal

Ceramic bust of an Anasazi
woman (about A.D. 950–1100)

One other important development was the introduction of a new weapon. The Anasazi got the bow and arrow, most likely from the north. The bow and arrow was more effective than the atlatl. The Anasazi became more skilled as hunters at the same time they were becoming more skilled as farmers.

The Anasazi by this time fit the pattern of other southwestern peoples. By A.D. 700 most of the peoples in the Southwest had similar ways of living. They knew about farming and the making of pottery. They lived in villages, most often in pit houses built in part below the surface of the ground. Their villages had a religious center. In addition, the bow and arrow, very likely a late arrival from Asia, had become the common weapon.

The Anasazi build houses above ground. The Anasazi Culture from A.D. 700 to 1050 was a Developmental Pueblo Culture. During this period the Anasazi began to build rows of adobe (mud-brick) houses above ground. Sometimes, they built their houses in U-shaped or L-shaped rows. These villages of surface houses in time came to be called *pueblos*. Pueblo is a Spanish word that means "town." Near the center of each group of houses was a pit house. This pit house was the religious room, a room known as a *kiva*. To enter and leave the kiva, the Anasazi used a ladder extended through an opening in the mud-covered roof.

As time passed, kivas became a more and more important part of the culture. Except on rare occasions, only men could enter the kivas. So a kiva became not only a religious center but also a special meeting place for men to plan ceremonies. Women may have been excluded from the kivas in spite of

pueblo: Spanish word that means town; used to name the adobe houses of the Anasazi and of the Indians also called Pueblos

kiva: religious center for the Anasazi and the Pueblo Indians; very important to the cultures that centered their religious ceremonies in a kiva

21

the fact that archaeologists believe that women were the property owners. Women apparently owned the houses and most of the furnishings. Property was then passed on from mother to daughter. Pueblo Bonito at Chaco Canyon is a good example of the kiva becoming more and more important to pueblo life. Kiva ceremonialism in New Mexico is still very much alive today.

This period seems to have been fairly peaceful. It was a time when the Anasazi became more skilled in a number of ways. They made finer pottery. They began to grow cotton and to weave cotton into cloth for summer clothing. They tamed the turkey and wove turkey feathers into blankets. Brought into the Anasazi Culture, most likely from the Mogollon area, was the hard cradleboard for holding babies. The use of this cradleboard caused the infants' heads to be flattened at the back. The flattened head became so popular that the whole physical appearance of the Anasazi changed within a few generations. The skulls of the Anasazi were normally long and narrow. Now the skulls looked short and wide and were flattened at the back.

The Anasazi Culture reaches its peak. The greatest achievements of the Anasazi occurred between A.D. 1050 and 1300. Archaeologists call this period the Classic Pueblo Period or the Great Pueblo Period. They also refer to it as the Golden Age. This was the period when the Anasazi used stone masonry to build multistoried apartment houses. It was a time as well of the great Anasazi cliff dwellings. During this period the Anasazi expanded to the south and the southeast. The Anasazi Culture became the dominant culture in what is today the American Southwest.

The Anasazi built their largest apartment house on the floor of Chaco Canyon in northwestern New Mexico. (See the map on page 19.) Pueblo Bonito, meaning "Pretty Town," was a huge structure. The Anasazi began work on it shortly after A.D. 900. They built the pueblo in stages and finished the work in about A.D. 1130. When completed, Pueblo Bonito covered more than 300 acres of land. It was a four-story complex, containing more than 800 well-plastered rooms. It housed perhaps as many as 1,200 people. Today you can see the ruins of Pueblo Bonito and other Chaco Canyon pueblos. Both Chaco Canyon and Aztec, another Anasazi site, are national monuments.

You can also see the ruins of the great cliff dwellings in Mesa Verde National Park. Mesa Verde, meaning "Green Table," is a flat-topped area, a *mesa*, that rises above rugged canyons in southwestern Colorado. There is evidence that the Anasazi moved to Mesa Verde sometime during the Modified Basketmaker Period (A.D. 500 to 700). At Mesa Verde they built large apartment houses on top of the mesa during the Classic Pueblo Period. But after A.D. 1200 most of the Anasazi left their community homes on top of the mesa. Some moved to caves. Others built cliff dwellings. Archaeologists believe that

mesa: flat-topped area that rises above the surrounding land

22

The ruins at Pueblo Bonito (1930s)

this move occurred because of pressure from enemies. The largest of the Mesa Verde cliff dwellings was Cliff Palace. It contained more than 200 rooms and some 23 kivas.

The Anasazi improve the quality of life. You can see, then, that one Anasazi achievement during this period was the great Anasazi skill of building. The Anasazi had other achievements as well. On Mesa Verde the Anasazi had already learned to control water. They had built reservoirs to store water and check dams to hold the water from summer rains. Now they began to dig ditches for irrigating their crops. (See Special Interest Feature.) Irrigation farming and better crops increased farm produce. This meant the people could spend less time growing food. They could devote more time to other matters. One such matter was religion. During this period, for example, the Anasazi built their great kivas in Chaco Canyon.

The Anasazi also spent more time on arts and crafts than they had in earlier periods. On their black-on-white pottery, they painted fine line designs. Each group of Anasazi, moreover, made pottery that was unique in both shape and pattern. The Anasazi painted murals, stories in pictures, on the walls of their kivas. They wove beautiful textiles. And they increasingly used personal ornaments made of shell, turquoise, and other materials. They imported parrots and macaws from Mexico.

The Classic Pueblo Period comes to an end. Despite these achievements, this Golden Age did not last forever. The beginning of the end of the Classic Pueblo Culture may have begun in Chaco Canyon as early as the late 1100s. Elsewhere the end came at the close of the 1200s. People abandoned one pueblo after another. No one knows for sure why this happened. Archaeologists do, however, think that there might have been several reasons. It is possible, for example, that roving Indian bands threatened the pueblos. Disease is another possibility. Still another possibility is that the pueblo peoples disagreed and perhaps even fought among themselves. What is known for sure is that farming had always been hard in the area of the northern pueblos. Then in 1276 a great drought hit the area. This drought lasted for 23 years. For most of these 23 years water was very scarce. Food was in short supply.

Water Control Systems and Roads at Chaco Canyon

If you visit Chaco Canyon, you will see a number of things. You will see the ruins of once great pueblos. You will also see examples of other Anasazi building skills. Two such skills were the building of water control systems and the building of roads.

At first the Anasazi could not really irrigate their crops. They had no constant supply of water. So the people of Chaco Canyon built a system of dams and walls that caught water as it ran down from higher places. The water control system then directed the water into ditches. Finally, the ditches carried the water through gates and into the fields.

The Anasazi also built a complex system of roads. Some roads were 30 feet wide. Other roads were 10 feet wide. The roads had borders and hard surfaces. They connected pueblos in the canyon with settlements outside the canyon. Stairways and ramps carried the people up and down the cliffs. Some roads even went beyond the settlements that were part of the Chaco area.

Clearly the Anasazi worked hard to build such roads as these. But no one knows for sure why so many and such big roads were built. Most likely the Anasazi at Chaco built their roads for a number of reasons. The Anasazi may have used these roads during their religious rites. They may have used these roads to carry on trade with other areas. And large numbers of workers may have traveled from one town to another over these roads.

Most likely, then, it was a combination of things that caused people to leave the great pueblos. Large numbers of people now moved around in search of new homes. The northern pueblo people generally moved southward. In doing so they moved into areas that already had a settled population. In New Mexico these areas were the Zuni country, the western mountainous region, and the Rio Grande Valley. These areas had a permanent water supply. Because they also had a settled population, the arrival of new settlers caused some problems. Some areas became overcrowded. Architecture, arts, and crafts suffered for a time until old and new settlers blended their skills together.

Cliff Dwellings at Bandelier National Monument

Early pottery: lower left, mud bowl (A.D. 450); upper right, black on white; lower right, black on red (A.D. 1000); and upper left, multicolored bowl (A.D. 1200)

New ways of living come into being. Archaeologists call this period after 1300 the Regressive Pueblo Period. External pressures had caused people to abandon Classic Pueblo sites. In moving to new areas, the Anasazi spent less time building their homes. Still, there were achievements during this period of change. The people again built large pueblos, mostly on the floors of valleys. Of these pueblos, Pecos, located just east of the Rio Grande, was the largest. These new pueblos had rows of buildings as high as five stories, often centered around open plazas. This marked a change from earlier pueblos, for this way of laying out pueblos became common only after 1300. The buildings in other pueblos stretched along streets. The open courtyards housed the kivas, but the kivas differed from pueblo to pueblo. Even the shapes were different. Some pueblos had round kivas. Others had rectangular kivas. The pottery also varied and was different from the pottery of the Classic Pueblo Period. Almost entirely gone was the black-on-white pottery. In its place was black and white-on-red pottery. This pottery by shape and by design varied widely from one pueblo to another.

26

Another major change in pueblo life took place after 1450. Once again there was abandonment of pueblos and movement of peoples. In 1500 New Mexico was left with two centers of population. One was the Zuni-Acoma area. The other was the Rio Grande Valley and the area eastward to Pecos. (See the map on page 19.) The people who lived in these population centers were the ancestors of the present-day Pueblo Indians.

The name Indians is not as old as the people we call this name. In fact, the name goes back not quite 500 years to the time of Christopher Columbus. In 1492 Columbus thought that he had reached the Far East spice islands called the Indies. Instead, he had landed in the Americas. Unaware of where he was, Columbus named the Caribbean Islands he had reached *Las Indias,* "the Indies," now known as the West Indies. The natives of these islands he called *Indios,* or "Indians." The name Indians stuck. In time the name Indians was given to all the people who lived in the Americas 400 and more years ago. This is why New Mexico's first settlers are known as Indians.

Section Review

1. (a) How many major cultures grew out of the Desert Culture?
    (b) Who were the Mogollon, and where did they live?
    (c) Describe their houses and villages.
    (d) What did the Mogollon do to feed themselves?
2. (a) Who were the Anasazi, and where did they live?
    (b) Why were the Anasazi called Basketmakers before A.D. 700?
    (c) How did the Basketmakers feed themselves?
3. (a) What changes took place in the Anasazi ways of living during the Modified Basketmaker Period?
    (b) By A.D. 700 what ways of living did the people of the Southwest have in common?
4. (a) Describe the first Anasazi pueblos.
    (b) What role did the kiva play in Anasazi Culture?
    (c) What do archaeologists believe may have been true of Anasazi women?
5. (a) Describe the homes of the Anasazi during the Classic Pueblo Period.
    (b) In what ways did the Anasazi improve the quality of their lives?
6. (a) What were some of the possible reasons for the abandonment of the northern pueblos in the late 1100s and the late 1200s?
    (b) How did the people change their ways of living after 1300?
    (c) By 1500 what were the two remaining population centers in present-day New Mexico?

Chapter Review

Words You Should Know

Find each word in your reading and explain its meaning.

1. geographical conditions
2. plains
3. plateau
4. basins
5. surface water
6. continental divide
7. irrigation
8. ground water
9. droughts
10. altitude
11. latitude
12. life zones
13. archaeologists
14. culture
15. kill sites
16. artifact
17. nomadic
18. sedentary
19. atlatl
20. metate
21. mano
22. pueblo
23. kiva
24. mesa

Places You Should Be Able to Locate

Be able to locate these places on the maps in your book.

1. four corners area
2. Great Plains
3. Llano Estacado
4. Rocky Mountains
5. Colorado Plateau
6. basin and range area
7. Rio Grande
8. Pecos River
9. Canadian River
10. San Juan River
11. Gila River
12. continental divide
13. archaeological sites

Facts You Should Remember

Answer the following questions by recalling information presented in this chapter.

1.   **(a)** What are the sources of water in New Mexico?

      (b) What does a supply of water allow people in New Mexico to do?

2.   **(a)** What did the very first people to arrive in New Mexico do to survive?

      (b) Once the big game disappeared, what ways of living were developed by the desert dwellers?

      (c) What items and skills did the Mogollon have that allowed them to take up a sedentary way of life?

3.   **(a)** What are the names archaeologists give to the different stages of the Anasazi ways of living?

(b) What were the major achievements of the Anasazi Culture during the Classic Pueblo Period?

(c) What became of the great Anasazi pueblos and the people who had lived in these pueblos?

Eyewitness to New Mexico's History
Coronado's Expedition Discovers Tiguex, 1540
From: George P. Hammond and Agapito Rey, eds., *Narratives of the Coronado Expedition, 1540–1542* (University of New Mexico Press, 1940), pp. 253–54.

Tiguex is a province of twelve pueblos, on the banks of a large and mighty river [Rio Grande near Bernalillo]. Some pueblos are on one bank, some on the other. It is a spacious valley two leagues wide. To the east there is a snow-covered sierra, very high and rough [Sandia Mountains]. At its foot, on the other side, there are seven pueblos, four in the plain and three sheltered on the slope of the sierra. . . . All of these pueblos have, in general, the same ceremonies and customs, although some have practices among them not observed elsewhere. They are governed by the counsel of their elders. They build their pueblo houses in common. The women mix the plaster and erect the walls; the men bring the timbers and set them in place. They have no lime, but they mix a mortar made with charcoal ash and dirt, which is almost as good as if it were made with lime. For although the houses are four stories high, their walls are built only half a yard thick. The people gather large amounts of brush and reeds, set fire to it, and when it is between charcoal and ash, they throw in a large amount of water and dirt and mix it, then make round balls with it, which they use as stones when dry. They set them with this same mixture, so that it becomes like a mortar.

CHAPTER 2

Indian Cultures the Spaniards Encountered

What you will learn in this chapter—

No group of people has better learned how to live on the land that is New Mexico than the Indians. These people, New Mexico's first settlers, adjusted to the land. They developed ways of living that fit what the land had to offer. By the 1500s most of New Mexico's Indians lived in the areas that allowed them to carry on whatever their ways of living were.

This is not, however, to say that all of New Mexico's Indians developed the same ways of living. You read at the end of the last chapter about the differences among New Mexico's first settlers. In this chapter you will learn about New Mexico's Indians. You will discover that some of the Indian peoples have much in common. You will also discover that there are differences among the Indians. As you read, keep in mind that New Mexico's Indians today have some ways of living that are like those of their ancestors who witnessed the start of Spanish exploration in New Mexico in 1539 and 1540. As you read, you will find answers to the following questions:

    1. Who are the Pueblo Indians?
    2. Who are the Navajos and the Apaches?

1. Who are the Pueblo Indians?

Pueblo Indians share a similar culture. You learned in Chapter 1 that pueblo is the Spanish word for town. Pueblo was the word the Spaniards traveling through the Southwest used to name the Indian villages they came across. Pueblos was the name the Spaniards gave to the people who lived in these villages. But the Pueblo Indians were not a single tribe in the 1500s, nor are they now. Rather, they are people who live today and have always lived in similar ways. Pueblo Indians were farmers in the 1500s. They are still basically farmers today. Pueblo Indians shared a similar culture in the 1500s. They shared similar living patterns, beliefs, customs, skills, and arts. They share a similar culture today.

Jemez Pueblo (about 1905)

Pueblo people do not share a common Pueblo language. There is one thing, however, that the Pueblo Indians have never shared. They have never shared a common Pueblo language. Among the Pueblos of the Southwest today, there are four different language groups. The New Mexico Pueblo people speak three of these. The Zuni Indians who live south of Gallup speak Zuni. Zuni is a language not closely related to any other language. The Indians who live in seven of the pueblos north of Bernalillo speak Keresan. Keresan is the language of Santo Domingo, Cochiti, Santa Ana, San Felipe, and Zia. It is also the language of two western pueblos—Laguna and Acoma.

The rest of New Mexico's Pueblo peoples speak one of three languages that fall within the Tanoan language family. They live mainly in the pueblos that extend from Taos southward to Isleta. Taos, Picuris, Sandia, and Isleta peoples speak Tiwa. Tewa is spoken in the pueblos of Santa Clara, San Ildefonso, San Juan, Pojoaque, Tesuque, and Nambe. Towa is the third of the Tanoan languages. The Jemez Indians alone speak Towa.

Such language differences date back over the centuries. These differences have helped keep the various pueblos separate from one another. The people of one pueblo have not been able to understand or to speak the language of other pueblos. Even people from different pueblos who speak the same Pueblo language may have trouble talking to one another in that language. Look at the map on page 33. Find the 19 pueblos that exist in New Mexico today. Think about the separation caused by language differences. Think as well about the separation caused by the fact that each pueblo group has long seen itself

New Mexico's Indians Today

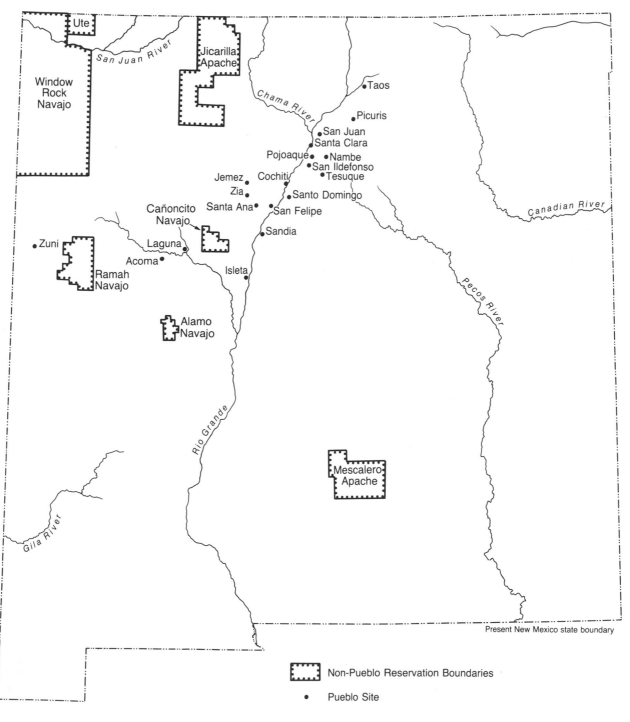

Ute

Jicarilla Apache

Window Rock Navajo

San Juan River

Chama River

Taos

Picuris

San Juan
Santa Clara
Pojoaque
Nambe
San Ildefonso
Jemez
Cochiti
Tesuque
Zia
Santo Domingo
Santa Ana
San Felipe
Cañoncito Navajo
Sandia

Zuni

Laguna
Acoma
Isleta

Ramah Navajo

Canadian River

Alamo Navajo

Rio Grande

Pecos River

Gila River

Mescalero Apache

Present New Mexico state boundary

Non-Pueblo Reservation Boundaries

• Pueblo Site

0 10 20 30 40 50 Miles

33

as a distinct and independent people. This same separation existed among the pueblos more than 400 years ago. Similarities among the pueblos also existed more than 400 years ago.

Pueblo Indians live in multistoried buildings. When the Spaniards arrived in the Southwest, they found some 75 to 80 pueblos. These pueblos stretched northward from Isleta to Taos. They extended westward to Acoma and Zuni and into Arizona, where the Hopis still live today. The Anasazi were the ancestors of the people who lived in the pueblos. They had settled in these areas after moving southward from such places as Mesa Verde and Chaco Canyon in the late 1100s and 1200s (page 24). Further movement of people after 1450 left New Mexico with two population centers (page 27). In these population centers were the pueblos the Spaniards described for us.

What first caught the Spaniards' attention was the way in which Indian people had built their houses. These houses were usually several stories high. Ranging from two to four or five stories, they were also terraced, or stepped. The rooms of one story rose above and behind the rooms of the next lower story. The buildings thus looked like giant stairways. It was the appearance of these multistoried structures that reminded the Spanish explorers of their towns back home. So the Spaniards named the Indian settlements pueblos ("towns").

The pueblo houses everyone in the community. The rooms in the pueblo had various functions. Lower-story rooms had no outside doorways or openings. People entered these rooms by climbing down pole ladders placed through narrow openings in the roof. These lower-story rooms served mainly as places for storing food and other items. Ladders placed on the outside of the building also led from one story to the next higher story. The upper-story

Taos Pueblo

rooms did have outside doorways. However, these doorways were small. They measured only 3 to 4 feet high and about 2 feet wide. The members of each family lived in one or two of the upper-story rooms. Because the pueblo was shaped like steps, each family had added living space outside in an area much like a balcony. Here the people could work. They could also cook their meals on the balcony.

None of the rooms set aside for living had much in them. At the center of a room was a clay- or stone-lined fire pit without a chimney. Smoke drifted out through roof and wall openings. The only other items in a living room might be a bench built along one wall and an area set aside for grinding corn. This same way of living was common to all who lived in each of the pueblos. Most pueblos housed between 200 and 300 people. Some pueblos were much larger. All totaled, about 30,000 Pueblo Indians lived in the Southwest in the 1500s.

The pueblos have other common features. Many of the pueblo buildings were faced in such a way that the south sun in the winter provided much of the needed heat. In other words, the Pueblo people made use of solar energy. They constructed the buildings with whatever material was available. The western Pueblo people used sandstone, a soft, often red rock. The Rio Grande Valley pueblos had no such supply of stone. So the people used *adobe*. Adobe is a building material made by mixing water with a soil mixture of clay and sand. The Indians made walls by spreading the adobe mixture over a framework of sticks and brush. Whether made of sandstone or adobe, the pueblos had a neat appearance. Outside walls were clean. In those pueblos built around plazas (page 26), religious murals or designs often covered the walls that enclosed the plazas.

adobe: building material made from mixing water with clay and sand

To provide for their animals, the Pueblo Indians designed special structures. Dug-out areas housed small, shaggy dogs. The dogs were domesticated (tame). They were not eaten. Large turkey pens held as many as 100 turkeys. The turkey, also domesticated, was valued for its feathers. Turkey feathers were a weaving material.

Religion is at the center of pueblo life. The kiva, or religious room, was another feature common to the pueblos. However, kivas differed in size and shape among the various pueblos (page 26). Pueblos built around plazas usually had two kivas in each plaza. These kivas were both social and religious centers. For example, they served as special meeting places for men. But more importantly, the kivas were the focal point of Pueblo religion. And Pueblo religion touched every part of a person's life. This religion was the basic set of beliefs that tied all the people of one pueblo together.

Pueblo religion was a religion grounded in nature. It was a religion in

36   Pueblo women plaster an adobe wall, 1936

Kiva wall paintings, Coronado State Monument

Pueblo Indian dancer

which the universe represented a system of order and harmony. It was a religion filled with ceremonies. The people appealed to the spiritual forces which they believed ruled the world they lived in from day to day. Basically, Pueblo religion was *polytheistic*. It recognized many gods. It recognized the sun and the earth as gods. It viewed the clouds, thunder, and wind as spirits. This religion is still important to the Pueblo peoples today.

Ceremonies celebrate Pueblo religion. In practicing their religion, Pueblo Indians held ceremonies at different times throughout the year. Certain groups within the pueblo took charge of the various religious rites. One or more priests (religious leaders) headed each group. The group might be a kiva, a dance society, or some other group. Each group made its preparations for the ceremony in secret. It had its own costumes. It had its own songs, dances, musical instruments, and whatever else was needed. During the summer months religious rites centered on the growing of crops. The people wanted rain and a good harvest. In the winter months religious rites dealt with such matters as hunting, curing, and sometimes with war.

In some pueblos religious rites revolved around *kachinas*. Kachinas were the spirits of ancestors. They were messengers of the Pueblo gods. The Pueblo people believed that the kachinas could control the weather and bring rain. They also believed that the kachinas could bring good health. Among the Pueblo peoples of New Mexico today kachinas are most associated with the Zunis.

Not all the pueblos practiced Pueblo religion in the exact same way. Some pueblos had special religious rites. These rites were designed to meet special needs. Then, too, the pueblos were independent. They were separate villages. Yet despite some differences in the rites themselves, Pueblo religion

polytheistic: word used to describe a religion that recognizes many gods; true of Pueblo Indian religion

kachina: spirits of an ancestor and messenger of a Pueblo Indian god; central to the Pueblo Indian religion

37

A garden at Zuni (1930s)

was the main force in Pueblo life. It helped define the ways of living that were and remain common to all Pueblo peoples.

The Pueblo peoples are farmers. Also common to Pueblo peoples and to their ways of living was farming. Farming defined the way in which people survived. The Pueblo peoples built their villages and located their fields near sources of water. This meant that in the Rio Grande Valley they planted their crops along the river. They used ditches dug with wooden tools to carry water to their crops. In other words, farming in the Rio Grande Valley depended on irrigation. This farming took a lot of work. All the members of the pueblo worked at irrigation farming as a community project. Both men and women dug and cleaned the irrigation ditches. The men alone then tilled the soil and planted the crops. The women joined the men in harvesting crops.

The Pueblo peoples who did not live in the Rio Grande Valley were also farmers. Limited rainfall and river water meant they had to practice a different type of farming—*dry farming.* To overcome the lack of water, the people tilled deep down so that the soil retained some moisture. They planted crops near dry washes (arroyos). These arroyos carried rain water and the runoff

dry farming: type of farming done in areas of little rainfall and little supply of water; requires special preparation of the soil and special farming methods

38

of the melting mountain snow to the crops. The farmers of the western pueblos practiced dry farming. So did the Pueblo peoples who lived east of the Manzano Mountains near present-day Albuquerque.

The Pueblo peoples are productive farmers. The Pueblo Indians 400 years ago were good farmers. They practiced *crop rotation*. They rotated, or changed on a regular basis, what crops were grown in what soil. By rotating their crops, they were less likely to wear out the soil. Their main crop was corn. It grew in many colors—blue, red, yellow, white, pink, and dark purple. Ground corn made into flat corncakes was the mainstay of the Pueblo diet. Different kinds of beans and squash also grew in the fields. At harvest time the people ate fresh vegetables. However, they carefully dried most of their crops on roof tops. They stored these dried foods for the rest of the year and for future years. These people were aware that little rainfall and perhaps even drought might lie ahead.

crop rotation: changing on a regular basis the crops that are grown in any one field

The Pueblo Indians hunt and gather foods. The Pueblo people added to their diet by hunting game and gathering wild fruits, nuts, and berries. The men did the hunting. They hunted mostly small game. Rabbits, for example, were in great supply. The hunters would round up rabbits by making a circle around a large area. They would then make the circle tighter and tighter, trapping and killing the rabbits inside. Groups of men and boys hunted rabbits in this way. Pueblo men also hunted deer, antelope, mountain sheep, squirrels, and gophers. Some Pueblo men went out onto the plains to hunt buffalo. The hunters returned to the pueblos with buffalo hides and dried buffalo meat, called jerky.

The Pueblo women ground the corn and did the cooking. They gathered the wild foodstuffs. They gathered wild plums, acorns, piñon nuts, and walnuts. They found ways to use cactus, yucca, sunflowers, dandelions, mustard plants, and cattails. In all, the Pueblo peoples used more than 70 plants for food, medicines, and dyes.

Pueblos have a structured society. All the people who lived in a pueblo had to work to insure their survival. Men did some of the work. Women did still other tasks. Because the pueblo way of life was hard, each village became a closely knit community. It followed the direction of one or more of the priests. It developed a social structure that made clear who owned what and who lived where.

Among most of the western pueblos, the *clan* was the most important social unit. A clan was a group of blood relatives. Clan members traced their blood relationships through their mothers. A society that traces its ancestral descent through the female line, or mothers, is called a *matrilineal society*. In these pueblos women owned the land. They owned the house, any furnishings,

clan: group of blood relatives; important Indian social unit, especially in western pueblos

matrilineal society: type of society in which people trace their blood relationships through their mothers; the society of the western pueblos

39

the fields, and the stored food. Family members who shared a household were the mother and her husband, their daughters, and their sons-in-law. In each household there were often three or more generations. Such a household was an *extended family*. It was a family extended beyond the two generations of parents and their children. In an extended family the oldest female was the most respected member of the household. In western pueblos, then, property was passed on through the female line. So, too, were certain positions within the pueblo. Among most western pueblos the social structure is much the same today.

Some of the eastern pueblos, those located in the Rio Grande Valley, had a different social structure. Among these pueblos clans were not so important. Rather, the people in each pueblo belonged to one of the two *moieties*. Moiety is a word that means a half, or either of two fairly equal parts. One moiety in some pueblos represented the summer people. The other moiety represented the winter people. In pueblos with this structure each moiety had a special chamber. A squash chamber existed for the summer people. A turquoise chamber existed for the winter people. Each moiety took charge of the religious rites that fell within its half of the year. Dancers from both moieties did, however, take part in these rites. Moieties are still part of the social structure within many of the middle Rio Grande pueblos today.

Some of the eastern pueblos also developed a *patrilineal society*. People traced their blood relationships through the male line, or their fathers. In addition, men controlled the property.

Pueblo Indians are skilled craftspeople. The land that is New Mexico proved hard to work for the people who lived on it. But the Pueblo peoples developed a way of life suited to the land. And they did more than merely survive. As part of the Pueblo Culture, the people created beautiful, handcrafted items. In the 1500s Pueblo peoples still practiced the ancient art of basketmaking. They also practiced the art of weaving. Pueblo men wove cloth out of cotton. Some of this cloth became the clothes worn every day. Women wore long cotton dresses. As part of these dresses, a piece of cloth crossed the right shoulder and passed under the left arm. The left shoulder was left bare. A long belt held the dress in place. Men wore cotton loincloths. Over these loincloths they wore a piece of material that was wrapped around the waist and hung down about a foot and a half. Woven cloth also became the clothes worn in the celebration of religious rites. It was in the 1200s and the 1300s that Pueblo peoples appear to have done their finest weaving.

Pueblo peoples also made fine pottery. They made and still make their pottery without the aid of a potter's wheel. The potters—who were the women—used what is called the coiling method. They began the pottery-making process

extended family: family including more than the two generations of parents and their children

moiety: social division within an eastern pueblo; group of people responsible for taking care of religious rites that fall within their half of the year

patrilineal society: type of society in which people trace their blood relationships through their fathers; the society of some eastern pueblos

by rolling clay into ropes. They wound these clay ropes around and around, forming their pottery into whatever size and shape pottery they wanted. The women then scraped, dried, and smoothed the pots. Next they might paint on designs with paint made from plants and minerals. Finally, they hardened their pottery by setting fire to wood and animal dung piled around the pottery. As the wood and dung burned away, the pots were fired. One other Pueblo art was beadmaking. Pueblo peoples strung together into beads sea shells obtained in trade with California Indians. They made other beads from stone and bone. Once the beads were strung, the bead workers finished the work by shaping and polishing the beads on sandstone slabs. This made the beads round and smooth. The skill of the Pueblo craftspeople did not escape the attention of the Spaniards. Spanish writers reported these artistic skills. Indeed, they reported many details of what they believed to be true about Pueblo ways of living and Pueblo Culture.

1. (a) What do the Pueblo Indians have in common?
   (b) Why have language differences among the Pueblo peoples been important?
2. (a) In what areas of the Southwest were the pueblos located in the 1500s?
   (b) Describe what these pueblos looked like from the outside.
   (c) What uses were made of the lower-story and the upper-story rooms?
3. Discuss the importance of religion to the Pueblo peoples.
4. (a) What kind of farming did the Pueblo Indians of the Rio Grande Valley practice?
   (b) In what ways did many of the western Pueblo Indians practice farming?
   (c) How did the Pueblo peoples take care of the soil, and what crops did they grow?
   (d) Besides farming, what did the Indians do to add to their food supply?
5. (a) How did the western Pueblo peoples trace their blood relationships?
   (b) What other ways of tracing blood relationships developed in some eastern pueblos?
6. What were the arts and crafts of the Pueblo peoples?

2. Who are the Navajos and the Apaches?

Non-Pueblo people live in New Mexico. When the Spaniards wrote about the Indians they met in New Mexico, they also wrote about those who did not live in pueblos. In fact, non-Pueblo peoples did not live in

Shiprock in the Navajo country

permanent homes. These Indians were to some degree nomadic. All of them spent at least part of the year on the move. Some of them even spent most of the year on the move. A somewhat nomadic existence was one way of living that non-Pueblo peoples had in common. These peoples were related in other ways as well.

The Navajos and Apaches share a common background. The largest groups of non-Pueblo people to move into the Southwest were the Navajos and the Apaches. They belonged to the same language family—the Athabascan. This means that the Navajos and the different Apache groups were and are still related to one another by language. The Navajos and the Apaches are, in turn, related by language to Indians who live today in Canada, in Alaska, and along the northern Pacific coast. Indeed, anthropologists believe that the Navajos and the Apaches originally lived in northwestern Canada. From there, they moved southward. Why the Navajos and the Apaches might have left their northern ancestral homes remains a mystery.

The Navajos and Apaches arrive in the Southwest. When the Navajos and the Apaches first reached the Southwest is another mystery. Some archaeologists believe that they arrived in the 1200s. These archaeologists suggest that the Navajos and the Apaches were at least partly responsible for upsetting life in the Southwest. It was at about this time, you may recall, that the Anasazi abandoned their cliff dwellings at Mesa Verde and their large pueblos at Chaco Canyon and elsewhere. Other archaeologists disagree. They believe that the Navajos and the Apaches did not reach the Southwest until the 1500s. They suggest that the Navajos and the Apaches arrived only a short time before the Spaniards entered the area. Spanish writers do tell us that there were some Apache groups living in the Southwest in the late 1500s and the early 1600s. This was the same time that the Spaniards began to make settlements of their own in present-day New Mexico. However, there is some physical evidence that places the Navajos in the Southwest before this time.

Of the Athabascan-speaking peoples who moved into the Southwest, members of three tribes live in New Mexico today. (1) The Navajos live in northwestern New Mexico and northeastern Arizona. (2) The Mescalero Apaches live east of the Rio Grande between Alamogordo and Roswell in the south-central part of New Mexico. (3) The Jicarilla Apaches live west of the Rio Grande in the north-central part of the state. Look at the map on page 33. Find where these Indian groups live today. A fourth Apache group, the Chiricahua, lived in New Mexico until the late 1800s. Through the centuries these non-Pueblo peoples have been separated by greater differences in cultures than the differences that separated the Pueblo peoples. Still, the Navajos and the southwestern Apaches arrived speaking similar tongues. They gave themselves the same name. They called themselves Diné, meaning "The People."

The Navajos adjust to the land. The largest group of Athabascan people are the Navajos. Today the Navajos number more than 125,000. They are the largest Indian tribe in the United States. Their reservation, also the largest in the country, covers about 16 million acres, or about 24,000 square miles. About one-third of the Navajos live in New Mexico. A small number live in Utah. The other Navajos, most of them, in fact, live in Arizona. However, 400 years ago, the Navajos were newcomers to the Southwest and to the land that is New Mexico. They had to develop ways of living on that land.

In developing their ways of living, the Navajos became hunter-gatherers. They also raided pueblos and, later on, Spanish settlements. In addition, they traded with the pueblos. From the Pueblo peoples the Navajos got corn, cotton cloth, and other needed items. In exchange, the Navajos gave the Pueblo peoples jerky (dried meat) and animal hides.

The Navajos build houses. In time the Navajos became a more settled people than the Apaches. The Navajos did not totally give up their nomadic way of life. They continued to move about, often moving with the seasons. But the Navajos did begin to build houses for their families. Sometimes a family had two or three houses. Each house was built in a place where the family lived during part of the year.

hogan: house of the Navajos

The earliest Navajo house was different from a modern Navajo house, or *hogan*. (A modern hogan may be round or rectangular, built of stone, and fitted with glass windows.) The Navajos built their earliest hogans around three wooden poles. These poles stood upright and formed the framework. The Navajos laid other logs horizontally over the framework. They then plastered the outside with mud. They completed their building task by adding a covered entryway. Some other early hogans had a different structure. Still, the hogans were usually round in shape, built of logs, and windowless.

The Navajos learn from the Pueblo Indians. Besides building hogans, the Navajos began to farm. They learned farming from the Pueblo Indians. Indeed, the name Navajo may come from a word in the Tewa language (page 32) that means "arroyo of cultivated fields." The Navajos mostly grew corn.

The Navajos' ways of living reflected some other aspects of Pueblo Culture. Like the western Pueblo peoples, the Navajos had a matrilineal society. They traced their blood relationships through their mothers. Married sons lived near their mothers. Hogans built close to one another usually housed a mother and her extended family. Hogans built close to one another were not, though, part of a village. The Navajos simply did not live in villages. In this respect they were different from the Pueblo Indians. The Navajos were again like the western Pueblo peoples in their division into clans. Each Navajo remained a lifelong member of the clan of his or her mother.

Religion is at the center of Navajo life. As the Navajos adjusted to the land of the Southwest, they expressed their religious beliefs. To the Navajos, religion was a part of all that they did. There were religious rites for curing the sick. There were religious rites for sending the men off to war or on raiding parties. The Navajos believed that supernatural (unearthly) beings had the power to do either good or bad. In charge of Navajo religious rites was the *shaman*. A shaman is also called a Navajo medicine man.

shaman: Navajo so-called medicine man; in charge of Navajo religious rites

One of the Navajos' main concerns was for the dead. If a Navajo died inside a hogan, the other family members would not again live in that hogan. Rather, they left the hogan, usually burning it to the ground. They then built a new hogan. The new hogan was on some other piece of ground. To save a hogan, the Navajos might move a dying person outside to die. When death occurred, the body was quickly buried. Burial took place in the ground. Or burial could also be in an opening among the rocks. The family buried the dead person's personal property alongside the body. Even after burial, the

Navajo women beside a hogan

Navajos believed that a deceased person's spirit could return at night to visit the living. This visit might be the result of a living person having done something to offend the dead person when he or she was still alive. This visit might be because the family had failed to bury the body in the right way or to bury everything the dead person had owned.

The curing ceremony is important. One of the most colorful features of Navajo religion was the sand painting. Pueblo Indians and Apaches also used sand paintings. But the Navajo sand painting was the most detailed of Indian sand paintings. It became more and more outstanding as time passed. The sand painting itself was part of a curing ceremony. The family of a person who was sick would choose the curing ceremony it wanted. Often the family's choice rested on the ability of the family to pay for the ceremony. Ceremonies could be costly. Some lasted as long as nine days. They might include dances, poems, sand paintings, and other rituals. The family had to pay the shaman and his helpers. They had to pay for the materials used in the ceremony. They

45

Navajo sand painting (from *Southwest Indian Drypainting,* by Leland Wyman, UNM Press)

also had to pay for the food served to all who came to the ceremony.

The shaman oversaw the sand painting ritual. He and from two to fifteen helpers did the work. They most often completed the sand painting on a layer of clean sand on the floor of the sick person's hogan. They used dry colors from ground-up plants and minerals. They painted by letting the dry colors sift between their thumbs and forefingers. Some sand paintings were only 1 or 2 feet across. Others were 15 to 20 feet across. The sand paintings showed events in the lives of the Holy People. They were painted from memory. They fit the curing ceremony the family had chosen. Each sand painting lasted only a short time. It had to be destroyed before the sun went down on the very day the shaman and his helpers created it. These same religious beliefs are still honored among Navajos today.

The Navajos and Apaches have similar religions. The other Athabascan people developed ways of living that were different from those of the Navajos. Still, the Apache religion was similar to the Navajo religion. The Apaches, too, believed in the good and evil powers of supernatural beings. They, too, showed special concern for the dead. They, too, had religious rites designed to go along with all that went on in their lives. These rites were events that brought people together.

Most of the Apache rites were curing ceremonies. A shaman directed each curing ceremony. The shaman used supernatural powers granted to him by the Mountain Spirits, or Gihán. A curing ceremony included masked dancers. Four in number, these dancers posed as the Mountain Spirits. In addition, it included songs sung by the shaman. These songs let the shaman ask the supernatural beings for help. The Apaches also had religious rites for events other than illness. One of these celebrated the passage of a female Apache from a girl into a woman. (See Special Interest Feature.) These same religious beliefs are still honored among Apaches today.

Apache tribes divide into separate groups. The Apaches adjusted to the land that is New Mexico. The Apache groups in New Mexico spread out. They lived far apart from one another. Indeed, no one group of Apaches even saw itself as a single, united tribe. For example, the Mescaleros had 5 tribal groups. The Chiricahuas had 3. Each separate tribal group, in turn, further divided itself into local groups. These local groups might consist of from 10 to 20 extended families. There was no central tribal organization. One of the tribal groups might act together in times of war. In such an event the strongest local leader acted as chief. This unity within a tribal group, however, rarely took place. At most times a local group acted as the hunting party, the raiding party, or the war party.

Mescalero
Reservation

An Apache Girl Comes of Age

The Apaches believe that a young woman's coming of age is cause for celebration. Once a young woman goes through a special ceremony, she can marry. The ceremony itself is complex. The earth and the sun are central to the rites. A brush tipi represents the universe. This tipi is said to be made of old hair and other things so that the young women may have long life. The young women who are coming of age represent White Painted Woman. She is an Apache priestess and the model for Apache women. The Apaches welcome the sun on the first and the last days of the rites.

Male dancers, most often four in number, portray the Mountain Spirits. They appear from different directions. One each comes from the north, south, east, and west. For every four dancers, there is a shaman to help prepare the dancers. Among other things, the dancers wear masks and beautiful headdresses. A fifth dancer acts the role of clown. He imitates the other dancers.

On the fourth night the young women dance all night. The next day they take part in footraces. They race to the east. They run around a basket that contains special items and then run back to deerskins placed in front of the brush tipi. They race to the east four times in all. Each time there are chants. Each time the basket is moved closer to the deerskins. Before the final race is over, the Apaches have taken down the special tipi. Gifts are thrown to those who have watched the rites. The girls return to their own homes. There they remain for the next four days and nights. Then and only then can a young man choose one of these women for his wife.

Mountain Spirit Dancers at Mescalero Apache ceremonial

tipi: cone-shaped tent of animal skins; shelter used by the Mescalero and Jicarilla Apaches

wickiup: grass and brush hut built on an oval-shaped frame; shelter used by the Chiricahua Apaches

mescal: agave plant with button-like tops that was a main staple of the Mescalero Apaches

For the most part the Apaches in New Mexico made their living by hunting and by gathering. They moved around almost all year long. Most of them did not take up farming as did the Navajos. They did not build any sort of permanent houses. Instead, they built shelters that could be moved. The Mescalero and Jicarilla Apaches lived in *tipis*. These tipis were cone-shaped tents of animal skins. They were similar to the shelters of the Plains Indians. The Chiricahua Apaches lived in *wickiups*. Wickiups were huts built around oval-shaped frames. The outside covering of the wickiups might be grass and brush in the summer and animal hides in the winter.

The Mescalero Apaches develop ways of living. The Mescaleros lived in the southern part of present-day New Mexico. Like other Apaches, they were mainly hunter-gatherers. They also ate *mescal*, or agave plant. Mescal has large leaves. It grew and still grows in the American Southwest and in northern Mexico. The fleshy cabbage or heart of the plant was the part of the mescal the Mescaleros ate. And it was because they ate mescal that the Mescalero Apaches most likely got the name by which we know them.

48

To prepare the mescal they gathered, the Mescaleros dug huge pits. Some of these pits measured from 3 to 5 feet deep and from 10 to 20 feet across. The Mescaleros next lined the pit with a layer of rocks. They added a layer of wood and yet another layer of rocks. They set fire to the wood and waited for the fire to burn down. They then placed the mescal on the top layer of rocks and covered it with damp grass, brush, and dirt. They left the mescal to cook in this way for a day or two. Finally, they uncovered the mescal. They ate some of it there and dried and stored what was left.

The Jicarilla Apaches develop ways of living. The Jicarillas lived in the northeastern part of present-day New Mexico. They also lived in the southeastern part of present-day Colorado. The Jicarillas were like other Apaches in their basic ways of living. They, too, were hunter-gatherers. They did differ from the other Apaches of New Mexico in one way. Some of the Jicarillas took up farming. They learned to farm from the Pueblo Indians just as the Navajos did. And like the Pueblo Indians and the Navajos, the Jicarillas centered their farming on corn. They did not, however, truly settle down. Most of them remained true to the nomadic way of life.

The Chiricahua Apaches also move into New Mexico. The Chiricahuas lived in an area to the west of the Mescalero Apaches. They moved over an area that is today southwestern New Mexico, northern Mexico, and southeastern Arizona. Called Gila Apaches by the Spaniards, the Chiricahuas were hunter-gatherers. In time they became one of the most skilled groups of Indian warriors anywhere in what is today the United States. In a later chapter you will learn the fate of the Chiricahuas. You will learn why they no longer live in New Mexico as a tribe.

The Navajos and Apaches develop as craftspeople. You can see on the map (page 124) that the Apaches and the Navajos lived within a large area rather than in just one place as did the Pueblo Indians. Indeed, it was the basic life-style of these people to stay on the move. They had little time for making handcrafted items. They did, of course, make the bows and arrows needed for hunting, raiding, and fighting. They made some baskets and pots. They also made their clothes, using deerskin. It was not until after the 1500s, however, that these people became truly skilled craftspeople.

The Navajos, like the Apaches, spent much of their time moving about. But they were more settled than the Apaches. The Navajos also lived in closer contact with the Pueblo Indians. They learned to make some of the same crafts as those made by their Pueblo neighbors. For example, they got cotton cloth from the Pueblo Indians. In time the Navajos used cotton cloth for making clothes and blankets. In addition, they learned how to make handcrafted items of their own. Still, the Navajos did not develop their special crafts of weaving and silverwork until much later than the 1500s. You will read about these artistic skills in a later chapter.

Other Indians live in New Mexico at a later date. In this chapter you have read about Indians who were in New Mexico by the 1500s. These were the people who lived on the land when the Spaniards entered the area more than 400 years ago. Two other groups of Indians also played a part in the history of New Mexico. These were the Comanches and the Utes. They did not enter present-day New Mexico until later. So the story of the Comanches and the Utes is told in later chapters. In later chapters as well are the stories of what changes have taken place in the Pueblo, Navajo, and Apache ways of living. These changes took place as life in New Mexico changed over the period of more than 400 years.

Section Review

1.　(a) Why is the way of life of the early non-Pueblo peoples of New Mexico described as nomadic?
　　(b) In what one way were the Navajos and the Apaches related to one another?
　　(c) When do archaeologists believe that the Athabascan peoples arrived in the Southwest?

2.　(a) How did the Navajos make their living?
　　(b) In what ways did the Navajos become a more settled people than the Apache groups of present-day New Mexico?
　　(c) What ways of living did the Navajos learn from the Pueblo Indians?

3.　(a) For what reasons did the Navajos hold religious rites?
　　(b) In what ways did the Navajos express their concern for the dead?
　　(c) Describe the Navajo sand painting ritual.

4.　(a) In what ways was the Apache religion similar to the Navajo religion?
　　(b) Into what two types of groups did each major Apache group divide itself?
　　(c) How, for the most part, did the Apaches of New Mexico make their living?
　　(d) Describe any special ways of living of the Mescaleros, the Jicarillas, and the Chiricahuas.

Chapter Review

Words You Should Know

Find each word in your reading and explain its meaning.

1. adobe
2. polytheistic
3. kachinas
4. dry farming

5. crop rotation	11. hogan
6. clan	12. shaman
7. matrilineal society	13. tipis
8. extended family	14. wickiups
9. moiety	15. mescal
10. patrilineal society	

Places You Should Be Able to Locate

Be able to locate these places on the maps in your book.

1. present-day pueblos
2. the present-day locations of the Navajos
3. the present-day locations of the Mescalero and Jicarilla Apaches

Facts You Should Remember

Answer the following questions by recalling information presented in this chapter.

1. (a) How did the Pueblo Indians live on the land that is New Mexico?
    (b) How did the Navajos live on the land?
    (c) How did the Apaches live on the land?
2. (a) How were the ways of living of the non-Pueblo Indians different from the ways of living of the Pueblo Indians?
    (b) How were the ways of living of these two Indian groups similar?
3. What part did religion play in the lives of the Pueblo Indians, the Navajos, and the Apaches?

Unit Summary

New Mexico, the fifth largest state in the Union, is located in the American Southwest. Because of its size and location, New Mexico has certain geographical conditions that have affected ways of living. The most important of these has been New Mexico's lack of water. Water has largely determined where and how people in New Mexico have lived. The very earliest people, however, lived in a New Mexico quite different in climate from the New Mexico of today. As long as big game roamed the land, early people could live their lives as big-game hunters. Once the climate became hotter and drier, the big game disappeared. Early people then had to hunt small game and to gather wild foodstuffs. Once the early people learned how to grow corn, squash, and beans and to make pottery, they could settle down.

New Mexico's first settled people lived in two different places. The Mogollon lived in what is now west-central New Mexico. To the north lived the people known as the Anasazi. During the height of their culture, the Anasazi built great pueblos in what is now the four corners area. They moved southward in the late 1100s and 1200s. With further resettlement after 1450, New Mexico was left with two centers of population. One was the Zuni-Acoma area. The other was the Rio Grande Valley.

In these two areas the Pueblo Indians developed their ways of living and their culture. The Pueblo peoples built and lived in multistoried pueblos. They farmed the land. And they developed a religion that was a part of all that they did. Still, each pueblo remained an independent unit. Language differences made such separation easier.

Moving into the Southwest at a later time were the Navajos and the Apaches. These Indians were nomadic. They hunted and gathered as their basic means of survival. The Navajos and the Apaches belonged to the same language family. Yet in most other ways, the Navajos and each group of Apaches were different from one another. Indeed, they differed more in their ways of living than did the Pueblo Indians. Of all the non-Pueblo Indians, the Navajos were the first to become really settled. They learned farming and other ways of living from the Pueblo peoples. They, too, had a religion that was a part of all that they did. Religion was equally important to the Apaches. The Indian cultures of present-day New Mexico have undergone changes over the centuries. Still, New Mexico's Indians today have some ways of living that are much like those of the Indians who lived in New Mexico more than 400 years ago.

Time Line:
Spanish Exploration and Settlement

Columbus reaches America ——— **1492**

Cortés invades Mexico ——— **1519**

Cabeza de Vaca reaches New Spain ——— **1536**
Fray Marcos explores northward ⹀ **1539**
Coronado explores New Mexico **1540**

Fray Agustin "rediscovers" New Mexico ——— **1581**

Oñate settles New Mexico ——— **1598**

New Mexico becomes a royal colony ⹀ **1609**
Santa Fe is founded **1610**

Church-state conflict peaks ——— **1640**

Pueblo Revolt occurs ——— **1680**

UNIT TWO

New Mexico Is Explored and Settled by Spaniards

After the Indians, the next group to arrive in New Mexico were the Spaniards. The first Spaniards here were explorers. Indeed, they explored the land that is today New Mexico quite thoroughly. To explore New Mexico, they had to journey across vast stretches of land. They did so, moreover, at a time when explorers from other European countries relied mainly on ships to explore along the northern Atlantic coastline of North America. Explorers from countries other than Spain did not, for the most part, travel over land into the interior of North America.

Besides exploring the land, the Spaniards built settlements in New Mexico. And like the Indians before them, the Spaniards adjusted to the land and to what the land had to offer. The first Spanish settlement in New Mexico came before the close of the 1500s. It came 9 years before Jamestown, the first permanent English settlement in the present-day United States. It came 10 years before Quebec, the first permanent French settlement in North America. In chapter 3 you will read about Spanish explorers in New Mexico. In chapter 4 you will learn about early Spanish settlements in New Mexico.

Eyewitness to New Mexico's History
Cabeza de Vaca's Walk Across Southern New Mexico, 1535
From: Álvar Núñez Cabeza de Vaca, *Adventures in the Unknown Interior of America*, trans. Cyclone Covey (University of New Mexico Press, 1983), pp. 111–12.

They [Indians from the Tularosa village] guided us [down the Tularosa then south] through more than fifty leagues [150 miles], mostly over rugged mountain desert so dry there was a dearth of game, and we suffered great hunger.

Many of the people began to sicken from the privation and exertion of negotiating those sterile, difficult ridges. Our escort, however, conducted us across a thirty-league plain [between the Sacramentos and the Huecos], and we found many persons had come a long distance on the trail to greet us and welcome us like those before. They brought double the quantity of goods for our escort than the latter could carry. I told the givers to reclaim what was left so it would not go to waste.

CHAPTER 3

The Spanish Explorers

What you will learn in this chapter—
Today you can travel across New Mexico quite easily. You can go by airplane, train, bus, or car. If traveling by car, you follow the highways that will take you to where you want to go. You know which highways to use because of the directions that road maps give. You can stop along the way at roadside rest areas to picnic or rest before starting off again. Or you can stop along the way in any number of towns, cities, or campgrounds. There you can find eating places and places to spend the night.

How different our travel today is from the travel through New Mexico 400 years ago and more. The Spanish explorers had only horses, some other animals, and their feet to carry them across New Mexico. They had only the often general directions given by explorers who had traveled into the area at some earlier time. What maps they had, if any, were unclear. What they could expect along the way was unknown. Much of what they saw was new and strange to them. In this chapter you will learn about the Spanish explorers and their journeys through New Mexico. As you read, you will find answers to the following questions:

    1. How did the Spaniards come to be in the Americas?
    2. Who were the first Spanish explorers to enter New Mexico?
    3. Who were the later Spanish explorers of New Mexico?

1. How did the Spaniards come to be in the Americas?

Europeans look for new trade routes to the Far East. Spain's presence in the Americas grew out of a series of events. The first of these was the desire of Europeans to trade with India and the Far East. From these areas Europeans could get spices, silks, perfumes, rugs, dyes, and medicines. They wanted and needed these items. They wanted and needed spices, for example, because spices both preserved their food and made it taste better. But trade with the Far East was not easy. People transported goods by going to the East

57

on both sea and land. This trade took many, many months. Then, too, this trade was under the control of merchants from Italian cities. If other Europeans wanted to profit from the Far East trade, they would have to find new trade routes that took them south or westward.

The first country to find a new trade route was Portugal. The Portuguese sent out ships to find an all-water route to the East. New and advanced navigation instruments made these voyages possible. (See Special Interest Feature.) Portuguese explorers sailed first south and then east. They explored along the west coast of Africa and in time reached the southern tip of the continent. Later, Portuguese explorers rounded the Cape of Good Hope. They sailed up the east coast of Africa and across to India. In 1498 Vasco da Gama was the first European to reach the Far East by sailing around Africa.

The Cross Staff

compass: tool used by sailors; shows direction by the use of a magnetic needle that points to magnetic north

astrolabe: tool used by sailors; helps pinpoint latitude by the position of the stars

cross staff: tool that consists of a long piece and a cross piece that slides up and down the long piece; used by sailors to show latitude by the position of the stars

Improvements in Navigation

The period of history covered in this part of the chapter is sometimes called the Age of Discovery. It was a time when Europeans discovered an area of the world that was new to them. Such discovery took place, in fact, only because long ocean voyages were possible. Long voyages, in turn, were the result of advances in navigation. Ships were longer and narrower than those that sailed the Mediterranean Sea. These ships were well suited to ride the long ocean swells. Maps, too, were getting better and better.

Other advances came in the form of new instruments of navigation. The *compass* had become widely known to Europeans at the start of the 1400s. The compass, a direction-finding instrument, used a magnetic needle to locate magnetic north. Other instruments helped sailors pinpoint latitude. In other words, sailors could use instruments to determine distance north and south from a given point. One of these instruments, the *astrolabe,* was not new. Arabs had invented the astrolabe about A.D. 700. Sailors used the astrolabe to help them locate their latitude according to the position of the stars. Another of these instruments was the *cross staff.* The cross staff also told latitude by the stars. It consisted of a long piece and a cross piece that slid up and down the long piece. The sailor looked down the length of the long piece, moving the cross piece until one end touched the north star and the other end touched the horizon. The scale on the long piece then allowed the sailor to determine latitude.

Christopher Columbus used the compass, the astrolabe, and the cross staff on his four voyages to the Americas. So, too, did other explorers who sailed at this time. Some of the crew who sailed from Spain in 1519 with Ferdinand Magellan returned to Spain in 1522. They had managed to sail around the world.

Spain seeks an all-water route to the East. Portugal was not alone in seeking an all-water route to India. Spain as well wanted to trade with the Far East. In fact, Spain became one of the first countries to seek such a route. By the time Spain took action, however, Portugal controlled the all-water trade route followed by ships sailing eastward from Europe. So the king and queen of Spain became interested in what might be another all-water route to the East. They turned in 1492 to a man who believed he could reach the Far East by sailing westward from Europe. This man was, of course, Christopher Columbus.

Columbus, an Italian by birth, had first told the Spanish rulers about his plans to reach the Far East by sailing westward in 1486. Queen Isabella of Castille and King Ferdinand of Aragon had turned him down at that time. Columbus then took his plans to other countries. He was turned down again and again. Neither Portugal, England, nor France would sponsor such a voyage. Yet Columbus held on to his dream. He reappeared before the Spanish court in 1491. Once more the Spanish rulers said no. However, in January 1492 they agreed to sponsor Columbus's voyage westward.

Columbus sails to America. Columbus and his crew sailed from Spain in early August 1492. The *Santa Maria*, the *Pinta*, and the *Niña* sailed westward but never reached the Far East. Rather, they crossed the Atlantic Ocean and landed in the Americas. Columbus had failed to reach the Far East because he was a poor geographer. All educated people of the day knew the world was round. What Columbus had misjudged was the amount of land and water on the earth's surface. He had also misjudged the very size of the earth itself. He insisted that water covered only 15 percent of the earth's surface. In fact, it covers 70 percent. He thought that the Far East spice islands called the Indies were about 2,400 miles west of Spain. By his figures, the Spice Islands should have been about where the crew of the *Pinta* first spotted land in the Caribbean Sea. That is why Columbus named the islands he sailed to the Indies, now called the West Indies. He named the first Caribbean island where he went ashore *San Salvador*, meaning "Holy Savior."

Columbus explores much new land. Christopher Columbus never knew how important the Americas were. He called the lands he had reached the "Other World." He believed until his death in 1506 that this other world was part of the Far East. He believed this even after he had sailed three more times to the Americas. Still, no other person explored so much land previously unknown to Europeans. On his four voyages Columbus explored the Caribbean islands and visited parts of Central and South America. (Look at the map on page 61.) On his second voyage (1493–94), he also founded the first permanent European settlement in the Americas. This settlement, made up of 1,500 people, was on the island of Hispaniola.

Yet the land Columbus explored was not even to bear his name. Instead, it became known as "America." In 1507 a German geographer and map maker gave it this name after reading Amerigo Vespucci's exaggerated account of his visits to what is now South America. The map done in 1507 was widely distributed and copied. Soon the name "America" was accepted everywhere. Whatever the name, the Americas were ready for further exploration and settlement. Columbus had made it all possible.

Spain expands into the Americas. The first European country to expand into the Americas was Spain. Spain had, of course, sponsored Columbus's voyages. But there were other reasons for Spain's expansion. One reason was that Spain had strong rulers and was a united country. The marriage of Isabella and Ferdinand had united all "the Spains" except for Moorish Granada. The Moors were a non-Christian people from northern Africa. They had invaded Spain in A.D. 711 and remained there for nearly 800 years. The Spaniards finally pushed the Moors out of Spain in 1492. After 1492 all Spain was united. Another reason for Spain's expansion was the Catholic Church. The Church had been active in the almost 600-year fight to expel the non-Christian Moors. With the Moors gone from Spain, the Church began to look for ways to extend the Catholic faith. Still another reason for Spain's expansion was the presence of people in Spain who were eager to go to new areas of the world. Members of the upper class knew they could keep some of the land they might conquer. This land would be a reward for service to the Spanish rulers. The promise of land made soldiers important in Spain and later on in Spanish America. Then, too, travel to the new lands of the Americas promised adventure to those who wished to go.

So the Spaniards began to move into the Americas. They first moved onto the Caribbean Islands. By 1513 they had established 17 towns in Hispaniola. They built other settlements in Cuba, Puerto Rico, and Jamaica. In time Havana, Cuba, became the center for further exploration.

The Spaniards lay claim to more of the Americas. From Havana, Juan Ponce de León in 1513 sailed to what is today Florida. Thus began the Spanish exploration of North America. Ponce de León looked for but did not find "the fountain of youth." Also from Havana, Francisco Hernández de Córdoba sailed to Yucatan in search of slaves. Yet another Spaniard who explored North America was Alonso Álvarez de Pineda. He sailed from Jamaica in 1519. In his travels he explored and mapped the coast of the Gulf of Mexico. He

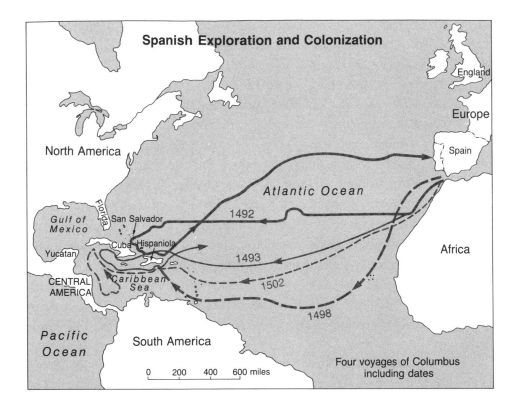

Spanish Exploration and Colonization

Four voyages of Columbus including dates

learned that Florida was part of a much larger mainland. He saw the coast of Texas and discovered the mouth of the Mississippi River. He looked for but did not find a way to the Pacific Ocean. (Vasco Núñez de Balboa had reached the Pacific Ocean in 1513. He and his men had spent more than four months cutting through the forest and climbing over the mountains of Panama.)

Besides exploring the Americas, the Spaniards moved onto and claimed for Spain vast areas of the North, Central, and South American mainlands. Córdoba, who had traveled to Yucatan, brought back tales of great wealth. He had heard stories of rich cities inland that were filled with gold. Based on these tales, the Spaniards began their conquest of present-day Mexico.

Cortés conquers Mexico. Hernando Cortés left Cuba for Mexico in 1519. He did so without official permission. Nonetheless, Cortés was destined to become one of the most famous of the *conquistadors.* The conquistadors were Spaniards who conquered for Spain vast areas in the Americas. Under the command of Cortés were 11 ships, 600 soldiers, and 16 horses. A number of priests also traveled with the expedition. In just over two years Cortés recorded a great victory for Spain. Stopping first on the Yucatan peninsula, he made his way to present-day Veracruz. He and his party then moved across Mexico. Helping him every step of the way was Marina (or Malinche), an exiled Aztec princess. She spoke both the Aztec and Mayan languages. She used her wits to

conquistador: Spaniard who conquered for Spain vast areas in the Americas

61

save Cortés from torture or even death more than one time. As Cortés moved through Mexico, he always made it his first duty to remove images from Indian temples. In their place he set up Christian altars.

In November 1519 Cortés entered Tenochtitlán, the capital of Moctezuma's great Aztec Empire. The next spring he learned that a Spanish army sent from Cuba was on its way to arrest him. He had, after all, undertaken the expedition without permission. Cortés kept his command by capturing the Spaniard sent to replace him. He then asked the members of the captured Spaniard's army to join him. Hearing of the vast Aztec wealth, the 800 newly arrived footsoldiers and 80 horsemen agreed. Even so, Cortés had to retreat from Tenochtitlán in June 1520. The Spaniards were short of supplies, and Cortés had become aware of the increased strength of the Aztec army. By December 1520 Cortés was again ready to move against the great Aztec city. He felt he could defeat the Aztecs once and for all if he destroyed the city itself. By August 1521 the Spaniards had defeated the Aztecs. They had, in the process, torn down three-fourths of what Cortés himself called the "most beautiful city in the world."

Cortés establishes New Spain. With the conquest of Mexico, Spain had added greatly to its American empire. (See the map of page 61.) The Spaniards named their new land "New Spain of the Ocean Sea" because of its great beauty. They rebuilt and renamed Tenochtitlán. They called it Mexico City after *Mexica,* the name the Aztecs called themselves. But New Spain did more than merely increase the size of the Spanish Empire. It also added people who could be converted to Christianity. It added untold wealth as well. New Spain was rich, especially in silver.

The Spaniards now ruled a part of the North American mainland. At the same time they ruled the Indians who had first lived on the land. The Spaniards replaced the Indian leaders. The Indians in New Spain and South America, moreover, accepted Spanish rule. For them, it was simply the replacement of one strong set of leaders with another. The Aztecs themselves had conquered most of the peoples of southern Mexico. They had ruled their people with an iron hand. The Incas had set up even stronger rule in Peru. (The Spaniards conquered the Incas in Peru in the 1530s.)

Still, life under Spanish rule was hard on the Indians. The Spaniards forced the Indians to work the mines and the land. Lacking immunity to diseases brought from Europe, Indians became ill and died in great numbers. Many others died from mercury poisoning. Mercury was used in Mexico to refine silver. Others died from lack of a good diet. Yet others died in mining and building accidents. From a population of 3 million or more in 1520, the

Indian population in New Spain would shrink to 1½ million in 1650. The story was much the same in Peru.

The Spanish Empire produces great wealth. The Spaniards did not set out to harm the native people of the Americas. Nonetheless, their search for wealth drove them to conquer the homelands of millions of Indians. These conquests meant hardships for the Indians, just as they meant great wealth for Spain. From the mines in New Spain and Peru, Spain got more gold and silver than all the other European countries combined got from the lands they controlled. The Spaniards did set out to convert (change over) the Indians to Christianity. Even the pope, the head of the Catholic Church, got involved. In 1537 the pope declared that the Indians were human and had immortal souls. The invitation to send missionaries to the Indians was clear. Spanish rulers made it their business to spread Christianity. They sent members of Catholic religious orders to serve as missionaries in the Americas. Dominicans, Franciscans, and later Jesuits came to the Americas to save souls.

As for the Spaniards in New Spain and elsewhere in the Americas, they adjusted well to the land. They grew and ate native foods. They adopted many Indian ways as their own. They headed the government and the Church. They ran the mines and the farms. To work in the mines and on the land, they used Indians. In some parts of Spanish America, Spaniards used black slaves imported from Africa to do the work. The Spaniards developed ways of living that allowed them to control the land and the people they had conquered.

Section Review

1. (a) Why did European countries seek new trade routes with the Far East?
    (b) Why did the king and queen of Spain agree in 1492 to sponsor Columbus's voyage?
    (c) Explain why Columbus landed in the Americas.
2. List the reasons for Spain's expansion into the Americas.
3. (a) In what ways was Spanish expansion into the Americas important to Spain?
    (b) What did life under Spanish rule mean to the Indians?
    (c) How did Spaniards adjust to life in Spanish America?

---

2. Who were the first Spanish explorers to enter New Mexico?
Spain explores eastern North America. Spain's good fortune in New Spain and elsewhere encouraged further exploration. The Spaniards turned once more toward Florida and eastern North America. They forgot about the

failures of Ponce de León and others. The dream of new wealth called. In time this dream would bring Spaniards into New Mexico.

In 1528 Pánfilo de Narváez sailed for Florida. With him were 400 men. Upon arrival, they began to hear tales of rich Indian villages in the interior of Florida. They found no gold or silver. Instead, many of them died from fevers or were killed by Indians. The 242 survivors then sailed for Spanish America. Their return trip was a disaster. Three of the five boats they had built sank at the mouth of the Mississippi River. The 80 survivors on the other two boats washed ashore near Galveston Bay in present-day Texas. There Indian villagers took the survivors in and cared for them. By the spring of 1529, however, only 15 remained alive. Among those who survived was Álvar Núñez Cabeza de Vaca. He had served the Narváez expedition as the royal treasurer.

Cabeza de Vaca journeys to New Spain. Cabeza de Vaca survived for a number of reasons. He learned to carry on trade between the inland and coastal Indians of southeast Texas. He insured his own safe passage among the Indians by acting as a healer. All the while, he hoped to find and free any Spaniards who had been made slaves by the Gulf Coast Indians. Cabeza de Vaca believed that he could in time make his way westward to some Spanish settlement.

Cabeza de Vaca's signature

Some time in September 1534 Cabeza de Vaca and three others who had been with Narváez began their march westward. They made their way from one Indian village to the next, acting as healers along the way. They traveled through Texas. They may have traveled through parts of present-day New Mexico and Arizona. Their journey came to an end in April 1536. They had at last reached the northern frontier of New Spain. This party of four brought back the first news of Narváez's ill-fated Florida expedition. They were, it seemed, the only survivors of that expedition. They had walked across two-thirds of the North American continent. Over eight years had passed from the time they had sailed for Florida.

Cabeza de Vaca tells the story of what he saw. Of the four survivors, two played a role in the history of New Mexico. One was Estevan, a black Moor. He would guide the first Spanish expedition into New Mexico. The other was Cabeza de Vaca. He told the Spaniards about the land north of New Spain. This land included New Mexico. Cabeza de Vaca said that in this land he had seen little farming and few settlements of any kind. He said that he had seen beads, turquoise, coral, and some arrowheads made out of "emeralds." He told of having heard about people who lived farther north of where he had traveled. He had heard that these people lived in large houses and traded in turquoise.

The tale told by Cabeza de Vaca was the tale of a poor land. But the Spaniards did not believe him. They had, after all, found great wealth in New

Romantic view of Cabeza de Vaca crossing the Southwest. Actually, the Spaniards wore deerskins

Spain. They had likewise found great wealth in Peru, a land they had just conquered. Might not a city said by Indians to hold great wealth lie farther inland in Florida than Narváez had thought? Might not the Indian villages with the large houses to the northeast of Mexico City be another Peru? The Spaniards asked such questions as they looked at the wealth they had already uncovered in the Americas.

Spaniards dream of finding the seven cities of gold. The Spaniards now began their search for the legendary seven cities of gold. The legend itself was an old one. In the 700s, when the Moors overran Portugal, seven bishops were believed to have fled westward by sea. Somewhere out in the Atlantic Ocean they were said to have set up new church districts in very rich lands. Added to this legend was an Aztec legend. The Aztecs believed that they as a people had come from seven caves far to the north. In addition, there were tales of a land of much gold and silver that lay some forty days' journey to the north. The Spaniards wanted to believe that these legends and tales were true. Acting on their beliefs, they sent out expeditions to solve the mystery of the seven cities.

Spaniards think about expansion northward. One of the people most interested in the lands north of New Spain was Don (a Spanish title of

viceroy: a king's or queen's agent in the New World; New Spain's highest ranking official

respect) Antonio de Mendoza. He was the *viceroy* of New Spain. As viceroy, he served as the king's agent. He was New Spain's highest ranking official. Mendoza had listened to Cabeza de Vaca's first story of what he had seen and heard. This story, the story of a poor land, was quite different from the one Cabeza de Vaca told upon his return to Spain in 1537. In Spain he found wealthy people eager to learn about North America. He began to spread fanciful tales. Soon Cabeza de Vaca had those who listened to him believing that the country he had seen was the richest in the world. Mendoza wanted to find out the truth about the northern lands. So he decided to send a small party northward to learn firsthand about the land there.

Besides the desire for more wealth, the Spaniards had other reasons for their interest in the land north of New Spain. One was the desire for land with people to work it. Land was wealth, and the promise of land appealed to younger sons of wealthy Spaniards. These younger sons could not under Spanish law inherit any land from their fathers. Another reason was the desire to save new souls for the Catholic Church. Still another reason was the desire for adventure.

Mendoza sends a party northward. In March 1539 Mendoza's small party set out. Its task was to gather specific facts about the land to the north. Depending on its report, Mendoza could decide whether or not to send a full-scale expedition northward. The leader of this party, Marcos de Niza, was a member of the Franciscan religious order. Fray (friar) Marcos had been with Francisco Pizarro during the conquest of Peru. Estevan, who had stayed in New Spain, served as guide. (See Special Interest Feature.) Some Indian helpers went along as well.

The party first traveled up the west side of New Spain. It then traveled northeast, across the desert of present-day Arizona. In time Fray Marcos decided to send Estevan on ahead. Fray Marcos told Estevan to mark a trail for the rest of the party. He also told Estevan to make friends with Indians along the way and to look for cities of gold. To keep Fray Marcos informed of his progress, Estevan was to send crosses back to the main party. These crosses, differing in size, were to signal what Estevan had found. A small cross would indicate that he had found nothing of value. A large cross would mean that he had found something of value.

Fray Marcos returns to New Spain with news of golden cities. While still in Arizona, Fray Marcos received from Estevan a very large cross. Fray Marcos was excited over the good news. But before he could catch up with Estevan, Fray Marcos learned that Estevan had been killed. Estevan had been some three days in advance of the main party. He had come upon and entered Hawikuh, one of the Zuni villages. Zuni was just inside present-day

New Mexico near Gallup. The Indians there had killed him. No one knows for sure why he was killed. Some historians believe Estevan may have demanded gifts and favors that the Zunis were not willing to give him. Some suggest he may have worn something offensive, perhaps a gourd rattle like that carried by enemies of the Zunis. Some suggest that Estevan, who was black and wore feathers and rattles, may have looked to the Zunis like a wizard.

No one knows for sure whether Fray Marcos then traveled on to Zuni. He never claimed that he entered Zuni. But he did later claim that he had seen Zuni. He said that Zuni was larger than Mexico City. He said that Zuni contained seven villages. It may have been that Fray Marcos never got close enough to see Zuni. Or it may have been that he saw what he wanted to see. New Mexico's sun shining brightly on the adobe villages at Zuni could have given them a "golden" look. Whatever happened, Fray Marcos rushed back to New Spain. He told Mendoza that he had seen the golden cities. These cities even had a name. They were, said Fray Marcos, called *Cíbola*. Cíbola is a Spanish word for "buffalo cow." It was now the name applied to that area north of New Spain, which the Spaniards believed was very rich.

Mendoza plans a full-scale expedition northward. With Fray Marcos's report in hand, Mendoza acted. The viceroy planned a full-scale expedition to the north. He hurriedly developed his plans. He did so because he knew that Hernando de Soto had sailed for Florida. De Soto was a veteran of

Cíbola: Spanish word that means "buffalo cow"; it was the name applied to the area north of New Spain, which the Spaniards believed was very rich

Ruins at Hawikuh

the conquest of Peru. He had also listened to the tales Cabeza de Vaca told once back in Spain. Excited by these tales, de Soto intended to explore eastern North America. What Mendoza feared was that Florida was close to Cíbola. He feared de Soto would get to Cíbola before Mendoza's own expedition.

The Legend of Estevan

Estevan, a black Moor from northern Africa, had arrived in the Americas as a slave. He had become a free man after showing up in New Spain with Álvar Núñez Cabeza de Vaca. As guide for the Fray Marcos party, Estevan must have enjoyed both his freedom and his role as advance man for the Spaniards who followed. He must have enjoyed as well the reception he received from the Indians he met on his journey northward. His reception at Zuni was, of course, quite different. No one knows exactly what happened there. Nonetheless, it is clear that the Zunis killed Estevan. It is equally clear that Estevan made a lasting impression, for the Zunis still tell the legend of Estevan. The legend goes like this:

> It is to be believed that a long time ago, when roofs lay over the walls of Kya-ki-me [Hawikuh], when smoke hung over the house-tops, and the ladder-rounds were still unbroken in Kya-ki-me [when the Indians still lived in Hawikuh], then the Black Mexicans came from their adobes in Everlasting Summerland [Mexico]. . . . Then and thus was killed by our ancients, right where the stone stands down by the arroyo of Kya-ki-me, one of the Black Mexicans [Estevan], a large man. . . . Then the rest ran away, chased by our grandfathers, and went back toward their country in the Land of Everlasting Summer.

George P. Hammond and Edgar F. Good, *The Adventures of Don Francisco Vásquez de Coronado* (Albuquerque: University of New Mexico Press, 1938), pp. 16 and 17.

Mendoza's choice as leader of his expedition was a young man from western New Spain. The man was Francisco Vásquez de Coronado. He was at that time governor of Nueva Galicia, a western province of New Spain. Both Mendoza and Coronado spent a lot of their own money on the expedition. They spent about 4 million dollars by today's standards. They outfitted the expedition

One section of a mural depicting the Coronado expedition

that Coronado would lead northward. They also outfitted a naval fleet. This fleet was to sail up the Gulf of California with support supplies. It was to look for a waterway to Cíbola.

Coronado reaches Zuni. The group that headed north in February 1540 was large. Fray Marcos served as guide. Five other friars went along as well. There were Indian helpers. There were about 250 horsemen and another 50 or more men on foot. All had weapons. Some had guns. The party took along extra horses, some mules, some cattle, and some sheep. Mendoza sent this party on its way with special orders. He told the members of the party that they were to Christianize rather than kill any Indians they met.

The Coronado expedition spent a hard six months traveling to Zuni. A scouting party, sent out in advance by Mendoza, reached Hawikuh in July 1540. Coronado and some of his men arrived shortly thereafter. One look was all it took for the Spaniards to know that they had not discovered the seven cities. The Indians fought the approaching Spaniards but were no match against Spanish weapons. Coronado took Hawikuh by force, and the Zunis made peace. Once into Zuni, the Spaniards discovered six villages, not seven. They found corn and beans, not gold and emeralds. Fray Marcos, who must have feared for his future, if not his life, scurried back to Mexico City. Coronado felt the only thing left to do was to look elsewhere for the seven cities of gold.

Spaniards explore the West. A disappointed Coronado now sent out small groups. Their task was to learn what they could about the land around them. Having heard of a land called Tusayan, he sent a group under Pedro de Tovar westward. Tovar met up with the Hopi Indians in present-day Arizona. These Spaniards captured the Hopi Villages. They then returned to Hawikuh with no news of riches, but with tales of a great river farther west. To learn about this river, Coronado sent out a group under García López de Cárdenas. These explorers saw a river and a deep canyon. Three in this group tried to climb down to the river. They turned back after going no more than a third of the way down. These were the first Europeans to see what today we know as the Colorado River and the Grand Canyon. Coronado sent a third group under Melchior Díaz to meet the supply ships. Díaz and his men reached the lower Colorado, but the fleet was gone. Under the command of Hernando de Alarcón, the fleet had entered the Colorado River. But when the Spaniards had found no waterway to Cíbola and no trace of Coronado, they had sailed for New Spain.

Coronado and the main party had remained in Hawikuh while all this activity was going on. Based on the reports he got back, Coronado decided

The Coronado expedition probably brought the first modern horses to New Mexico in 1540

70

Ruins at Pecos Pueblo

that no wealth lay to the west. News about the land to the east also helped him decide to look elsewhere. This news came from a resident of the Pecos Pueblo. This man, called by the Spaniards *Bigotes,* meaning "Whiskers," had heard about the Spaniards at Hawikuh. He went to Hawikuh to see them. While there, he told Coronado about the plains and the buffalo to the east. He also told him about Acoma Pueblo and about Tiguex Pueblo on the Rio Grande.

Coronado winters on the Rio Grande. To learn about the things Bigotes had described, Coronado sent out Pedro de Alvarado. Alvarado saw Acoma, Tiguex, Pecos, and the plains. He returned to Hawikuh and suggested that the expedition spend the winter of 1540–41 at Tiguex, a pueblo near present-day Bernalillo. Taking Alvarado's advice, Coronado and his party moved to Tiguex. There they heard new tales of a rich land to the east called Quivira. The teller of these tales was a man from Quivira whom the Spaniards called *El Turco,* meaning "the Turk." El Turco was a captive of the Pecos when Alvarado found him. According to El Turco, Quivira was so rich in gold and silver that the Spaniards would have trouble carrying it home. But with winter setting in, Coronado knew he would have to wait for spring before heading eastward. In the meantime, the Spaniards settled in the earthen houses at Alcanfor, the southernmost Tiguex village.

The Spaniards did not have an easy time there. The Tiguex Indians had been forced to leave Alcanfor. They had been forced to supply the Spaniards with food and blankets. They may have been forced to grant still other favors.

71

Under the weight of these demands, the Tiguex Indians revolted. The fighting was fierce but short-lived. The Indians could not overcome Spanish weapons. The end result was tragic. Two villages lay in ruins, and most of the people in them had died. Coronado had gone against Mendoza's orders. He had killed rather than Christianized the Indians.

The Coronado expedition comes to an end. When spring came, Coronado and some of his men headed eastward across the plains. Their guides were El Turco and Isopete, a Wichita Indian woman. Coronado and his army pushed across the Texas panhandle and into present-day Kansas. In central Kansas they came to the end of their journey. They were near what is now the town of Lyons. There stood the grass houses of the Wichita Indians. Their chief wore a copper plate around his neck because it was the only metal he had. El Turco admitted to having tricked the Spaniards in an effort to help the people of New Mexico get rid of their unwanted guests. He had also, Coronado learned, begun plotting against the Spaniards once he was among the Wichitas. So the Spaniards killed him. Isopete escaped and later met up with de Soto's men. As for Coronado, he now knew he had failed.

Coronado and his men made their way back to the Rio Grande. There they spent the winter of 1541–42. The weather was cold. The sense of failure was great. Coronado himself fell from his horse when the saddle girth broke. A second horse trampled him, leaving him with a serious head injury. By the spring of 1542, Coronado was well enough to travel. So he and his party returned to Mexico City. Three priests remained behind. They hoped to save new souls for the Catholic Church. Instead, all three likely died at the hands of Indians.

The Coronado expedition both fails and succeeds. After a brief stay in Mexico City, Coronado resumed his post as governor of Nueva Galicia. His troubles, however, were far from over. In 1544 he went to court in New Spain on charges that he had mismanaged the expedition. Among other things, the government charged him with great cruelties upon the natives of the land he had explored. It also charged him with misusing government funds and gambling. He was convicted of "general neglect of duty . . . rank favoritism and numerous irregularities." His punishment was a fine. During his legal troubles Coronado had spent some time in jail. The highest court in New Spain in time overturned this conviction. Cleared of the charges against him, Coronado then held a minor post in Mexico City. But he was a broken man. His health gave way. In 1556 Coronado died. He went to his grave knowing that he had failed to find Cíbola or any new riches for Spain.

Still, Coronado and his men had accomplished a number of important things. They were the first Europeans to see the Colorado River and the Grand

Signature of Francisco Vasquez de Coronado.

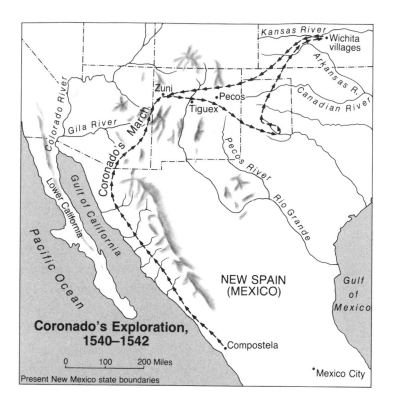

Coronado's Exploration, 1540–1542

0   100   200 Miles

Present New Mexico state boundaries

Canyon. They were the first Europeans to travel through the land of the Pueblos. They were the first Europeans to recognize the continental divide as the watershed it is (page 7). In addition, they explored vast stretches of land north of New Spain. In so doing they added greatly to the geographical knowledge about North America. The information Coronado gathered helped Spaniards plan further advances into New Mexico. Look at the map on this page. There you can see the route that Coronado followed.

Section Review

1. **(a)** How did Cabeza de Vaca make his way back to New Spain after being washed ashore in present-day Texas?
   (b) How did Cabeza de Vaca first describe the land he had seen and heard about?
   (c) How did he describe this land once he returned to Spain?
2. **(a)** Explain the legends and tales of the seven cities of gold.
   (b) Besides wealth, what other reasons did the Spaniards have for wanting to move into the land north of New Spain?
3. **(a)** What was the purpose of Fray Marcos's journey northward, and what did Fray Marcos report back to Mendoza?
   (b) How was the Coronado expedition a failure?
   (c) What did the Coronado expedition accomplish?

73

3. Who were the later Spanish explorers of New Mexico?

The Spaniards take a break from expeditions northward. After Coronado's return to New Spain, the Spaniards did not send any new expeditions northward for 40 years. Coronado's failure to find new riches was part of the reason. There were other reasons as well. For one thing, Spaniards got caught up in a silver rush. New sources of silver were found northwest of Mexico City. People eagerly moved to the north in search of even more silver. For another thing, settlers began to farm lands in northern New Spain. They pushed farther and farther to the north and west.

Yet even in the absence of new expeditions, the Spaniards had never fully lost their interest in the lands still farther north. There were, after all, people with souls living in those lands. The Catholic Church wanted to save their souls. There might also be a water passage through North America somewhere in those northern lands. Europeans had long looked for a waterway to carry them between the Atlantic and Pacific oceans. The Spaniards hoped to be first in finding such a waterway. Finally, the dream of riches in those lands had not totally died out. The recent silver discovery in New Spain merely brought that dream back into the open. Perhaps, some said, there was a rich "new" Mexico somewhere in the interior of the northern lands. More and more, the Spaniards called the northern lands "new Mexico" because of the riches they hoped the lands would hold. The name New Mexico stuck.

Spaniards again head northward. Because of the renewed interest in the northern lands, four expeditions got underway in the 1580s and 1590s. They did not follow the same routes that Fray Marcos had taken. There were two basic reasons for this. (1) The Spaniards had decided that the deserts of eastern Arizona had nothing to offer. So those who traveled northward avoided the path through Arizona. (2) The Spaniards had recently learned of a route that went up the Rio Grande. So most of those who traveled northward after 1580 followed the Rio Grande Valley route.

The first of the four expeditions headed northward in 1581. Its leader was Fray Agustín Rodríguez. Fray Agustín had been stationed at Santa Barbara on the northern edge of Spanish settlement. There he had heard of land to the north with souls to save. Fray Agustín asked for and received permission from the viceroy of New Spain to lead an expedition. He planned to explore the land along the Rio Grande. He further planned to expand the work of the Catholic Church into this area. This area would thus be a new missionary field.

Fray Agustín visits the pueblos of New Mexico. Fray Agustín and his party set out from Santa Barbara. In the party were Fray Agustín and 2 other priests. A military man, Francisco Sánchez Chamuscado, led the 9 soldiers who went along to protect the priests. An Indian servant traveled with

Acoma Pueblo (1900s)

each member of the escort party. Other Indians accompanied the friars. Traveling up the Conchas River and then up the Rio Grande, the party visited the Rio Grande pueblos. They went northward to Taos. To the west, they visited Acoma and Zuni. To the east, they crossed onto the plains and saw the buffalo.

Some members of the party became excited by their findings. One priest left the others to carry news of the expedition's findings back to New Spain. He, however, was killed by the Pueblo Indians. So, too, were the two priests, Fray Agustín and Fray Francisco, who had decided to remain at one of the Tiguex pueblos. The Indians killed them after the soldiers had left. As for the soldiers, some made it home. Chamuscado was not one of them. He died along the way. Those who survived reached New Spain in April 1582. They told about the priests who had stayed behind. They did not, of course, know the fate of these priests. They told about all that they had seen. Their stories stirred the interest of others who thought about going to New Mexico.

The Espejo expedition takes place. Within a year another group of Spaniards headed northward. Leading them was Antonio de Espejo. Espejo had himself put up the money for the expedition. He had hired 14 soldiers to go along. The expedition's first concern was to learn about the well-being of the 2 priests who had stayed in New Mexico the year before. Indeed, Fray Bernardino Beltrán had worked to see that such a search took place. Fray Bernardino traveled with Espejo. Espejo also had his own reasons for leading a group into New Mexico. He hoped to find mines and what he had heard was "a lake of gold."

Espejo and his party soon learned that Fray Agustín and Fray Francisco had been killed. They then searched for mines and the golden lake. They did not find either one, but their search took them westward into present-day Arizona. There they found copper and some silver. All in all, the Espejo party had failed. Nonetheless, Espejo told a good story. His story grew more and more colorful in the telling. It was a story of riches. It was a story that got the attention of those who wanted to search for wealth.

New Mexico attracts more expeditions. The Fray Agustín and Espejo expeditions had excited many Spaniards about the land of New Mexico. They had also attracted the attention of the Spanish ruler. In 1583 King Philip II issued a royal law. This law told the viceroy of New Spain to take actions that would lead to the Spanish settlement of New Mexico. The viceroy was to find someone to settle and to bring peace to New Mexico. This person would, at the same time, oversee the conversion of the Indians to the Catholic faith. But before the official settlement of New Mexico could take place, two other groups entered New Mexico. The first was the group that Gaspar Castaño de Sosa led northward.

Castaño de Sosa decided in 1590 to settle New Mexico on his own. In the absence of the governor of Nuevo Leon, Castaño de Sosa as lieutenant governor had taken charge of that province. He planned the settlement of New

76

Mexico even though he did not have a direct *grant* from the king to do so. A grant meant that the king gave his permission for a certain person to settle certain lands. Still, the letter of the law at that time seemed to require a grant only to settle new lands. Reasoning that New Mexico had been crossed and recrossed by many Spaniards, Castaño de Sosa simply told officials in New Spain of his plans. Then in July 1590 he headed northward.

grant: permission from the king or queen for a certain person to settle certain lands

Castaño de Sosa took with him the people from the small silver-mining town of Almadén. The silver in that town was mostly gone. So Castaño de Sosa tricked the 170 townspeople into believing they would find silver in New Mexico. He allowed them to bring whatever animals they owned. The members of the Castaño de Sosa party reached the Pecos River in October. Two months later they arrived at Pecos Pueblo. Early in January 1591 Castaño de Sosa's soldiers engaged the Pecos people in battle. Even though the Pecos had greater numbers, they were no match for Spanish horses and weapons. After the victory the Castaño de Sosa party explored the Rio Grande pueblos.

New Mexico is at last ready for settlement. Castaño de Sosa saw much of New Mexico. Still, his expedition had from the outset made some officials in New Spain jealous. Fifty soldiers sent to New Mexico by these officials arrested Castaño de Sosa in March 1591. They placed him in chains and returned him to Mexico City. There he stood trial. The government charged him with taking over land inhabited by friendly people and with raising an army. It charged him with trying to settle New Mexico without a direct grant from the king to do so. The court in New Spain found him guilty. As punishment, Castaño de Sosa had to leave the Americas. He died in a shipboard uprising in 1593 while being taken to his place of exile, the Far East. Officials in Spain later cleared Castaño de Sosa, but too late. Had he lived, he might have returned to New Mexico in the official role of governor of that land.

Castaño de Sosa and his party had nonetheless made history. Carts had

77

carried the goods of the would-be settlers over the land that is today New Mexico. They were the first wheeled vehicles to travel over land that would one day be a part of the United States. The Castaño de Sosa party also helped support an ever-more popular idea about New Mexico. This was the idea that New Mexico might be a land worth settling.

The fourth expedition into New Mexico in the late 1500s took place in 1593–94. Its leader was Captain Francisco Leyva de Bonilla. Leyva's motives were not the same as Castaño de Sosa's had been. Rather, Leyva headed northward in pursuit of the age-old dream of wealth. He and his men traveled up the Rio Grande to San Ildefonso, a pueblo near present-day Santa Fe. They stayed at San Ildefonso, living off the Indians. To get rid of their unwanted guests, the Indians there did what other Indians before them had done. They tricked the Spaniards into leaving by telling them of riches elsewhere. The Indians told the story of rich cities on the plains to the east. In other words, they retold the old story about Quivira. The Leyva party fell for the trick and traveled to the east. On the plains the Spaniards in this party met their deaths, most at the hands of Indians. Their journey had come to an end perhaps near where Coronado had ended his travels.

At some later time an Indian servant who had been with Leyva made his way to New Mexico. He told the Spaniards about the fate of the Leyva de Bonilla party. He told his tale, moreover, to the man who led the first official group of Spanish settlers into New Mexico. But the story of settlement belongs in the next chapter. This chapter has been about the Spanish explorers. These explorers were the people who had traveled through New Mexico. They had helped advance the idea that New Mexico was worthy of Spanish settlement.

Section Review

1. (a) Why did the Spaniards not send any new expeditions northward for 40 years?
   (b) Why had the Spaniards remained interested in the land that came to be called New Mexico?

2. (a) What was the purpose of the Fray Agustín expedition, and what was its fate?
   (b) Why did Espejo head northward, and what story did he tell upon his return?

3. (a) What did the royal law of 1583 say?
   (b) What did Castaño de Sosa hope to do, and what became of him?
   (c) What did Leyva hope to do, and what became of his party?
   (d) What idea about New Mexico had the Spanish explorers helped to advance?

Words You Should Know

Find each word in your reading and explain its meaning.

1. compass
2. astrolabe
3. cross staff
4. conquistador
5. viceroy
6. Cíbola
7. grant

Places You Should Be Able to Locate

Be able to locate these places on maps in your book.

1. islands in the Caribbean Sea
2. Central America
3. South America
4. North America
5. Florida
6. Yucatan
7. Gulf of California
8. Mississippi River
9. Pacific Ocean
10. New Spain (Mexico)
11. Mexico City
12. Zuni
13. Colorado River
14. Tiguex
15. Pecos

Facts You Should Remember

Answer the following questions by recalling information presented in this chapter.

1. (a) How was Spain able to claim such a large empire in the Americas?
    (b) How did this empire benefit both the country of Spain and individual Spaniards?

2. (a) What interest did the Catholic Church take in the Indians who lived in Spain's American empire?
    (b) What role did the Spanish rulers play in the spread of Christianity to these Indians?

3. (a) What did the Spanish dreams of the seven cities, Cíbola, Quivira, and a "new" Mexico have in common?
    (b) Where did the Spaniards explore in pursuit of these dreams?
    (c) What did the explorers who traveled into present-day New Mexico actually find?
    (d) How did these explorers help advance the idea that New Mexico was a land worth settling?

4. Who are the following people, and why are they important?

   (a) Christopher Columbus;

   (b) Queen Isabella and King Ferdinand;

   (c) Alonso Álvarez de Pineda;

   (d) Hernando Cortés;

   (e) Álvar Núñez Cabeza de Vaca;

   (f) Estevan;

   (g) Don Antonio de Mendoza;

   (h) Fray Marcos de Niza;

   (i) Francisco Vásquez de Coronado.

Eyewitness to New Mexico's History
A Former Captain General Describes New Mexico, 1639
From: Francisco Martínez de Baeza, "Contributions Are Small" in *Foreigners in their Native Land,* ed. David J. Weber (University of New Mexico Press, 1973), p. 28.

The provinces of New Mexico are distant four hundred leagues, a little more or less from this city [Mexico City]—two hundred of them [containing] settlements of Spaniards and of peaceable Indians [and extending] until one reaches the mines of El Parral, which is the last settlement. The other two hundred leagues, traveling always toward the north, [extend] through unsettled country. It is a land that is very cold in winter and very hot in summer, [that is,] until one reaches the first settlement of the said provinces, which is the pueblo of San Antonio de Senecú. It is distant from the villa of Santa Fé, the capital of these provinces, fifty leagues—all settled with Indians reduced to our holy faith. In this distance there are ten or twelve farms of Spaniards, who plant wheat and maize by irrigating with water which is obtained from the Río del Norte. In the villa of Santa Fé, where the governors live, there are few more than fifty inhabitants, with established homes and families, who form a moderate-sized settlement.

CHAPTER 4

Early Spanish Settlement, 1598–1680

What you will learn in this chapter—

Today people who live in New Mexico are closely tied to people who live in other parts of this country and in far distant places throughout the world. New Mexicans can go to stores and buy foods and other products brought into the state from all over. They can receive mail in a fairly short period of time from people who live thousands of miles away. They can turn on their television sets or their radios and learn instantly what is going on in the rest of the world.

How different life in New Mexico is today from life in New Mexico 300 years ago. Then New Mexico was a remote place. It stood apart from other populated places because of both distance and time. The Indians did not, of course, mind the separation from other groups of people. Indeed, each group of Pueblo Indians had long remained separate even from other Pueblo peoples. The Navajos and the Apache groups had also developed separate and distinct ways of living. But for the Spanish settlers who early came to New Mexico, the separation from other Spaniards removed them from the ways of living they had known. To be sure, the settlers brought their culture with them. Yet New Mexico was neither New Spain nor Spain.

Contacts with New Spain were few and with Spain fewer still. Royal supply caravans from New Spain arrived in Santa Fe with foodstuffs and other products. They brought mail and news from friends and relatives left behind when the settlers moved to New Mexico. They brought visitors. Supply caravans arrived, but a round trip from New Spain took many months. Travel each way lasted 5 to 6 months. A new caravan was supposed to arrive in Santa Fe every 3 years. At times 4 and even 5 years might pass between caravans. So Spanish settlers had to adjust to what they found in New Mexico. They had to be self-sufficient to survive. In this chapter you will learn about these early Spanish settlers and their settlements. As you read, you will find answers to the following questions:

1. What were the first Spanish settlements in New Mexico?
2. What happened during the great missionary period in New Mexico?
3. What was the Pueblo Revolt of 1680?

1. What were the first Spanish settlements in New Mexico?

Oñate is chosen to make the first Spanish settlement. You read in the last chapter about Spanish interest in New Mexico. The Spaniards had, of course, long been interested in the land north of New Spain. They dreamed of finding new riches. They wanted to save souls for the Catholic Church. For these reasons interest grew in New Mexico as a land worthy of settlement. You may recall that the Spanish king had in 1583 told the viceroy of New Spain to find someone to settle New Mexico (page 76). The man chosen to do just that was Don Juan de Oñate.

There were several reasons why Oñate became the person chosen for the first official settlement of New Mexico. For one thing, he came from a wealthy and distinguished family. He had been born in 1552 in New Spain, likely in Zacatecas, a city in the silver-mining district northwest of Mexico City. His father had become rich from the silver mines located nearby. Don Juan de Oñate in time married into a wealthy and powerful family. His wife, Doña

Don Juan de Oñate's coat of arms

Isabel Cortés Tolaso, was a descendant of Hernando Cortés, the conqueror of Mexico. For another thing, Oñate had military experience. He had spent 20 years as a soldier. He had fought many battles against Indians who had resisted the Spanish advances northward from Mexico City. Finally, Oñate was looking for something new and challenging to do. His life had seemed empty since the death of his wife in the 1580s.

Oñate prepares for the settlement of New Mexico. Oñate first asked the viceroy for a contract to settle New Mexico in 1595. After a wait of more than 2 years, Oñate in 1597 got his grant. Along with this grant, he received the titles of governor and captain general of New Mexico. He received as well the right to give out land among the settlers. Oñate could not, however, have undertaken the settlement of New Mexico had he not been wealthy. He had to agree to finance the expedition. He was to pay the expenses of the soldiers and the families. He also had to buy the supplies and the livestock. The government paid only the expenses of those people whose main purpose was to convert Indians to Christianity. This showed that Spain's officials thought that Oñate's first duty was to spread the Catholic faith.

Besides settling New Mexico and saving souls, Oñate had other duties to perform for Spain. He was to explore and map the coasts and harbors of New Mexico. The Spaniards still believed that the Pacific Ocean lay only a short distance westward of the land covered by earlier explorers. He was also to search for an all-water passage through the Americas.

Spaniards settle in New Mexico. Oñate and his party set out from Santa Barbara in northern New Spain. The date was January 26, 1598. In the party were about 400 men. Of these, 130 had wives and children, and 129 were soldiers. In the party as well were 10 Franciscan friars. Two-fifths of these people were originally from Spain. Nearly one-third had been born in New Spain. The rest came from places either not identified or located in other parts of Europe or America. The expedition included 7,000 head of livestock and 83 carts.

Slowly the party pushed toward the Rio Grande. Then they followed its course northward. By the middle of April 1598, they were within 25 miles of present-day El Paso. In time they reached the land of the Piros Indians, who gave them much-needed food and water. The Spaniards named this place *Socorro*. Socorro is a Spanish word that means "succor," or "aid given in time of need or distress." Here Oñate left the main party and moved on with an advance group. This group traveled northward, visiting several Indian villages. Among these villages was San Juan, which stood north of present-day Española. The people of San Juan, said by earlier explorers to be friendly, welcomed the Spaniards.

Site of San Gabriel near Española.
Base reads: "Onate's Capital, 1598,
First in U.S."

San Juan was located in a small valley near the point where the Chama
River flows into the Rio Grande. At San Juan Oñate made the first Spanish
settlement in New Mexico. The date was July 11, 1598. The name given to
this settlement was *San Juan de los Caballeros,* or "San Juan of the gentlemen."
This was the way in which Oñate and the other members of his group saw
themselves. Oñate's main party at last reached San Juan in the middle of August.
Within two weeks the Spaniards had laid the foundation for a church. Within
six months they had moved from San Juan to the west side of the Rio Grande.
This move put some distance between them and the San Juan people. It gave
them a site with room for expansion. On this site the Spaniards built their
second settlement in New Mexico. They called this settlement San Gabriel.
Look at the map on page 87. There you can see the location of the first Spanish
settlements in New Mexico. You can also see the route taken by Oñate.

Life in New Mexico is troubled. From the very outset Spanish
settlers found the land of New Mexico uninviting. Many of them had likely
hoped to find riches. Oñate himself had brought mining equipment along, just
in case he found gold and silver. In fact, the settlers spent much of their time
looking for wealth that was nowhere to be found. They should instead have
worked at living on the land as it was. This story was not, however, a uniquely

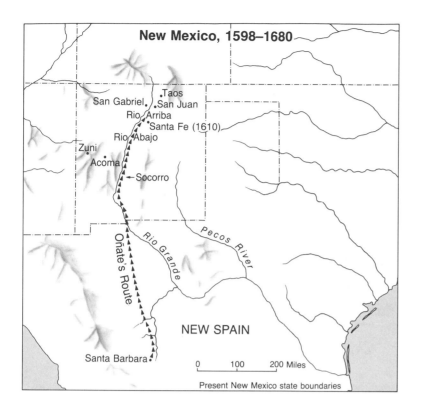

New Mexico, 1598–1680

San Gabriel
Taos
San Juan
Rio Arriba
Santa Fe (1610)
Rio Abajo
Zuni
Acoma
← Socorro

Oñate's Route
Rio Grande
Pecos River

NEW SPAIN

Santa Barbara

0   100   200 Miles

Present New Mexico state boundaries

Spanish story. The story was much the same at Jamestown, Virginia. English settlers in 1607 established Jamestown as the first permanent English settlement in the Americas. There, too, settlers spent their time searching for riches. Captain John Smith saved Jamestown, but only after setting down strict rules by which the settlers would live. Nearly 2,000 miles west of Jamestown, Oñate had acted to save the Spanish settlement in much the same way. He, too, found it necessary to govern the settlers with strict rules. Oñate's rules angered many of the settlers.

The settlers in New Mexico also had early troubles with some of the Indians. The San Juan people remained friendly and helpful. The Acomas, on the other hand, were anything but friendly. They lived in a "sky" village at the top of sheer walls several hundred feet above the plain. The only paths to the top were toeholds dug into the sheer walls. The Acoma people must have felt safe and secure from all other peoples. Late in 1598 they tested the Spaniards. They spied a small group of soldiers heading toward Zuni. Leading this group was Juan de Zaldívar, Oñate's nephew. Zaldívar, on orders from Oñate, was riding to join up with Oñate. Oñate, having visited some of the pueblos east of the Manzanos, had decided to ride westward toward the Pacific Ocean. Now he was riding home, and he wished to meet his nephew on the way. Zaldívar

87

The cliffs at Acoma

and his men never reached Oñate, for the Acomas decided to test Zaldívar's power. They lured most of Zaldívar's men to their sky village, where a fight broke out. Zaldívar was killed. The other Spaniards either died in the fighting or were forced to jump 360 feet to the plain below. At least one died in the fall. As many as three others survived when they landed in the wind-swept sand at the base of the walls.

The Spaniards get revenge. When Oñate got the news, he wept at the loss of his nephew and 10 others. Oñate felt he had no choice but to attack Acoma. If he failed to act, other Indians would feel that the Spaniards were weak. Life in New Mexico would then be impossible. So, on January 12, 1599, the Spanish force got underway. Ten days later 70 soldiers attacked Acoma. On the advice of others Oñate had remained behind at San Gabriel.

Commanding the Spanish forces was Vicente de Zaldívar. His brother had been the leader of those Spaniards killed at Acoma. The fighting on both sides was fierce. The Spaniards overcame the obstacle of having to scale sheer walls to reach the village. However, the Acomas could not overcome Spanish weapons. When the fighting ended, between 600 and 800 Acomas lay dead. Those who survived were taken to Oñate to stand trial. The fate of these captives was terrible indeed. Men and women alike were sentenced to 20 years of work under Spanish supervision. Males over the age of 25 also had one foot cut off. Sixty young girls were sent to Mexico City to live out their lives in Catholic convents. Young people under age 12 escaped punishment but were placed in the care of Catholic priests.

The Oñate venture slowly falls apart. The trouble with the Acomas had begun within 6 months of the Spanish settlement at San Juan. Added to this problem was the failure of the settlers to find riches. A further problem was food. Even though the settlers did some farming, they never produced enough food to supply themselves. Oñate received some additional help from New Spain. Soldiers, some friars, and supplies arrived at San Gabriel in the winter of 1600. This help allowed Oñate to undertake new explorations. Unfortunately, neither the help from New Spain nor Oñate's explorations insured the success of Spanish settlement in New Mexico.

Oñate and his men first explored the land east of San Gabriel. They followed much the same path as that taken by Coronado and Leyva de Bonilla before him. Indeed, their guide was Jusepe, the Indian who told Oñate about the fate of the Leyva party (page 78). Oñate and his 80 men traveled northeast across Oklahoma and into Kansas. They came to the land of Quivira. Quivira had not changed from earlier days. It again failed to yield the wealth promised in the legends. When Oñate returned to San Gabriel, he found the settlement nearly deserted. The settlers had taken advantage of Oñate's 5-month absence. Tired of the hard life and the governor's strict rule, the settlers had made their escape down the Rio Grande.

New Mexico becomes a royal colony. Oñate did not give up yet. He sought support from Spain and New Spain. He again set off to explore the area around New Mexico. This time he went westward. In 1604 Oñate and 30 men expected to find the Pacific Ocean and perhaps the water passage through the Americas. Instead, they reached the Colorado River, which they followed to the Gulf of California. Other hard times followed. At last Oñate gave up. His service in New Mexico had not fulfilled his dreams. He had settled New Mexico. He had not, however, become either famous or rich in the process. Greatly disappointed and much poorer than at the start of his venture, Oñate left office under suspension from the king. He officially resigned as governor and captain general of New Mexico on August 24, 1607.

Nine years had passed from the date of the first Spanish settlement in New Mexico. Spanish officials now looked with dismay at the state of affairs in the colony. For a brief time the king even thought about giving up on New Mexico once and for all. But then came word that the Franciscan friars were having some success. They could already count 8,000 Indian converts to Christianity. To give up on the new converts was out of the question. So on November 1, 1609, the king made New Mexico a *royal colony*. As a royal colony, New

Don Juan de Oñate's signature

royal colony: colony under direct control of the Spanish rulers; New Mexico was a royal colony of Spain beginning in 1609

89

Oñate's carving at Inscription Rock near Grants

Mexico would be under the direct control of the Spanish rulers. They would pay all the expenses of the colony. They would control its future direction. Henceforth, New Mexico would be a colony turned over to the efforts of the friars to save the souls of the Indians. It would be a field for missionary work. The days of looking for riches were gone forever.

Santa Fe becomes the capital of New Mexico. Despite his sense of failure, Oñate had left behind many accomplishments. Chief among them was a Spanish settlement in New Mexico. It was to this settlement that New Mexico's first royal governor, Don Pedro de Peralta, traveled in early 1610. Shortly after his arrival, he moved the settlers from San Gabriel. He moved them to the site where the Spaniards built a new capital—Santa Fe, meaning "Holy Faith" (see the map on page 87). Peralta probably chose the location of Santa Fe for several reasons. (1) It was at the center of many of New Mexico's pueblos. Yet it was far enough removed from all the pueblos that there would be no conflict over who owned the land. (2) It was located along a stream. This stream, the Santa Fe River, brought water down from the Sangre de Cristo ("Blood of Christ") Mountains. (3) The site was attractive. At 7,000 feet the air was clear and cool. The Sangre de Cristos provided the backdrop. The Jemez Mountains stood at the edge of the wide-open view to the west.

Once built, Santa Fe would remain on its original site. It would long remain the center of the non-Indian population of New Mexico. It is today more than 375 years old. It stands as the oldest capital city in the present-day United States. Spanish settlers had had their troubles in New Mexico. Nonetheless, the Spaniards had settled in New Mexico, and in New Mexico they meant to stay.

Section Review

1.   **(a)** Why was Oñate chosen as the person to settle New Mexico?
    (b) What were Oñate's titles, and what duties did he have?
2.   **(a)** Where did the Spaniards make their first settlement in New Mexico?
    (b) When and why did the Spaniards move their settlement to the west side of the Rio Grande?
3.   **(a)** Describe the conflict between the Acoma Indians and the Spaniards.
    (b) What other troubles did the early Spanish settlers in New Mexico have?
4.   **(a)** What events led to Oñate's resignation from office?
    (b) What did it mean for New Mexico to be a royal colony, and what was New Mexico's future as a royal colony expected to be?
    (c) Who was New Mexico's first royal governor, and why did he build Santa Fe on its present-day site?

---

2. What happened during the great missionary period in New Mexico?

The great missionary period begins. From 1610 to 1680 the history of New Mexico was the story of Spanish efforts to Christianize the Indians. In a larger sense the Spaniards tried to remake Indian culture in the Spanish image. They felt that they had a duty to make the Indians practice certain ways of living. According to the Spaniards, the Indians would have to live under Spanish law. They would have to work in the same manner that the Spaniards worked. They would have to dress in the Spanish manner. This meant Indian males would have to wear shirts and pants. Females would have to wear skirts and clothing on their upper bodies. They would have to practice *monogamy,* marriage to one person. Furthermore, they would have to marry in formal Catholic ceremonies. And, of course, the Indians would have to become Christians.

monogamy: marriage to one person; a practice the Spaniards required of New Mexico's Indians

In wanting to change Indian ways of living, the Spaniards never took a close look at Indian life. They never thought that the Indians might have a culture of their own. They never stopped to think, for example, that the Indians' own religion might be as important to them as the Catholic faith was to the Spaniards. In time the Spanish way of ruling New Mexico's Indians would backfire. Indian resentment of their Spanish conquerors would burn like slow embers until finally bursting into flames.

The Spaniards set up missions. The Indians' main contact with Spanish culture came through the *mission*. The mission was a community of Indians who were supposed to obey the mission priest. They were to follow his instructions in matters of religion. They were to obey him as well in worldly matters. Because the Pueblo Indians already lived in towns, the missions grew up at the pueblos. The mission priest moved to the pueblo. He wished to make the Indians who lived in the pueblo turn their attention toward him.

To begin his work, a mission priest first did some preaching of the Catholic faith. He baptized those children who were brought to him. He then viewed these children and the other members of their families as the core of the mission's congregation. Once he had made some converts to Christianity, the mission priest oversaw the building of a church. The first such church might be a temporary structure. In time a more permanent church building appeared in each mission. So, too, living quarters for the priest and other Spaniards were built in each mission.

New Mexico's mission communities are unique. The church and the priest's living quarters at most of the pueblos were located at one side. The pueblos were, of course, already compact living units. There was no place at the center of the pueblo for a large church. The New Mexico mission community, then, differed from most other Spanish missions in North America. Elsewhere the church was at the very center of the mission community. New Mexico's mission priests, though, remained somewhat apart from the Indians. Adding to this separation was another factor. At many of the pueblos a wall was built between the mission buildings and the pueblo. This wall separated the church and the Spanish living quarters from the living space of the Indians.

Despite the location of the mission buildings, the very size of these buildings allowed them to dominate most pueblos. And despite the separation of the mission priests from the Indians, the priests gained control of the pueblos. These priests were Franciscans. New Mexico was one of the Franciscan missionary fields. With each priest lived Spanish soldiers. Together they moved into their living quarters at the pueblo. Together they worked to control the lives of the Indians.

The Franciscans teach religion. The first duty of the priest was to

mission: community of Indians who were supposed to obey the mission priest; a mission system was set up within New Mexico by the Spaniards

Franciscan priest

Mission ruins at Quarai (Salinas National Monument), 1936

teach religion. The priest started out with a few converts. He then expanded his work. He looked for Indians who would memorize parts of the Catholic catechism. This catechism was a handbook of questions and answers for teaching the basic beliefs of the Catholic faith. These Indians were expected to teach others. The priest appointed one Indian to be the catechist. The priest taught this Indian enough Spanish to be able to understand the catechism. This Indian, in turn, helped the priest translate the catechism into the Indian language. For the most part, Franciscan priests made little real effort to learn the language of the Indians. They learned only the words they needed for their work.

In time the mission priest established a religious routine for the pueblo. He led regular prayer sessions. He oversaw the teaching of the basic beliefs of Christianity. He held masses on Sunday. He preached about such Christian moral standards as the importance of formal marriage. He also used visual images to show basic Christian beliefs to the Indians. The Indians saw images of Jesus Christ, the Virgin Mary, and the saints. The priest then asked them to do Christian paintings on the walls of the church. He asked them to put on religious plays. In one group of plays the Indians reenacted the Easter Story. Selected Indians served in a church choir.

The Franciscans oversee Indian labor. Besides teaching religion, the mission priest oversaw the day-to-day life of the mission. He selected one or more Indians to take care of the church. He appointed one or more Indians to make sure that the other Indians came to mass. There were Indians who looked after the horses and the livestock. Other Indians trained as blacksmiths and carpenters. Indians were also assigned to weave cloth, to cook, to garden, and to be servants to the Spaniards.

The mission interior at Isleta Pueblo (about 1950)

The Pueblo Indians were used to hard work. Their irrigation farming had always taken a lot of work. But some of the jobs given them by mission priests must have seemed to be too much work. Under the direction of the priests, for example, the Indians built huge churches. These churches took many adobe bricks made in the Spanish manner. These adobes were molded and quite large. They measured 10 inches wide by 18 inches long and were five inches thick. Each adobe weighed 50 to 60 pounds. With these adobes the Indians built high walls. On top of these walls they laid huge beams called vigas. The vigas supported a roof covered with adobes and topped by a bell tower. These churches took a great deal of hard work. They often took years to build. Other work required by priests must have seemed not only hard but also degrading. Many Indians were forced to work as servants. Still other work was in conflict with Pueblo Indian culture. The priests told Pueblo males to build walls. Wall building was a female task. Those males who obeyed the priests were made fun of by the other Pueblo Indians. Those who refused were punished.

The Franciscans punish those who disobey. Indeed, it must have seemed to the Indians that their work was never done. Besides their work for the mission, the Indians had their own work. They had their fields to care for. They had their families to feed and clothe. Yet the Indians knew that their Spanish conquerors had the upper hand. They knew they would be punished if they disobeyed.

The punishment at the missions in New Mexico tended, in fact, to be quite harsh. It was harsher than at most Spanish missions located elsewhere in North America. For the most part the Spaniards enforced their own rules. Either the priest or the soldiers carried out the punishment. They whipped some of those who broke the rules. Others who disobeyed were placed in stocks. Made of wood, these stocks held the legs of the person being punished. And until stopped by the viceroy in 1620, priests shaved the heads of some males who broke the rules. This punishment was harsh indeed. For Pueblo Indians loss of hair meant loss of self-respect. Some Indians who had their heads shaved ran away from the pueblos.

Franciscans outlaw Pueblo religion. The priests may have acted harshly. Nonetheless, they did what they did in the joint names of Christianity and Spanish culture. They believed in their causes. They enjoyed some success. Pueblo Indians accepted much of the new religion. They adjusted to the rituals. They adopted the saints. Yet, at the same time, the Pueblo Indians fully intended to keep their own religion. After all, Pueblo religion was a part of everything the Pueblo Indians were and did. Had the Franciscans let the Pueblo

Acoma Mission was built with Indian labor

The church bell at
Zia Mission

Indians practice their religion, New Mexico's history might have been different.
But the Franciscans did not.

What the Franciscans did, in effect, was to outlaw Pueblo religion.
They outlawed kachinas. They outlawed religious dancing and singing. Indeed,
they outlawed all Pueblo religious rites. To the Franciscans, Pueblo religion
was devil worship. The Franciscans felt it their right to destroy Pueblo religious
objects. They destroyed kachina masks, costumes, and prayer sticks. They
destroyed religious murals on the walls of kivas and even the kivas themselves.
They reserved their harshest punishment for Pueblo religious leaders. The
Franciscans tried hard to wipe out Pueblo religion. Try as they might, they
succeeded only in driving Pueblo religion into hiding.

Church government grows up in New Mexico. From 1610 to
1680, then, the great mission work in New Mexico went on. A total of about
250 Franciscans served in New Mexico. They began their work among the
northern Rio Grande pueblos. In time they extended their work south along
the Rio Grande. They also extended their work westward to include the Zunis
and, in present-day Arizona, the Hopis.

As a royal colony New Mexico's role as a missionary field was clear.
The missions allowed the Spaniards to bring both Christianity and Spanish
culture to New Mexico. Just as clear was the fact that New Mexico was a large
and distant mission field. It required a great deal of management. It needed
someone to oversee the work of the mission priests. It needed someone to
oversee the Spanish settlers who lived apart from the missions. As a result, two
types of government grew up in New Mexico. One was religious government.
The other was nonreligious, or civil, government. This government oversaw
the day-to-day management of New Mexico as a royal colony. The religious
manager was the *custodio.* The custodio ("custodian") was in charge of all church

custodio: religious manager
of New Mexico during the
Spanish period; in charge of
all church matters

matters. His office was at Santo Domingo. The civil manager was the royal governor. He, of course, had his office in Santa Fe.

Civil government grows up in New Mexico. The royal governor came to his office under appointment from the king or the viceroy. He was in charge of governing the Spanish settlers of New Mexico. He was also in charge of the defense of the area. Because of the distance of Santa Fe from Mexico City, a strong governor could become quite powerful. Under the governor served a number of officials. One was the secretary to the governor. After 1660 another was the lieutenant governor. He served in the region south of Santa Fe. At the local level were officials called *alcaldes mayores*. Their number increased as the Spanish population of New Mexico grew. These local officials acted as judges. They tried to keep the peace by hearing and settling minor disputes. The alcaldes mayores handled problems that developed between the settlers and Indians. They carried out laws that came down from above.

alcalde mayor: local official during the Spanish period; acted as judge and handled local affairs

There were other governmental bodies in Spanish New Mexico besides those discussed above. Two such bodies deserve special mention. One was the *cabildo,* or town council. There were cabildos in many parts of New Spain. New Mexico's one cabildo was in Santa Fe. The people of Santa Fe elected four men to serve in the cabildo. The cabildo advised the governor about matters of concern to the people. The second government body was the *república.* It was the only body under Spanish rule in which the citizens themselves could take part in politics. The república had come to New Mexico with Oñate. Having found no one leader in a pueblo able to speak for all the people, Oñate set up a república in each pueblo. He had allowed the people of each pueblo to elect their own governor and some other officials. He had allowed the Indians to manage some of their local affairs. The king of Spain in 1620 continued this practice. He said that a pueblo would have a governor and other officials. Once picked, each pueblo governor received a cane of office from Spanish officials. (See Special Interest Feature.)

cabildo: town council during the Spanish period; advised the governor about matters of concern to the people

república: government body during the Spanish period; the only body under Spanish rule in which the citizens themselves could take part in politics

A conflict develops between church and state. As a royal colony, then, New Mexico had two kinds of government. One was religious. The other was civil. The two had separate areas of concern. They really had little to do with each other. But the two nonetheless began to fight. The basic fight began over the question of who should control the Indians. The fight grew into a struggle for power. The sticky problem was whether religious leaders or civil leaders would have more power in New Mexico.

To learn more about this conflict, we need to look at the position of the Indians within Spanish New Mexico. Pueblo people were at that time under the control of mission priests. They had to do what the mission priests told them to do. At the same time Indians were subject to Spanish law. And under

The walls of two Franciscan missions at Gran Quivira (Salinas National Monument)

encomienda: system under which Spanish soldiers were given Indians to care for and to oversee; in exchange for this the soldiers received favors from the Indians

tribute: payment by Indians to the Spaniards; often one bushel of corn and one blanket each year

Spanish law they had basic duties to perform. These duties were the result of the *encomienda* system. Under this system certain settlers were given Indians to care for and to oversee. In return, these settlers served the Spanish rulers. The Spanish rulers used the encomienda system as a way to defend New Mexico. The persons granted encomiendas became part-time soldiers. In return for their military service, they collected *tribute* from the Indians rather than pay from the king. Indians in the Rio Grande Valley had to pay tribute after they had been under Spanish rule for 10 years. The Zunis and Hopis did not pay tribute. They had received this freedom from the king in 1621 because they lived on the edge of Spanish missionary work. The first mission priest did not arrive in Zuni until 1629. In time tribute became the payment each year of one bushel of corn and one other item such as a blanket. During good years the Indians had few problems paying such a tax. In bad years the tax was a real hardship for the Indians.

The Pueblo Governors' Canes

During the 1600s a practice began that continues to this very day. The person who served as governor of each pueblo had a cane. This cane showed that person's authority to serve as governor. Under Spanish rule, the governor of each pueblo received a cane from the Spanish government.

The Spanish cane had a metal top. In this metal was carved the Spanish cross.

In time New Mexico became a territory first of Mexico and then of the United States. Under Mexican rule the pueblo governors received new canes. The Mexican government wanted the office of pueblo governor to continue as it had under Spanish rule. The Mexican canes were topped with silver. Now pueblo governors had two canes to show their authority. A third cane was the gift of President Abraham Lincoln. At that time New Mexico had been a territory of the United States for more than 10 years. This new cane was ebony black. Its top, made of silver, bore the president's name, "A. Lincoln."

Today pueblo governors still use their canes of office to show their authority. They bring their canes to public events. Most pueblo governors, however, have only two of the three canes. They have kept the Spanish and Lincoln canes. The Mexican canes were apparently either given to lieutenant governors or were simply lost.

A second duty of Indians under the encomienda system was a kind of forced labor. Persons granted encomiendas could make Indians work for them on the land that the Spaniards owned. Under the law Spaniards were to pay for this labor. The labor was to be for a limited time. In practice many Spaniards paid Indians little or nothing for their labor. Also they either demanded too much time or wanted the Indians when they needed to be working on their own land.

Spanish control over the Indians is weakened. The Franciscans accepted these two duties put upon the Indians. They had to. Both were a part of Spanish law. What the Franciscans did not willingly accept was what they saw as a threat to their power. The priests disliked any efforts by civil officials to influence pueblo affairs. They objected, for example, when civil officials played an active part in pueblo elections. They felt civil officials were trying to insure that the Indians elected pueblo officeholders friendly to them. The Franciscans were right. Civil officials did try to sway the outcomes of pueblo elections. But then, so did the Franciscans. The fact is that the Franciscans wanted total control over the pueblos. In 1620 the viceroy ordered a halt to any outside interference in pueblo elections. Nobody in New Mexico paid much attention to this order.

The conflict between church and state officials was not good for the peaceful rule of New Mexico. It also confused the Indians. How could the Indians believe their priest when the royal governor called him a liar? This happened during the late 1630s. Early in 1640 the royal governor expelled all churchmen from Santa Fe. He then attacked 2 priests who returned to Santa Fe in peace. He beat them with a stick. He later vandalized some of the Franciscan churches. This same governor and some later royal governors abused the tribute system. They made the Indians produce more tribute than that required by the king. They made Indians weave cloth and gather piñon nuts, salt, and other goods for the governor's private trade. They made Pueblo people trade with other Indians for buffalo hides.

Some royal governors, then, used their power unwisely. They created tension between the Spanish and Indian populations. But even more damaging to Spanish-Indian relations was the conflict between church and state. This conflict led the Pueblo Indians to believe that Spanish power was weak. This conflict in time helped cause a breakdown in Spanish control over the Indian population of New Mexico.

Section Review

1. (a) Explain how the Spaniards tried to remake Indian culture.
    (b) How much attention did the Spaniards pay to the Indians' own culture?

2. (a) What was a mission, and why were the missions important to the Spaniards?
    (b) How did New Mexico's missions differ from other Spanish missions?

3. (a) How did the Franciscans teach religion to New Mexico's Indians?
    (b) What labor were Indians required to do for mission priests?
    (c) How were Indians who refused to obey the priests punished?
    (d) What was the reaction of the Franciscans to the Pueblo Indian religion?

4. (a) Describe church government in New Mexico at this time.
    (b) Describe civil government.

5. (a) Under Spanish law what could Spaniards who had been granted encomiendas require of the Indians?
    (b) Why did church officials and state officials fight with each other?
    (c) What did the conflict between church and state lead to?

3. What was the Pueblo Revolt of 1680?

Indians suffer under Spanish rule. Life in New Mexico during the 1600s was hard. No group of people had an easy time. Still, the Indians had the hardest time. There were several reasons for this. One was that Indian people had to work not only for themselves but also for the Spaniards. Another was that the Pueblo peoples were not immune to the diseases that came with the priests and new settlers. Smallpox, measles, whooping cough, and other diseases took an awful toll. In 1640 alone, about 3,000 Pueblo Indians died from smallpox. This was more than 10 percent of the total Pueblo population. Another reason was a change in the weather. After 1650 New Mexico became much drier. As time passed, conditions grew worse and worse. From 1667 to 1672, there was an extended period of drought and bad crops. Starvation became commonplace among the Indians. In the 1670s entire pueblos, like the one at Humanas, were abandoned. At Humanas 450 Indians had died from starvation. Today Salinas National Monument reminds us that there once was a Humanas Pueblo. Still another reason was the raids of Athabascan peoples on the pueblos. The Spaniards were not able to stop these raids.

So the Indians suffered. Under the watchful eyes of the Franciscans, they could not even do their rain dances, rites basic to their religion. At first they made little effort to regain control of their own lives. To act effectively the Pueblo Indians would have to unite. They would have to find a way to work together. This would not be easy for the pueblos. After all, each pueblo had long remained separate and independent from the other pueblos. And yet the pueblos finally did unite. They united at last because of renewed efforts by the Spaniards to destroy anything and anyone that was a part of Pueblo Indian religion.

Spaniards crack down on Pueblo religion. The new attacks on Pueblo religion came in the 1670s. The leaders of church and state had put aside their quarrels. This meant the priests could focus their attention on religion and on the pueblos. It also meant that the priests could rely on civil officials to help them with their work. The priests were determined that the Pueblo peoples would practice the Catholic faith and only the Catholic faith.

To enforce their religion the mission priests did whatever they thought was needed. In 1673, for example, they called upon the royal governor to arrest certain Pueblo Indian religious leaders. To the Spaniards, of course, these men were devil worshippers. The royal governor did what he was asked. He sent soldiers into the pueblos and arrested 47 Pueblo medicine men. The soldiers took the captives to Santa Fe. There Spaniards dealt harshly with the medicine men. They hanged 3. (One Indian hanged himself.) They then whipped and jailed the rest.

The Pueblo Revolt is planned. After they had returned with their captives to Santa Fe, the soldiers rode off to fight the Apaches. In the absence of these soldiers, some Indians from pueblos north of the capital took bold action. They came into Santa Fe. They demanded the release of the Pueblo

religious leaders. With no soldiers to support him the governor gave in. He released the captives. Among those released was a young San Juan Pueblo man, Popé.

Over the next five years, Pueblo peoples would think about what they had learned. United they could likely defeat the Spaniards. United they could likely drive these newcomers out of New Mexico. A united action against these people would take careful planning. It would take secrecy. It would take leadership. Popé, who moved to Taos after being freed from prison, became one of the leaders. There were other leaders as well. Together they planned a Pueblo war against the Spaniards.

Spaniards learn of the plans. The day the Pueblo leaders chose for the start of this war was August 11, 1680. To let each pueblo know the date, runners carried knotted yucca cords among the pueblos. Each day one of the knots would be untied. The number of knots left would tell how many days remained until the start of the fighting. Secrecy was vital. Popé even killed his own son-in-law when he began to doubt the young man's loyalty to the Indian cause.

Pueblo people as far south as Isleta got the message. So, too, in time did the Spaniards. Some settlers learned about the plans for the revolt on August 9. However, they got the date wrong. Whatever the date was to have been, it was already too late for the settlers. The Pueblo Indians attacked before the settlers could find the means to defend themselves.

The revolt begins. Knowing that the Spaniards had learned of their plans, the Pueblo Indians began their attack before August 11. One Spaniard was killed on August 9. The full fury of the revolt then began to be felt on August 10. Everywhere the Indians struck out at the Spaniards the story was the same. The Tesuque people quickly killed 30 Spanish settlers. Indians from Taos killed about 70 Spaniards, including settlers and mission priests in Taos Valley. Some settlers from Galisteo Valley took refuge in Galisteo Pueblo, a pueblo that had not joined in the revolt. But even these settlers died in the revolt. Other settlers from Galisteo Valley and some from north of Tesuque Pueblo fled to Santa Fe.

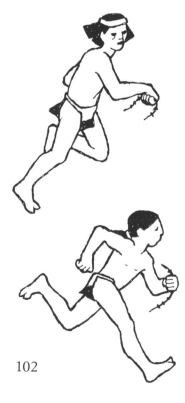

Settlers who lived in the area of the Rio Arriba suffered the greatest losses. The Rio Arriba was the area "up the river" from Santa Fe. There were other settlers who lived south of the lava cliff named La Bajada, meaning "the descent." These people lived in the area of the Rio Abajo. They lived "down the river" from Santa Fe. Look at the map on page 87. There you can see the locations of the Rio Arriba and the Rio Abajo. The Rio Abajo settlers also suffered loss of life and property. But the survivors from the Rio Abajo found a way out of the fighting. More than 1,000 refugees gathered at Isleta, a pueblo that had not joined the revolt. They remained at Isleta for a time. Their leader was Alonzo S. García, the lieutenant governor of New Mexico.

The Spaniards are defeated. In the meantime, fighting in the north centered around Santa Fe. Santa Fe in 1680 was the only real Spanish town in New Mexico. By August 15 the Indians had the town surrounded, but the Spaniards did not give up. Under the leadership of Governor Antonio de Otermín, they fought hard. Some of the Spaniards went out from the town a number of times. They went out to fight. They went out to get water once the Indians cut off the town's water supply. Each time the Spaniards ventured forth, they defeated the Indians. Still, the Spanish position seemed hopeless. The news about settlers living in the Rio Abajo was bad. There was no hope of getting new supplies or more soldiers. So on August 22 Governor Otermín decided to give up Santa Fe.

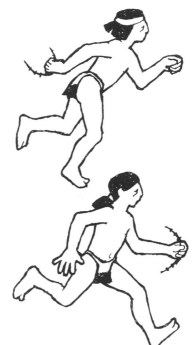

The Spaniards left Santa Fe and headed south. The Indians let the Spaniards go. The Indians' goal had been to get rid of the newcomers. They had accomplished their purpose. Meanwhile, Lieutenant Governor García and his party left Isleta. They headed toward El Paso. In early September the García party learned two things. (1) They heard that a supply train had left El Paso on August 20 and was heading toward them. (2) They learned that Spanish survivors from Santa Fe were also heading toward them. Indeed, Governor Otermín sent word that the García party was to wait for the group from Santa Fe.

The Spaniards leave New Mexico. By this time the party led by García had traveled to a point far south of Socorro. García left the main party there. He and a few soldiers went northward until they met up with Otermín just north of Socorro. Otermín at first placed García under arrest. He felt García had too quickly vacated the Rio Abajo. Once he knew the whole story, Otermín agreed that García had done the right thing. Soon the two groups of survivors joined forces. Together they traveled to El Paso and out of present-day New Mexico.

The Pueblo Revolt had taken quite a toll. At the outbreak of the revolt nearly 2,900 Spanish colonists lived in New Mexico. Of these, almost 400 settlers had lost their lives in the fighting. Twenty-one out of the 33 mission priests were killed. Some 375 settlers also died. More than two-thirds of the Spaniards who died in the revolt had lived in the Rio Arriba. The total would have been higher had the Pueblo peoples not been content with merely driving the Spaniards from New Mexico. It was the missions and their churches that felt the full anger of the Indians. The missions had stood as the proud achievement of the Spaniards. They had been the reason why the Spaniards had stayed in New Mexico. Within a matter of days the Pueblo Indians had destroyed nearly all the missions. The great missionary period had come to an end.

The first attempt at reconquest fails. Once in El Paso, Otermín waited for orders from the viceroy. The question for the Spaniards was whether they would try to regain control of New Mexico. With the Spaniards gone from New Mexico, the Pueblo peoples lost their need and desire for unity. Each pueblo once again became a separate unit. Changes in pueblo life did, nonetheless, take place. The Pueblo people in the Galisteo Valley moved from the valley because of Apache raids. Some Pueblo peoples in the Rio Grande Valley left their villages. Aware of the likely return of the Spaniards, these Indians resettled on mesas.

In 1681 Otermín received his orders. He was to return to New Mexico. In the party that headed northward were 146 soldiers. Many of the pueblos Otermín visited were abandoned. The Spaniards, then, had to be content with burning kivas and destroying whatever the Indians had left behind. At Zia Pueblo the people put up a fight but were easily defeated. Otermín's party then moved southward to Isleta, a pueblo that had remained loyal to Spanish rule. They burned Isleta. They allowed friendly Indians to go with them to El Paso. Among these Indian refugees were the Piros, who had also remained loyal to Spanish rule. The refugees never returned to their former homes in New Mexico. Instead, they began new lives for themselves near El Paso. One of the four settlements built to house them was named Isleta del Sur, meaning "Isleta of the South."

Otermín had failed to reconquer New Mexico. Two expeditions later in the 1680s failed as well. For the Spaniards the Pueblo Revolt had been a major defeat. Nowhere else in the Americas did the Indians succeed in driving out their European conquerors. The reconquest of New Mexico would have to await some other day.

Section Review

1. In what ways had the lives of the Pueblo people been hard during the 1600s?

2. **(a)** What actions by the Spaniards caused the Pueblo people to unite?
   (b) How did the leaders of the revolt let the pueblos know when the revolt was to begin?

3. **(a)** What did the settlers from the Rio Abajo do to get away from the fighting?
   (b) At what point did Governor Otermín and the people from the Rio Arriba abandon Santa Fe?

4. **(a)** Describe the Spanish attempts to reconquer New Mexico during the 1680s.
   (b) Why was the Pueblo Revolt a major defeat for the Spaniards?

Words You Should Know

Find each word in your reading and explain its meaning.

1. royal colony
2. monogamy
3. mission
4. *custodio*
5. *alcaldes mayores*

6. *cabildo*
7. *república*
8. *encomienda*
9. tribute

Places You Should Be Able to Locate

Be able to locate these places on the maps in your book.

1. Santa Barbara
2. Socorro
3. San Juan
4. San Gabriel
5. Acoma Pueblo

6. Santa Fe
7. Zuni Pueblo
8. Taos Pueblo
9. Rio Arriba
10. Rio Abajo

Facts You Should Remember

Answer the following questions by recalling information presented in this chapter.

1.   **(a)** What were the first 3 Spanish settlements in New Mexico, and where were they located?
   (b) Why did the king of Spain make New Mexico a royal colony?
2.   Give a brief description of the mission system in New Mexico as set up and controlled by the Franciscans.
3.   Why was the conflict between church and state bad for Spanish rule in New Mexico?
4.   **(a)** How had Pueblo Indian ways of living changed under Spanish rule?
   (b) What did the Pueblo people accomplish by their revolt?
5.   Who are the following people, and why are they important?
   (a) Don Juan de Oñate;
   (b) Juan and Vicente de Zaldívar;
   (c) Don Pedro de Peralta;
   (d) Popé;
   (e) Alonzo S. García;
   (f) Antonio de Otermín.

105

Unit Summary

Soon after Christopher Columbus reached the Americas, Spain began to build an American empire. This empire included the islands in the Caribbean, Central America, and most of South America. It also included parts of North America, first Mexico and then parts of the present-day United States. Spain's American empire produced much wealth. It produced as well a mission field for Catholic priests. They worked hard to convert the Indians of America to Catholic Christianity.

Having found great wealth in lands already conquered, the Spaniards hoped to find even more riches elsewhere. Spanish explorers first led expeditions into Florida and, in time, into present-day New Mexico. One Spaniard, Alvar Núñez Cabeza de Vaca, had seen much of the land to the north of New Spain. The land he had seen held no riches. Nonetheless, the Spaniards still believed that the northern lands held gold and silver and perhaps even the legendary "seven cities of gold."

The viceroy of New Spain, Don Antonio de Mendoza, sent two expeditions northward. The first, headed by Marcos de Niza, set out in 1539. This party crossed Arizona and traveled to Zuni just inside New Mexico. Fray Marcos mistakenly reported to Mendoza that he had found Cíbola, a land of riches. The second, headed by Francisco Vásquez de Coronado, was a much larger expedition. Coronado left New Spain in 1540 and did not return until 1542. Coronado explored much of New Mexico and Arizona and marched across the plains into present-day Kansas. Coronado had accomplished much. Still, he had failed to find new riches. Later explorers similarly failed to find the legendary wealth that the Spaniards so very much wanted.

At last the Spaniards settled New Mexico. Don Juan de Oñate and his party made the first Spanish settlement at San Juan in 1598. They later moved to a site that they named San Gabriel. But life in New Mexico was hard. The Spaniards had trouble with the Acoma Indians. They found no gold or silver. The settlers also resented Oñate's strict rule, and most of them returned to New Spain in his absence.

In 1609 the king declared New Mexico a royal colony. As a royal colony, it was to be a great mission field. Santa Fe became the new capital. Franciscan mission priests went about the work of converting the Indians to the Catholic faith. The great missionary period lasted from 1610 to 1680.

The Franciscan priests during this period set up missions at pueblos throughout New Mexico. In time they controlled the lives of the Indians. But two major problems also surfaced. One was the conflict between the officials of the church and the officials of the state. The other was the harsh crackdown on Pueblo religion. The result was the Pueblo Revolt of 1680. The Indians defeated their conquerors and drove them from New Mexico.

Time Line:
New Mexico Is the Home of Hispanic Culture

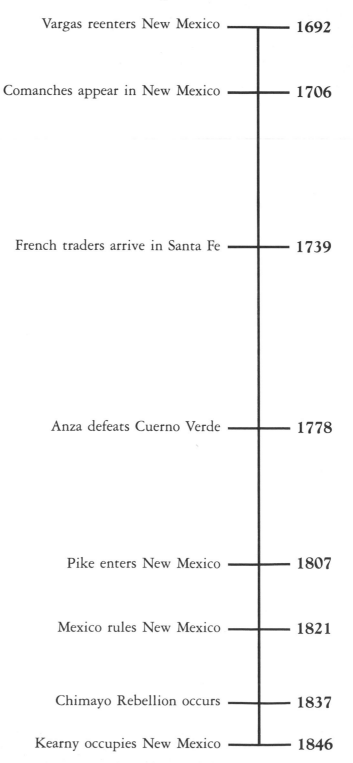

Vargas reenters New Mexico —— **1692**

Comanches appear in New Mexico —— **1706**

French traders arrive in Santa Fe —— **1739**

Anza defeats Cuerno Verde —— **1778**

Pike enters New Mexico —— **1807**

Mexico rules New Mexico —— **1821**

Chimayo Rebellion occurs —— **1837**

Kearny occupies New Mexico —— **1846**

UNIT THREE

New Mexico Is the Home of Hispanic Culture

New Mexico has long been a land of different cultures. It has been a land where people from different cultures have helped shape the state that we know today. In Unit One you learned about New Mexico's Indian cultures. In Unit Two you learned about the culture brought to New Mexico by early Spanish settlers. In this unit you will study the Hispanic culture in New Mexico from 1692 until well into the 1800s. By Hispanic culture we mean the ways of living introduced into New Mexico by people whose ancestors came from Spain. With the passage of time, these ways of living became uniquely New Mexican. These ways of living helped define the heritage that belongs to all the people who live in New Mexico today. In chapter 5 you will read about New Mexico under Spanish rule following the Spaniards' return to New Mexico after the Pueblo Revolt. In chapter 6 you will read about life in New Mexico's Spanish communities. In chapter 7 you will read about New Mexico under Mexican rule after it became part of a newly independent Mexico.

Eyewitness to New Mexico's History
Vargas's Account of the Reconquest of Taos, 1692

From: J. Manuel Espinosa, *First Expedition of Vargas into New Mexico, 1692* (University of New Mexico Press, 1940), pp. 150–51.

After about an hour had passed, an Indian, sent by the said Don Luis, came to notify me that the inhabitants of this pueblo of Taos had been discovered and that they were in an *embudo* [a canyon shaped like a funnel] which is located in the center and at the entrance to the said mountain, on the peaks of which some of the said Taos rebels were stationed as sentinels. With this information, and without further waiting for the horses, I and the troops, on the same horses, immediately set out for the said place. At the foot of the said sierra, an intelligent rebel Indian arrived; having been asked his name he said that it was Josephillo and that he was nicknamed "the Spaniard." I embraced him and gave him my hand, telling him that the people of his pueblo had done wrong in having gone to the sierra to suffer much cold and snow, abandoning their homes, and that he should tell them this; that I had come to pardon them, and that the king, our lord, had sent me for this purpose, and that was why I had brought with me the image of the Blessed Virgin on the royal banner; that he should tell them this; that I had come only for this reason and that they again become Christians, which was the reason why I had brought with me the fathers to absolve them and baptize their children and such other persons as had not been baptized. He understood everything. After I had told him many other things, I told him to go and tell all this to them. In order that they might more readily believe him, I gave him a rosary, which I placed about his neck, and he left.

CHAPTER 5

New Mexico under Spanish Rule, 1692–1821

What you will learn in this chapter—

Today we know that the Spaniards returned to New Mexico after the Pueblo Revolt. We know this because of the constant reminders of Spanish influence in New Mexico. People, place names, building styles, and so many of our ways of living remind us daily of New Mexico's Hispanic heritage.

Near the end of the 1600s, however, New Mexico's future under Spanish rule was not at all certain. In their revolt against the Spaniards, the Pueblo Indians reclaimed the land that is New Mexico. The Spaniards had to decide whether it was worth the effort to reconquer the area. They had to decide what the future of New Mexico as a Spanish colony would be, if indeed the reconquest took place. In this chapter you will learn about the Spanish reconquest of New Mexico and about New Mexico as a Spanish colony from 1692 to 1821. As you read, you will find answers to the following questions:

1. How did the Spaniards reconquer New Mexico?
2. How was New Mexico threatened by outside forces?

1. How did the Spaniards reconquer New Mexico?

The Spaniards decide to return to New Mexico. At the end of the last chapter, you read about the first attempts by the Spaniards to reconquer New Mexico (page 104). Otermín's attempt failed. Two later expeditions in the 1680s likewise failed. For the Spaniards, the question became one of whether to try again to reconquer the area. In time the Spaniards decided that such a reconquest would have to take place.

The Spaniards based their decision to return to New Mexico on a number of factors. First, the Spaniards needed a *buffer zone*. This buffer zone would add an outer layer of protection to New Spain. It would help protect settlements in what is today northern Mexico against Indian raids. Second, there was the long-standing Spanish desire to Christianize the Indians. The Spaniards felt the need to return the Indians of New Mexico to the Catholic faith. Third,

buffer zone: outer layer of protection for a people or country; New Mexico was a buffer zone for New Spain

111

Spain's standing in the Americas was threatened. Spanish pride called for a return to New Mexico. There was also a growing fear that other European nations might threaten Spanish settlements in North America. A French explorer, René Robert Cavelier, Sieur de la Salle, traveled down the Mississippi River to its mouth in 1682. La Salle claimed for France the entire Mississippi River. This river runs, of course, through the heart of the present-day United States. The French claim to the Mississippi divided Spanish Florida from other lands claimed by Spain in what is today the United States. These lands, extending from present-day Texas westward to the Pacific Ocean, included New Mexico.

Vargas becomes governor of New Mexico. The man destined to reconquer New Mexico was Don Diego de Vargas. Vargas received his appointment as governor and captain general of New Mexico in 1688. He arrived in El Paso and took over his office in early 1691. To his new office Vargas brought both honor and courage. He was the head of one of Spain's leading families. He had fought with Spanish armies in Europe before moving to the Americas. In New Spain he held a series of political offices. As the new governor of New Mexico, he began his term of office by working to make El Paso a safe place to live for its 1,000 residents. Vargas did this by defeating the Indians who raided the settlement. He then set about his next goal. This was the task of reconquering New Mexico.

Vargas headed north from El Paso in August 1692. With him were 60 soldiers and 100 Indian helpers. Vargas's plan was to retake the Pueblo country by peaceful means. Under this plan his party would approach each pueblo. No shots would be fired. Instead, the party would announce its presence and ask the Indians to join again the Catholic Church and to live again under Spanish rule. The priests in the party would then forgive the Indians' sins. They would baptize any children born since the Pueblo Revolt. If each pueblo, in turn, accepted the peaceful terms offered by the Spaniards, the reconquest would be bloodless. Resistance by the pueblos would mean bloodshed. Vargas brought two cannons along. He was fully prepared to fight if forced to do so.

The reconquest is peaceful. As the Spaniards pushed up the Rio Grande, they found one abandoned pueblo after another. The Indians had moved to better-protected areas. The Spaniards then traveled on to Santa Fe. They arrived there after dark on September 13. They found that Santa Fe was occupied by a group of Pueblo Indians. The Spaniards announced who they were, but the Indians did not at first believe them. The Indians feared that the party outside the gates was an Apache or Pecos party. Even after they knew that the Spaniards had indeed returned, the Indians shouted out their intentions to fight. At dawn Vargas rode forward. He offered peace and a full pardon. He

Don Diego de Vargas

told the Indians they would be returned to the Catholic faith. The Indians still were ready to resist. So the Spaniards trained their cannons on the town and lined up to attack. Only then did the Indians agree to peaceful surrender. By nightfall the Spaniards had completed their reconquest of New Mexico's capital.

The next morning Vargas and the friars entered Santa Fe. Three times the Spaniards raised the royal banner. It was the same banner brought into New Mexico by Oñate in 1598 and carried out of New Mexico by Otermín in 1680. Each time the banner was raised, the Indians repeated after Vargas, "Long live the king." The friars then forgave the Indians their sins.

In the days that followed, the Spaniards saw more signs of Indian acceptance of renewed Spanish rule. Some of the governors from nearby pueblos arrived in Santa Fe to pledge their loyalty. Then in late September, Vargas and his men left Santa Fe. They visited all the northern pueblos. They made peace with each pueblo, although there were some tense moments. The reconquest of the Rio Grande Valley was now complete. Near the end of October Vargas sent the main party southward to El Paso. In this party were the cannons, the

carts, and some of the soldiers. Also going along were Spaniards that Vargas had freed from captivity. These Spaniards had been held captive since the Pueblo Revolt.

Once the main party had left, Vargas and some of his men headed to the western pueblos. These people were said to be preparing to fight the Spaniards. Each pueblo put up some resistance, but no major fighting broke out. With great courage Vargas walked among and talked to the Pueblo peoples of western New Mexico. He got them to agree to Spanish presence in New Mexico.

Vargas plans the resettlement of New Mexico. Vargas and his men at last returned to El Paso. On their way back they were attacked by a group of Apaches. The Spaniards captured and killed two Apaches. One of them died after he had converted to Christianity. These Apaches were the only two Indians to die in this first effort by Vargas to reconquer New Mexico. During the 4-month adventure, not a single soldier had been killed. Vargas had showed what a wise leader he was in other ways as well. He had reconquered 23 pueblos without firing a shot. He had burned not a single kiva or pueblo storehouse. Having apparently reconquered the area, Vargas now planned the resettlement of New Mexico.

Vargas and his men returned to El Paso on December 20, 1692. Almost 10 months later Vargas led a group of settlers northward. They left El Paso on October 4, 1693. Vargas had wanted to set up a presidio (fort) of 100 soldiers and a colony of 500 settlers at Santa Fe. In the actual party that traveled northward were 100 soldiers, 70 families, and 18 friars. There were, in addition, some 2,000 horses, 1,000 mules, and 900 head of cattle. There were also 3 cannons this time, instead of 2, and a total of 18 carts. A large number of friendly Indians went along as well.

Vargas reconquers New Mexico a second time. As the settlers advanced northward, Vargas and a small group rode ahead of the main party. They wanted to find out what mood the Indians were in. During the almost year-long absence of the Spaniards, most of the pueblos had become unfriendly. Learning this, Vargas returned to the main party. He found that 30 women and children had died. They had died as the party crossed the area south of Socorro named the Jornada del Muerto, meaning "Journey of the Dead Man." (See Special Interest Feature.) The party pushed on to Santa Fe. They arrived there on December 16. Finding some Indians inside the town, Vargas entered the capital and formally reclaimed it for Spain. The Spaniards then camped outside the town. They waited for the Indians to leave.

It soon became clear that the Indians planned to stay in Santa Fe. During the two weeks that followed the arrival of the Vargas party, 21 Spaniards died. The cold, snowy camp outside the town had taken its toll. During the same period the Indians inside Santa Fe had made preparations to defend their position. On December 28 the Indians dared the Spaniards to attack. The Spaniards accepted the challenge. They attacked and on December 30 captured the town. A total of 81 Indians died in the fighting. Another 70 were executed on orders from Vargas. Still another 400 Indians were taken captive. The Spaniards reentered Santa Fe. They had a capital city. But beyond Santa Fe the land and its people would have to be conquered once again.

Jornada del Muerto

To those who traveled into New Mexico from the south, the journey was both long and hard. But one part of the journey was especially difficult. This was the crossing of a stretch of land the Spaniards named Jornada del Muerto. This Spanish name translates as the "Journey of the Dead Man."

The Jornada lay in what is today southern New Mexico. It was part of the trail that stretched from Chihuahua to Santa Fe. The Jornada was almost 90 miles long. It ran from present-day Rincon to present-day San Marcial. On the east were the San Andres Mountains. On the west were the Caballo and Fray Cristobal ranges. The main geographical feature of the area was its total lack of water.

Travelers heading north into New Mexico could avoid the Jornada. However, few travelers did so. To bypass the Jornada added at least an extra day to the already long trip. Crossing the Jornada under the best of conditions was hard. Under the worst of conditions the crossing took a heavy toll in lives. Many men, women, and children died as a result of the harsh nature of the land. Some others died at the hands of Indians who hid in the mountains or arroyos along the trail. All told, hundreds lost their lives in the Jornada del Muerto. The memory of those lost lives lingers on. Historians and other writers have recorded the stories of those brave people who died. And even present-day maps carry a reminder of that difficult journey. The name that is still applied to the stretch of land in southern New Mexico is Jornada del Muerto.

The Pueblo Indians resist Spanish rule. Bringing peace to the land was not an easy task. The Spaniards learned this fact in the years that followed. For 9 months in 1694, for example, a group of Pueblo people defied Spanish rule. From their headquarters on the Black Mesa near San Ildefonso,

Black Mesa near San Ildefonso

they raided Santa Fe. In time most of these Indians suffered defeat. They again pledged their loyalty to the Spaniards. Also in 1694 the Jemez people killed their mission priest. Joined by people from Zuni and Acoma, the Jemez people then fought the Spaniards. The Spaniards, with the help of people from Zia, Santa Ana, and San Felipe, once again prevailed. They drove the people of Jemez into the mountains. Many Jemez Indians went to live among the Navajos or among the Hopis. Pueblo people had begun living with the Navajos after the Pueblo Revolt. It was during this time that the Navajos probably began to weave. They most likely learned the art of weaving from the Pueblo Indians who lived among them. Today Navajo women are the most skilled weavers in the Southwest.

Yet another revolt against Spanish rule broke out in 1696. Involved in this revolt were Indians from several pueblos. Six mission priests and 21 other Spaniards died in this revolt. There was defiance of Spanish rule as well at San Ildefonso. There the Indians killed two mission priests. The Spaniards and their Pueblo allies again won out in the end. They defeated those Indians who had resisted Spanish rule. After 1696 Spanish control of the Indians along the Rio Grande was complete. The Rio Grande pueblos never again took up arms against the Spaniards.

The Spanish reconquest disrupts the pueblos. The Spanish victory over the pueblos was not without costs. This victory disrupted life along the Rio Grande. For the next 20 years the people of the same pueblo often did not trust each other. The people of one pueblo did not trust the people of other pueblos. The basic question that divided the Pueblo peoples was the question of loyalty to the Spaniards. Most but not all pueblos experienced this strife.

Besides strife within and among the pueblos, the lives of the Pueblo peoples underwent other changes. Perhaps as many as 400 Indians taken captive by Vargas at Santa Fe were given as slaves to Spanish settlers. Many of the Rio Grande Pueblo Indians left their homes. Some went to live among the Hopis. Altogether several thousand Pueblo Indians left the Rio Grande Valley during the early 1700s. They refused to accept Spanish rule. To the Spaniards these Indians were a threat. They were a threat in part because of their influence on the Hopis. The Spaniards called these Pueblo refugees *apostates.* In 1716 the Spaniards returned some of the apostates to the area of the Rio Grande. Fifty years would pass before other apostates returned to their homeland. As for the Hopis, they were never reconquered by the Spaniards.

The Pueblo Indians readjust to Spanish rule. In time most of the Pueblo peoples settled down under Spanish rule. The Spaniards sent out more and more mission priests. By 1740 40 mission priests were living and working among the Pueblo Indians. These mission priests directed the building of new churches. They worked to restore some aspects of pueblo life to what it had been during the great missionary period. However, the Spaniards made no further raids on the kivas. They stopped destroying the objects of Pueblo religion. They did not punish so harshly those Indians who failed to attend Catholic services. For their part, the Pueblo peoples, on the surface at least, accepted Christianity. They apparently took great care to hide their own religious rites from the Spaniards.

Contact with Spaniards brought many desirable items into the Pueblo culture. From the Spaniards the Pueblo peoples received cattle, sheep, and horses. They received wheat, melons, peaches, chili peppers, and other new foods. Nonetheless, life was hard for the Pueblo Indians during the 1700s, just as it had been during the 1600s.

The Pueblo Indian population declines. The Pueblo population at the end of the 1700s was only half of what it had been 100 years before. In fact, the population was just one-fourth of what it had been when the Spaniards arrived in New Mexico. By the end of the 1700s, there were also many fewer pueblos. Of the more than 60 pueblos located in the drainage area of the Rio Grande in the middle of the 1500s, only 19 still stood. Of these 19, only 4 were on the same spot they had occupied in the mid-1500s. The 4 were Isleta,

apostates: the name Spaniards gave the Pueblo Indians who left the Rio Grande Valley during the early 1700s; these Pueblo Indians refused to obey Spanish rule and moved away from their homes

117

Isleta Pueblo (about 1890)

Acoma, Taos, and Picuris. Besides declining in size and number, the Pueblo population shifted. By the end of the 1700s, many Pueblo Indians had abandoned their homelands altogether and had moved elsewhere. One group from Santo Domingo even built a new pueblo in 1699. This was the pueblo of Laguna near Acoma. Some pueblos were not affected as greatly as others. Yet even these pueblos were smaller by the end of the 1700s than they had been in the 1500s.

The Pueblo population declined during the 1700s for a number of reasons. Of these, two were of particular importance. The first was disease. Outbreaks of smallpox especially cost many lives. Smallpox hit New Mexico once every 10 years on the average. The second was the attacks on the pueblos by groups of Indian raiders. These raids took a toll in both Pueblo lives and property. Contributing to the Pueblo population decline to a lesser degree were the movements of Pueblo Indians to other places.

The Spanish population grows. The story of the Spaniards in New Mexico was quite different. From the time of the reconquest to the end of Spanish rule in New Mexico, the Spanish population grew at a steady pace. The number of Spanish *villas* (towns) also grew. In April 1695 Vargas led 44 families from Santa Fe to what is today the Española Valley. These settlers set up the villa of Santa Cruz de la Cañada, better known as La Cañada. Thirty-five Spanish families set up yet another villa in 1706. The spot chosen was south of Santa Fe on the banks of the Rio Grande. A steady water supply, good soil, grasslands, and timber made the spot attractive. This villa was the Villa

villa: kind of Spanish town that grew up in New Mexico

118

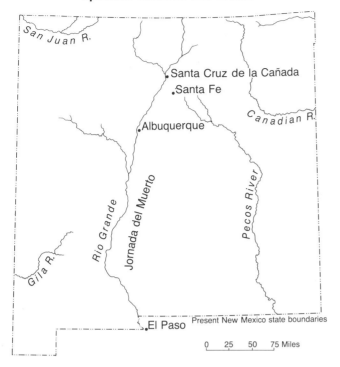

Spanish Villas in the 1700s

de Albuquerque. La Cañada and Albuquerque joined Santa Fe and El Paso as the official villas of the land the Spaniards called New Mexico. Spaniards founded all four villas under grants from the Spanish government. These were the only four villas founded while New Mexico was a colony of Spain. You can see the location of these villas on the map on this page.

The villas were the centers of New Mexico's population during the Spanish period. Fertile land near the villas attracted more settlers. The population both in and around the villas grew throughout the 1700s. Vargas had brought 100 soldiers and 70 families with him in 1693. By 1752 3,402 settlers, not including those at El Paso, called New Mexico their home. This number nearly doubled over the next 25 years. It more than doubled once more between 1776 and 1789. The number of Spanish settlers in New Mexico climbed to more than 10,000 during the 1790s. New Mexico had by 1800 become one of New Spain's most populous outer provinces. More people lived in New Mexico in 1817 than lived in the whole area that is today California, Baja California, Arizona, and Texas.

1. **(a)** Why did the Spaniards decide that they had to reconquer New Mexico?

Section Review

(b) How did Don Diego de Vargas plan to reconquer the pueblos?

(c) Describe the efforts of Vargas to reconquer New Mexico in 1692.

2. (a) What was the mood of the Pueblo Indians when Vargas returned to New Mexico in 1693?

(b) What incidents showed that some Pueblo peoples resisted Spanish rule?

(c) When did the Spaniards finally gain control over the Rio Grande pueblos?

3. (a) How did the Spanish reconquest disrupt the pueblos?

(b) From the 1500s to the end of the 1700s, what changes took place in the lives of the Pueblo peoples?

4. (a) What villas did the Spaniards found in New Mexico?

(b) Describe the growth of the Spanish-speaking population in New Mexico.

---

2. How was New Mexico threatened by outside forces?

France threatens Spain's American empire. You read in the last section about the French claim to the Mississippi River. You also read that French presence in the interior of North America had encouraged the Spanish reconquest of New Mexico (page 112). In time the French began to settle on the Gulf of Mexico and along the Mississippi. These settlements both threatened and divided lands claimed by Spain. In response to this threat, the Spaniards built missions and forts in eastern Texas. In south Texas they built the Alamo mission and the town of San Antonio. The Spaniards founded San Antonio in 1718. That same year the French founded New Orleans near the mouth of the Mississippi. San Antonio soon became a rest center and a place of protection for Spaniards carrying supplies from New Spain to eastern Texas. By about 1740 San Antonio had become the main settlement in Texas.

French presence along the Mississippi never directly threatened New Mexico. More than 1,000 miles separated French settlements from Spanish New Mexico. Nonetheless, New Mexico became more and more important to the Spaniards as a buffer zone (page 111). It was supposed to protect the rich mining areas of what is today northern Mexico from all outside threats. New Mexico was to help keep foreigners out of Spanish territory.

French traders eye New Mexico. Spanish officials in New Mexico had a hard time trying to keep foreigners out of their territory. In part this was because of the activities of French traders. French traders moved into the areas of North America claimed by France. These traders began to trade with many of the Indians who lived in the interior of North America. Before long

Spanish officials heard that the French were trading with the Plains Indians. Some Plains Indians moved along the outer border of New Mexico. If French traders were indeed trading with these Indians, then New Mexico was threatened. Spanish officials feared that French traders might soon try to trade with people who lived in New Mexico.

From the time of the earliest Spanish settlements in the Americas, the Spanish government had strictly controlled its American trade. By law Spaniards in the Americas could legally trade only within the Spanish empire. They could not trade with any foreign nations. Aware of increasing French trade in North America, Spanish officials in the early 1700s restated this policy. They warned New Mexico's governor to look out for any French activity on the outer border of Spanish territory. They further advised Spaniards living along the Rio Grande not to trade with foreigners. In effect, officials reminded the people in New Mexico of long-standing Spanish rules.

Some outside trade does occur. In trying to head off French advances, Spanish officials took some direct action. New Mexico's governor sent out a small armed force in 1720. He directed this force to find out if in fact the French were trading with the Pawnee Indians. The Pawnee Indians were very strong. They had the upper hand in the central plains area. Trade with the Pawnees would show that French activity had spread westward. The Spanish force left New Mexico and headed for the Platte River in present-day Nebraska. Its leader was Don Pedro de Villasur, a young lieutenant from the presidio at Santa Fe. With Villasur were 42 Spanish soldiers and some Pueblo soldiers. A few non-soldiers went along as well. The force traveled to the Platte. There they clashed with the Pawnees. Armed with French muskets and their own bows and arrows, the Pawnees overran Villasur's force. More than 30 soldiers from New Mexico died. So did their leader and their scout. The wounded returned to Santa Fe with news of the disaster.

The French were surely trading with the Pawnees. Before long they were trading with the nomadic Indians who lived on the plains of eastern New Mexico. And in 1739 the first French traders arrived in Santa Fe. The people of Santa Fe welcomed these traders. In fact, Spanish settlers were starved for outside goods. They promptly bought what goods the traders offered for sale. The governor watched while the settlers broke Spanish law. He then wrote the viceroy of New Spain. He asked the viceroy to relax the Spanish rules on trade. The governor hoped that trade could be opened between the Spaniards in New Mexico and the French in the Mississippi Valley. The viceroy's reply to the governor's request was brief. He simply restated the Spanish position. No trade was to be carried on with foreigners. Nonetheless, French traders continued to enter New Mexico in the years that followed. They knew they could be arrested, but they came anyway. They did so because their trade with New Mexicans brought them great profits.

Indians threaten the Spanish empire. Clearly the Spaniards had trouble keeping French traders out. In part this was because New Mexico never had enough soldiers to patrol its borders. The soldiers were also too few to stop another threat to Spanish New Mexico. This threat came from groups of nomadic Indians who raided Spanish settlements and Indian villages. The first of these nomadic groups were the Apaches and the Navajos. You will recall that the Apaches and the Navajos were probably in New Mexico when the Spaniards arrived. It was not, however, until 25 years after the first Spanish settlement in New Mexico that the Spaniards began to take notice of these Indians. By the 1620s the settlers had become aware that there were some Indians in New Mexico who did not live in villages. These Indians spoke languages and practiced ways of living that differed from those of the Pueblo peoples.

The Spaniards began to call these nomadic Indians "Apaches." In their records the Spaniards in time gave the separate bands of Apaches special names. It was only later in history that the various Apache bands formed tribes. They then came to be known by the names you learned in chapter 2—the Jicarillas, the Mescaleros, and the Chiricahuas. As for the Navajos, they were related to the different bands of Apaches by language. In fact, the Spaniards at first listed the Navajos as one of the Apachean bands. But, you will recall, the Navajos became a somewhat settled people. They learned how to farm, for example, from the Pueblo Indians. Nonetheless, the Apaches and the Navajos alike threatened Spanish New Mexico because they made their living in part by raiding. Before the Spaniards introduced horses into New Mexico, neither the Apaches nor the Navajos bothered the settlers. With horses they could strike quickly and ride away. Nomadic Indians who moved into New Mexico at a later time likewise threatened the area.

The Spaniards fail to make peace with the Apaches. When the Spaniards settled in New Mexico, they hoped to bring all the Indians in the area under peaceful control. They tried to group the nomadic Indians together. They failed. They tried to Christianize these Indians. They failed again. In the 1600s the nomadic Indians of New Mexico lived outside Spanish control. The Navajos roamed the mountains and mesas on the west. The ancestors of the Jicarillas lived in the northeast. The ancestors of the Mescaleros lived in the southeastern region. To the south and west lived the ancestors of the Chiricahuas.

In their raids on settlements in the 1600s, the Navajos and the Apaches disrupted life. They disrupted life both in New Spain's northern provinces in present-day Mexico and in New Spain's outer province of New Mexico. In the 1670s, for example, the ancestors of the Mescaleros forced people to leave the pueblos east of the Manzano Mountains. And at the end of the 1600s Indians the Spaniards simply called Apaches had taken control of a large area. By the early 1700s Spanish records said that the Apaches controlled the area from present-day northern Mexico all the way northward to Zuni.

Indian raids continue after the reconquest. After the Pueblo Revolt and the Spanish reconquest, a new group of nomadic Indians appeared in New Mexico. They, too, upset the lives of those who lived along the Rio Grande. These Indians were the Comanches. They arrived from the northern plains. In 1706 the Comanches raided the present-day Jicarillas. The Comanches saw the plains northeast of Taos, and they liked what they saw. For a time thereafter the Comanches camped alongside the Ute Indians, a people who lived in the mountains to the north. The Comanches and Utes stayed awhile in the San Luis Valley near the head waters of the Rio Grande. From this area they launched raids on the Jicarillas. At times they also raided pueblos and Spanish settlements.

Then in the 1730s and 1740s, the Comanches took control of New Mexico's eastern plains. They forced Apache bands to leave the region. For the next 50 years the Comanches kept up their raids on the people of New Mexico. (See the map on page 124.)

The Spaniards and the Pueblo Indians unite. During the 1700s, then, Indian raids disrupted life in New Mexico. Comanches, Utes, Apaches, and Navajos alike raided Spanish and Pueblo settlements in the Rio Grande Valley. These Indians took horses, sheep, and other livestock. They took food and other goods. Some Indian raids destroyed lives as well as property. In 1760, for example, the Comanches raided Taos. From Taos they carried off 50 Spanish women and children. A few were ransomed. Others were later taken to St. Louis and New Orleans.

Indian raids so threatened the people of New Mexico that the Spaniards and the Pueblo peoples joined forces. This cooperation was possible because of changes in Spanish policy. Spaniards had become less harsh in their treatment of the Pueblo Indians after the reconquest (page 117). The Spaniards now formed Pueblo militias. As militiamen (citizen soldiers), the Pueblo peoples helped protect the area. The Spaniards and their Pueblo allies mostly tried to defend settlements against Indian raids. At times they gave chase to bands of raiders. They fought few formal battles, mainly because the raiders did not want to fight. Raiders preferred hit-and-run tactics.

Yearly trade fairs take place. Yet despite frequent raids, the Spaniards found time to trade with the very people who raided their settlements.

Nomadic Indian Groups in the 1700s

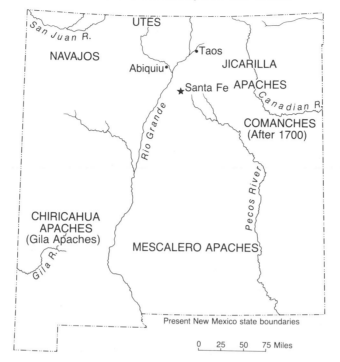

Once a year a trade fair was held in Taos. The Spaniards traveled up the Rio Grande to the fair. They were joined in Taos by different Indian groups—Comanches, some Apaches, and perhaps some Navajos. Sometimes one or more French traders showed up. A Catholic Church official attended one of these fairs in 1760. He described the fair in this way.

> They [the Indians] bring captives to sell, buckskins,
> many buffalo hides, and booty they have taken in other
> parts—horses, guns, muskets, ammunition, knives,
> meat, and various other things. No money circulates in
> these fairs, but articles are traded for each other and in
> this way those people provide themselves.

Some of the goods the Indians brought to Taos had come in the first place from French traders. The French traded with the Indians of the Great Plains. These Indians, in turn, traded with the Comanches who traveled to the fair at Taos. By the 1770s a second fair took place at Abiquiu. Held in the fall, the Abiquiu fair was mainly for trade with the Ute Indians. From the Spaniards at Taos and Abiquiu, the Comanches, the Utes, and the other Indians got goods they needed or wanted. They traded for horses, knives, bridles, saddle blankets, clothing, and corn.

Anza becomes governor of New Mexico. The trade fairs brought a moment of peace to the people of New Mexico. But the moment soon passed as Indian raids quickly began again. In the 1770s these raids became so bad that they threatened the very survival of New Mexico as a Spanish colony. Many settlers along the Rio Grande left their homes in the country. Some moved into the villas. Some moved into the Indian pueblos. Lives were lost among both Spanish and Pueblo peoples. Then in 1776 the Spanish king responded to the crisis in New Mexico. He set up a new military region for northern New Spain. He appointed an able military leader, General Teodoro de Croix, to head that region. General Croix concluded that New Mexico would have to be saved as a buffer zone. Otherwise, Indian raiders would soon control the area along the border of present-day Mexico.

The person chosen to save New Mexico was Juan Bautista de Anza. Anza had fought Indians in Sonora, one of New Spain's northern provinces. In the 1770s he had opened the westward land route from Sonora to Upper California. And in 1776 some of his men had founded San Francisco. Then in 1778 Anza made his way to Santa Fe to assume the office of governor of New Mexico. His instructions were to bring the Comanches under control. He was to convince the Comanches to join the Spaniards in a war against the Apaches. But in order to defeat the Comanches, Anza would have to fight them on their home ground. He would have to fight them on the plains that stretch across Colorado and eastern New Mexico. He would have to overcome the famous Comanche chief, Cuerno Verde, meaning "Green Horn." Cuerno Verde wore a headdress with a buffalo horn painted green.

Governor Juan Bautista de Anza

Anza makes peace with the Comanches. To fight Cuerno Verde and the Comanches, Anza gathered a force of 600 soldiers. Some were regular soldiers. Most, however, were volunteers, both Spanish and Pueblo Indian. This force headed northward in the late summer of 1779. In pushing toward Colorado, Anza took a new route. He avoided the pass east of Taos taken by earlier groups going to fight the Comanches. Instead, he traveled up the western side of the Rocky Mountains. Hidden from the Comanches by the mountains, Anza and his soldiers in time crossed the Rockies. They surprised and defeated one group of Comanches. Anza then learned from his captives that Cuerno Verde was on his way back from a raid into New Mexico. The Comanche chief would soon return to his camp west of the Arkansas River. Moving southward, Anza and his men arrived below the Arkansas in time to ambush Cuerno Verde. Surrounded and outnumbered by the Spaniards, Cuerno Verde made his last stand. He and his followers killed their horses and fought from behind the horses' bodies. With greater numbers Anza and his soldiers prevailed. Cuerno Verde and a number of Comanche leaders died in the fighting.

Anza's victory was a great victory for the Spaniards, but it brought no immediate peace with the Comanches. Nonetheless, it lessened the number of Comanche raids. These raids had troubled New Mexico for more than 50 years. Anza's victory also laid the groundwork for a permanent peace with the Comanches. Anza brought about this peace after years of skilled and patient talks with various Comanche leaders. At last the peace was made. Comanche and Spanish leaders met at Pecos Pueblo in February 1786. There the two sides declared peace—a lasting peace. From then on the Comanches left the people of New Mexico alone. The Spaniards and Comanches now traded with one another on a regular basis rather than only at yearly trade fairs. At the same time the Comanches joined the Spaniards in their fight against the Apaches.

The United States becomes an independent nation. The Indian wars in New Mexico and elsewhere in New Spain took place at a time when no other nation greatly threatened Spain's American colonies. French presence in North America stopped being a problem after the 1760s. In 1762 France transferred the Louisiana area west of the Mississippi River to Spain. The nations were at the time on friendly terms. Then in 1763, after losing a war to the British, France was forced out of North America altogether. Great Britain received Canada and Louisana east of the Mississippi from France. Britain also received Florida from Spain as a result of Spain's friendship with France. Even then Britain posed no real threat to Spanish America. This was mainly because Great Britain began to struggle with its own 13 American colonies, colonies located along the Atlantic Coast.

In 1776 this struggle between Britain and its colonies formally became

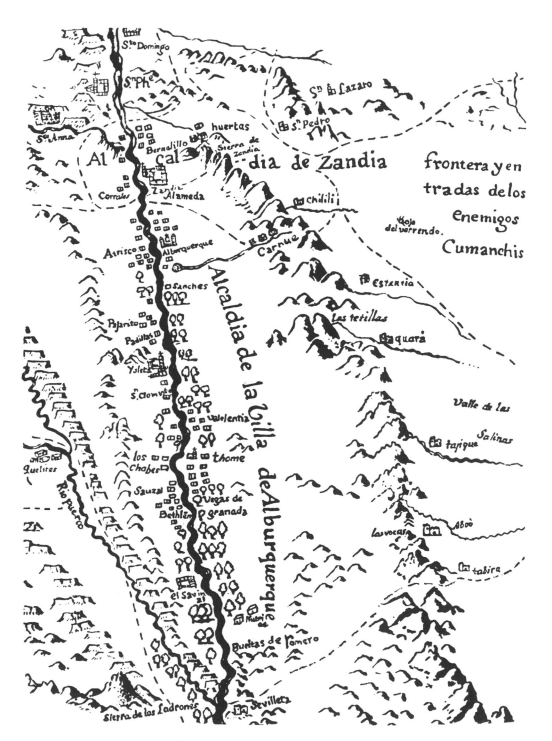

Spanish settlements in the Middle Rio Grande Valley, 1779 (from *Albuquerque,* by Marc Simmons, UNM Press)

the War for American Independence. France and, to a lesser degree, Spain helped those colonists who fought against Great Britain. In time the colonists won. A treaty in 1783 recognized the independence of the United States. It recognized the territory of the United States as extending from the Atlantic Ocean to the Mississippi River. For Spain the American victory was a blessing. The treaty returned Florida to Spain. However, a new young nation, the United States, now stood as a possible threat to Spain's American colonies.

The United States purchases Louisiana. As a young nation, the United States after 1783 was mainly concerned with its problems at home. Americans had no great urge to expand beyond the land that was already theirs. Certain events took place, however, that changed that picture. In 1800 Spain under pressure from France gave Louisiana back to France. Napoleon, the leader of France, promised Spain that Louisiana would never be given to a third country. Three years later Napoleon broke his promise. He sold all of the Louisiana territory to the United States.

The first concern for Spain was the question of boundaries. What boundaries would the United States claim for its new land? The American president, Thomas Jefferson, soon replied. He claimed that the Louisiana territory extended all the way across Texas to the Rio Grande. Jefferson's claim challenged Spanish land claims. Neither the United States nor Spain, however, was prepared to fight over this boundary. Still, American presence west of the Mississippi worried Spain's leaders. So, too, did American expeditions sent out to explore the new territory of the United States. Of concern as well were reports that the Americans were trying to turn the Plains Indians against the Spaniards.

The first American expedition, that of Meriwether Lewis and William Clark, traveled all the way to the Pacific Ocean and back to St. Louis in the years 1804 to 1806. It did not come near Spanish America. However, a Spanish party sent to learn more about the expedition found that Americans had made alliances with some of the central Plains Indians. A second expedition, that of Zebulon Pike, in fact entered Spanish territory. Sent out in 1806, Pike's orders were to look for the headwaters of the Arkansas and Red rivers. He was to explore the southwestern part of the land called Louisiana.

The Spaniards respond to the American challenge. Word of Pike's expedition reached Santa Fe in 1806. To meet the challenge to Spanish authority in the area, the Spaniards responded. They sent a force eastward to the plains boundary that Spain claimed was the true western boundary of Louisiana. The force was under orders to make friends with Plains Indians and to form alliances against the United States. It was also supposed to find Pike. Included in the force of 400 men were 100 Spanish soldiers. The rest were militia. The force left New Mexico in June 1806. It carried enough supplies for a 6-month journey.

In October the force was back in Santa Fe. It had not found Pike. Pike's party had already traveled across the Colorado plains. The party had spent a hard winter at the base of the Rocky Mountains. The name Pike's Peak is a reminder of the explorations of this early explorer. In the late winter of 1807, Pike and his men entered the Rockies. On a small river that they thought was the Red River, the Anglo-Americans built a stockade. As it turned out, the stockade was in Spanish territory. Pike may or may not have known this.

Shortly afterward, Spanish troops arrived. They escorted Pike and his men to Santa Fe. Pike was able to view a settlement long closed to the eyes of outsiders. The Spaniards treated Pike in a pleasant manner. Still, they took from him his notes and his maps. Some time later in 1807 they took him first to Chihuahua, then to the Louisiana border. There the Spaniards released Pike. Once back in the United States, Pike found that people wanted to know more about his adventures. So Pike wrote from memory what he had seen during his visit in New Mexico. He provided the outside world with the first view of life in Spanish settlements along the upper Rio Grande. Published in 1810, Pike's writings were of special interest to Anglo-American traders. Perhaps they could find a way to penetrate Spanish New Mexico.

Section Review

1. **(a)** How did the Spaniards respond to the building of French settlements on the Gulf Coast and along the Mississippi?
   (b) How did Spanish officials restate Spanish trade policy in the face of French advances toward Spanish America?
   (c) How did the people of New Mexico respond to French traders, and why did French traders continue their illegal trade in New Mexico?

2. **(a)** What groups of nomadic Indians first threatened settlements in New Spain's northern provinces in present-day Mexico and New Spain's outer province of New Mexico?
   (b) How successful were the Spaniards at making peace with and Christianizing nomadic Indians?

3. **(a)** Where did the Comanches come from, and when did they take over the eastern plains of New Mexico?
   (b) What Indian groups raided settlements in New Mexico, and what did they take in these raids?

4. **(a)** Why was it possible for Spaniards and Pueblo Indians to unite, and in what ways did they join forces?
   (b) Describe the trade fairs at Taos and Abiquiu.

5. **(a)** How did Juan Bautista de Anza defeat the Comanches, and why was his victory important?

   (b) When did the Spaniards and Comanches make peace, and how did the Comanches then help the Spaniards?

6. **(a)** What boundary did the United States claim for its new territory of Louisiana?

   (b) How did Anglo-Americans and Spaniards try to use the Plains Indians against one another?

   (c) Why did the Spaniards arrest Zebulon Pike, and why were Americans eager to read about his adventures?

Chapter Review

Words You Should Know

Find each word in your reading and explain its meaning.

   1. buffer zone   2. apostates   3. villas

Places You Should Be Able to Locate

Be able to locate these places on the maps in your book.

1. El Paso
2. Jornada del Muerto
3. Santa Fe
4. Santa Cruz de la Cañada
5. Albuquerque
6. Taos
7. Abiquiu

Facts You Should Remember

Answer the following questions by recalling information presented in this chapter.

1. **(a)** Why did the Spaniards think it important first to reconquer New Mexico and then to make sure it survived as a colony?

   (b) Why did Vargas have to reconquer New Mexico not once but twice?

2. Compare and contrast what happened to the Pueblo and Spanish populations and settlements in New Mexico from the 1500s to the end of the 1700s.

3. **(a)** In what ways did Spanish officials try to keep New Mexico closed to foreigners?

   (b) How did the French and later the Americans pose a threat to Spanish New Mexico?

4. **(a)** What groups of nomadic Indians raided settlements in New Mexico?

   (b) In what ways did the Spaniards deal with these Indians?

5. Who are the following people, and why are they important?

(a) Don Diego de Vargas;

(b) Don Pedro de Villasur;

(c) Juan Bautista de Anza;

(d) Cuerno Verde;

(e) Zebulon Pike.

Eyewitness to New Mexico's History
A Dance in the 1800s

From: Fabiola Cabeza de Baca, *We Fed Them Cactus* (University of New Mexico Press, 1954), pp. 32–33.

By eight o'clock, the dance hall was filled and the *baile* [dance] had started. . . . There were many beautiful senoritas at the dance and good dancers as well. The girls were well chaperoned and it was not easy for lovers to have much opportunity for courtship, yet they managed, and after one of these *bailes,* the families of many prospective grooms went in search of brides for their sons. It was still the custom for the parents to make matches, but American influence was becoming more and more evident as the years rolled on, and the young folks were more at liberty to choose their mates.

The dance was a beautiful sight. The senoritas in voluminous skirts, tight waists and elegant jewelry, were swung around by the cowboys of two languages, in fancy boots, bright shirts and bandannas. The tiny feet of the women were lost in the fast rhythm of the polkas, schottisches, waltzes and varsovianas, and only the boots could be seen and heard.

CHAPTER 6

Life in New Mexico's Spanish Communities

What you will learn in this chapter—

Even today New Mexico's towns and cities are fairly distant from one another and from towns and cities in other states. In some cases stretches of flat, often straight roads separate towns and cities from one another. In other cases mountain roads, roads that are steep and curved, are the only way to reach these communities. In a sense, then, some New Mexicans are subject to a greater degree of isolation than are people who live in many other parts of the United States.

While New Mexico was a colony of Spain, the people who settled the land were likewise separated from other people. They, too, were subject to isolation. This isolation—separation from others—meant that the people of New Mexico could largely develop their own life-style. They could develop their own ways of living. They could develop their own cultural traditions.

The people who came to New Mexico did not, however, develop an entirely new life-style. These people were, after all, Spanish settlers. They brought certain ways of living and certain cultural traditions with them. So the story of life in Spanish New Mexico is one of people learning to live in their new homeland. In this chapter you will learn how the settlers adjusted their cultural traditions to the land. As you read, you will find answers to the following questions:

1. What ways of living were developed by the people who lived in New Mexico's Spanish communities?
2. How did New Mexicans blend their Spanish culture with the land that is New Mexico?

1. What ways of living were developed by the people who lived in New Mexico's Spanish communities?

Spanish settlements begin to grow. You will recall that Don Juan de Oñate founded the first Spanish settlement in New Mexico in 1598. But because Oñate's settlement largely failed, the king of Spain changed New Mexico's role within the Spanish empire. In 1609 he declared New Mexico a royal colony. He had decided that it should serve as a missionary field. Life in New Mexico from 1610 to 1680, then, centered on the work of the mission priests. The great missionary period was a time of converting the Pueblo Indians to the Catholic faith. It was a time of building missions. It was not a time of settlement. As a result, the number of Spanish settlers never increased very much during the 1600s. Indeed, there were not quite 2,900 Spanish settlers living in New Mexico at the time of the Pueblo Revolt of 1680.

You will further recall that Don Diego de Vargas reconquered New Mexico in the 1690s. By late 1693 Santa Fe was once again a villa and New Mexico's capital city. By 1696 the Spaniards had brought the Pueblo peoples in the Rio Grande Valley back under peaceful control. From the 1690s on, New Mexico's Spanish-speaking population grew fairly rapidly. There were ten times as many Spanish settlers living in New Mexico by the late 1700s as there had been in 1680.

Spanish settlers become native New Mexicans. Vargas had, of course, brought settlers with him in 1693. Some were full-blooded Spaniards. Others were of mixed blood. Marriage between Spaniards and Indians had followed the Spanish conquest of Mexico in 1521. The children of such marriages were called *mestizos*. Other people of mixed blood also lived in New Spain and in time lived in New Mexico. They were the children of still other groups of people who had intermarried.

mestizo: child of a marriage between a Spaniard and an Indian

As time passed, New Mexico's Spanish-speaking population became more and more a mixed population. It became more and more a population of people born in New Mexico. The 1790 census for the colony, not including Indians, listed only 49 people who had been born outside New Mexico. Of these, 22 were natives of El Paso and 25 had been born in one of New Spain's other provinces. Only 2 had been born somewhere outside the Viceroyalty of New Spain. New Mexico's Spanish-speaking settlers had by the late 1790s become New Mexicans.

New Mexico's society is isolated. Perhaps the main reason why this native population developed was New Mexico's isolation. New Mexico was far removed from the population centers of New Spain. In addition, the Spanish government had laws which controlled the movements of its citizens. It restricted the movement of people from one settlement to another. It did so by requiring special travel permits. The government allowed groups of settlers to go to New Mexico in the years after the reconquest. Then the arrival of new settlers largely stopped. So the growth of New Mexico's population and settlements was the result of what the people themselves did. Spanish settlers in

Church at Las Trampas

New Mexico intermarried with other groups and had children. These New Mexicans, in turn, had more children.

As the population of New Mexico grew, so did the number of settlements. You read in the last chapter about the founding of two new villas, Santa Cruz de la Cañada and Albuquerque (page 118). Each was founded under a special grant from the government. Settlers in time moved into other places as well. They first scattered over the Rio Grande Valley. They then moved away from the river. They moved to what became Abiquiu, Laguna, and San Miguel del Vado. They formed communities in the Sangre de Cristo Mountains. The map on page 136 shows these areas of settlement. Isolated from the outside world, the people who lived in these settlements adjusted to the land that is New Mexico.

New Mexico has an open society. Besides being isolated, New

135

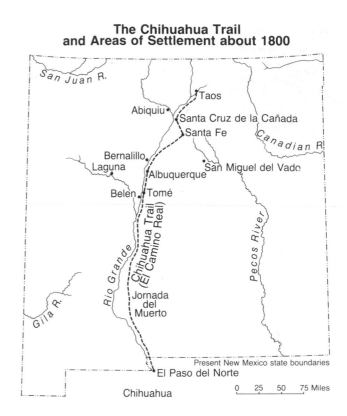

**The Chihuahua Trail
and Areas of Settlement about 1800**

San Juan R.

Taos

Abiquiu

Santa Cruz de la Cañada

Santa Fe

Canadian R.

Bernalillo

Laguna

San Miguel del Vado

Albuquerque

Belén

Tomé

Chihuahua Trail
(El Camino Real)

Rio Grande

Pecos River

Gila R.

Jornada
del
Muerto

Present New Mexico state boundaries

El Paso del Norte

Chihuahua

0   25   50   75 Miles

frontier area: area that marked the advance of settlement; New Mexico was the area that marked the northernmost advance of Spanish settlement

castes: name given to people of mixed blood; castes were listed in the census figures for New Mexico's Spanish communities in the 1700s

genízaros: Indians who belonged for the most part to Indian nations other than those usually found in New Mexico; they were Indians captured or freed from captivity by New Mexicans

Mexico was also a *frontier area*. It was an area that marked the northernmost advance of Spanish settlement. Life on the frontier was hard. It was dangerous as well. So in the frontier area of New Mexico, all people were treated more or less the same. It did not matter as much about a person's social class as it did, for example, in Mexico City. In New Mexico Spaniards and people of mixed blood alike could become officeholders. They could rise to high rank as soldiers. They could become landowners. Indeed, census figures for New Mexico's Spanish communities in the late 1700s listed only two groups of people. Listed as the first group were "Spaniards and castes." The *castes* were people of mixed blood. The second group listed were "Indians."

The term Indians included the Pueblo, Navajo, Apache, Comanche, and Ute people. It also included people called *genízaros.* The genízaros were Indians whose people did not usually live in New Mexico. They were Indians captured or freed from captivity by Hispanic New Mexicans. They were then employed by those who had taken charge of them. Or they were allowed to settle in one of New Mexico's communities. New Mexico society was remarkable in part because of the many castes and the ability of people of mixed blood to become influential members of that society. But it was also remarkable because Indians were accepted into New Mexico's Spanish communities. Indians who lived in Spanish communities earned their livings in much the same ways as did the Spanish settlers. Some Indians married Spaniards and castes. Accepted as well into Spanish communities were blacks and *mulattoes*. Mulattoes were children born of black and white parents.

Spanish settlers become landowners. On arriving in New Mexico, most Spanish settlers were granted land. All the land belonged at first to the Spanish ruler. The monarch, in turn, gave away pieces of land. Or the monarch allowed someone else to give away the land. This person might be the viceroy or the governor of a province. This person might be someone who had been given the authority to start a settlement. Pieces of land given away in this manner were called *land grants*. Some land grants were made to individuals. Other land grants were made to a whole community of people.

The promise of land attracted settlers to the frontier area of New Mexico. Settlers were given not only land but also seed, livestock, tools, and some financial support from the government. The person granted the land had to live on and farm the land for 4 years. After this period that person formally owned the land. No one was supposed to settle on land that the Indians lived on and farmed. Under Spanish law such land belonged to the Indians. Nor were settlers supposed to get a permit to graze livestock so near to Indian lands that Indian crops were damaged. Unfortunately, Spanish settlers at times violated Spanish law. They trespassed on Indian lands both north and west of Santa Fe.

Most New Mexicans are farmers. Land ownership was important because farming was New Mexico's main occupation. There was no encomienda system (page 98) in New Mexico in the 1700s. And while there were some large landowners who employed others to do the work, most New Mexicans were small farmers. They were *subsistence farmers*. They grew crops mainly to feed their own families. Mostly they grew corn, wheat, beans, chili, other vegetables, and some fruits. They grew cotton as well. Cotton was used along with the wool from sheep to make blankets and clothes.

New Mexico's farmers had little metal. As a result, they relied mainly on wooden tools. Their plow, for example, was made from a short tree trunk. A large branch was left attached for use as a plow's handle. At the sharpened end of the plow, farmers fastened metal. In this way they made the point of the plow. Farmers also had a way of adjusting the angle of the plow. By adjusting the plow's angle, they could make deep furrows or shallow furrows. The plow itself was tied to a pole that spanned the horns of two oxen. The oxen, of course, pulled the plow.

Farmers irrigate their crops. Both men and women worked at farming. Joined by their children, they planted the seeds, weeded the fields, and

mulatto: child of a black and a white parent

land grant: tract of land awarded by the Spanish monarch or some other person; made to individuals and to whole communities of people

subsistence farming: type of farming in which farmers grow crops mainly to feed their own families

137

An acequia

acequia: irrigation ditch dug by Spanish farmers

carreta: wooden, two-wheeled cart used in New Mexico during the Spanish and Mexican periods

harvested the crops. Men alone did the heavy work. For example, they did the plowing. In addition, men did the work connected with irrigation. Irrigation was as much needed by Spanish farmers in New Mexico as it had been by Pueblo farmers. The men dug and cleaned the irrigation ditches, ditches called *acequias*. From New Mexico's rivers the acequias carried water to the communities that had grown up along the rivers. The acequias that carried water from the Rio Grande to the fields around Albuquerque were fairly wide. They were so wide that small bridges had to be placed across them. Men also did the actual irrigating of the fields.

The men were the tool makers as well. They made the plows. They made wooden hoes and shovels. Indeed, the men did all the work in wood. They made the wooden, two-wheeled carts called *carretas*. (See Special Interest Feature.) They made the wooden parts of the houses and the furniture. They even made the wooden utensils used in the kitchens.

The Carreta

The carreta was a two-wheeled cart, or wagon, made almost entirely of wood. Made by Spaniards, the carreta had early played a role in the history of New Mexico. Don Juan de Oñate and the first Spanish settlers had brought 83 of these carts into New Mexico in 1598. These carts, 32 in number, had carried the supplies to the missions during New Mexico's great missionary period. They had done so as part of the royal supply caravan that arrived in New Mexico every 3 years during this period.

In the 1700s and early 1800s, the carreta remained the only vehicle in use in New Mexico. From the very beginning the only materials used in making the carreta were wood and leather. Spanish settlers had little metal. This meant that in the place of nails they had to use wooden pegs and leather thongs to assemble their carts. In the place of metal-rimmed wheels they had to use wooden wheels.

In making the floor bed of some carretas, cart makers used pine planks or pine planks and leather. For other carts they used thick slabs of cottonwood cut from tree trunks. Floor beds measured about 1 foot thick, 4 feet long, and 2$^1/_2$ feet wide. The cart makers bored a hole through the pine planks or cottonwood slabs. Through this hole they inserted a pine axle on which they placed wheels made from cottonwood. The wheels measured about 4 feet in diameter.

Once the floor beds were finished, the cart makers built up the cart's sides with light-weight poles. They fastened a wooden tongue to the front of the cart. The carts were then ready for use. They were pulled by oxen. Most carretas were owned by traders. Carretas were also used to haul grain. For the most part they were used for long trips. They jolted and lurched along narrow and rough trails. Now and then they got stuck in mud and sand. They made a horrible noise as they screeched along on wooden wheels that were never oiled well enough. Nonetheless, the carretas were a marvel of construction. They met the needs of a people who had no other way of hauling heavy loads.

New Mexicans live in adobe houses. The houses themselves were built of adobe. The men and the women alike were the house builders, but here, too, the tasks were divided. The men did the heavy work. They began their work by making the adobe bricks. The men used their feet to blend the desired mixture of clay, sand, and straw. They then scooped this mixture into wooden molds that had no top or bottom. They next removed the molds from the newly formed adobes and left them to dry for several days. The straw kept the adobes from cracking as they dried. Each adobe commonly measured 10 inches wide, 18 inches long, and 5 inches thick. It weighed about 50 pounds.

On a foundation of stones the men laid the adobes for the walls. They used thick mud between the adobes and between each layer of adobes to hold the walls in place. At the corners they alternated the adobes, laying them first one way and then the other. When they had finished the walls, they laid vigas (wooden beams) across the width of the house. In some places vigas were laid so that they stuck out on both sides of the houses. The men made the roofs in layers. They first placed short, flat wooden boards across the beams. These pieces of wood formed the ceilings. The men next built up the roofs. On top of the pieces of wood the men placed brush, then a layer of adobe, and finally eight or more inches of dirt. The roofs were flat. Still, they provided some drainage when built with vigas that varied slightly in size and were arranged in order from smallest to largest. The women added the finishing touches on the houses. They plastered the outside of the houses with clay plaster. Depending on the clay available, this plaster might be red, a distinctive shade of brown, or white. The women also plastered the insides of the houses. Using sheepskin pads, they spread a white or earth-colored mixture on the walls.

The houses are plain. Most New Mexican houses in the 1700s were small. Some were built around a patio or in an L shape. Some were built with rooms in a straight row. Each room opened to the outside. Seldom did rooms have connecting doorways. The doorways were small, measuring only 5 feet in

Making adobe

height. The doors themselves were made of wooden planks fastened together with wooden pegs and goathide glue. Holding the doors to the door frames were all-wood hinges. The houses had few windows, and what windows there were were quite small. Early settlers hung animal skins across the window openings to keep out rain, snow, and wind-blown dust. Later settlers stretched scraped animal hides across the window openings. Or they made a crude type of window glass using layers of mica.

The light inside the houses was dim. And the interiors were plain. There were earth floors and by the 1800s some brick floors. To make their earth floors stronger, New Mexicans often soaked the ground with animal blood. Across the floors they usually spread animal hides and hand-woven woolen carpets. Houses were heated with wood-burning, corner fireplaces. The house walls formed two sides of each fireplace and chimney. The fireplace itself was shaped like a bell and had a horseshoe-shaped opening. A house often began with a single room. The family then added rooms to meet new needs or to shelter new family members. When a son married, he and his bride lived in

Collection of Spanish colonial furnishings

a room added to his family's house. At times families stopped living in certain rooms. These rooms, in turn, became storage rooms.

Furnishings are simple. Most New Mexicans had very few furnishings inside their homes. The most common was the bench-like seat that ran along a wall. Most seats consisted of rolled-up bedding pushed up against the wall. Some seats were made of split logs or adobe and were a permanent part of the wall. Still other seats, made of wooden planks, were movable. In time New Mexicans began to add backs to the seats and to decorate them with carvings. There were beds, but the beds of early settlers were not pieces of furniture. At night the family members simply unrolled their beds of sheepskin or buffalo hides. During the day the rolled-up beds served as seats. There were also shelves for candles and other items. Individual chairs were scarce. So family members sat on the floors to eat their meals. What tables there were were small and had wooden aprons. These aprons hung down and prevented people from sitting with their legs under the tables. What little light was used at night came from candles.

In most houses, then, there was very little furniture. Part of the reason for this was because every room was for living and sleeping. There was not, for example, a separate room for dining. As a result, there was no need for special dining room furniture. Even the kitchen was both a living and sleeping room. What furniture makers tried to do was to design furniture that served a practical function. They used the materials that were close at hand. That is why they made furniture out of pine, a tree that grows well in the mountains of New Mexico. At the same time pine is a soft wood that splinters easily. So with pine as their main material, the men made furniture that was heavy and had straight lines.

Women do the cooking. The food, like the building materials for houses and furniture, was suited to New Mexico. Corn was the main food. The women ground the corn into meal using the mano and the metate (page 20). From the meal they made tortillas, a round, flat bread. Another main food was beans. Many meals consisted of tortillas and beans. Having few if any plates or eating utensils, the people used the tortillas as a sort of spoon to dip beans out of a common pot. To add flavor and spice to their meals, the settlers used chili peppers. Chili was first grown in the Americas. The Spaniards, once they settled in the New World, began to cook with chili. They in time sent the chili seeds to Spain for planting there.

The women did the cooking. They cooked many of the meals in the corner fireplace. When the weather was pleasant, they might cook over a fire built outside. Because metal was scarce, New Mexicans had few metal cooking pots. Most of the women had only a sheet of metal on which to cook their tortillas. Their other cooking pots were made of materials other than metal. To meet some of their needs, the women got clay pots from the Pueblo Indians. They had pots for cooking, pots for carrying water, and pots for storing food. To meet other cooking and eating needs, the settlers made non-metal utensils. Using wood the men carved spoons, stirring sticks, bowls, cheese presses, and bread-dough trays.

Women do the baking. The women did their baking in outdoor ovens they made themselves. These ovens, called *hornos,* were dome-shaped. On one side was a rounded opening that served as the oven door. The floor of the oven was smooth, and the inside was plastered with fire-resistant clay. A small hole at the top was left to let the smoke out. Another small hole at the base of the oven let in the air needed for a good fire. When ready to bake, the women built fires in the oven. They kept the fires burning until the walls of the oven had stored heat enough for baking. Once the fire had burned out, they removed the coals. They then slid the bread dough or other item to be baked into the oven. For this purpose they used long-handled wooden paddles. To conserve fuel, some women built as many as three ovens. Each was a different

horno: dome-shaped, outdoor oven in which the Indian and Hispanic women of New Mexico did their baking

143

Ovens outside an adobe home

size and served different baking needs. The horno is sometimes simply called the beehive oven. The Pueblo Indians learned how to make this oven from the Spaniards.

The clothing is colorful. Most settlers had only one change of clothing, but what clothing they had was colorful. The men commonly wore shirts and pants woven of cotton or wool. Some men also had leather shirts and pants. The pants were worn tight around the hips and were often open from the knee down. As an outer garment men wore brightly colored woolen blankets. Worn in the style of ponchos, these blankets had openings in the middle so that the blankets slid down over the wearers' heads and onto their shoulders. On their heads the men wore sombreros made of straw. On their feet they wore leather boots with hard soles and pointed toes. Their hair was worn long and fastened in a single braid. Beards and moustaches were fashionable.

Women's clothing consisted of two basic pieces. One, made of cotton, served as both a blouse and a slip. It had a low neckline and short sleeves and hung down to the knees. The other, made of heavy woven cloth, was a very full, ankle-length skirt. Often red in color, this skirt had a sash that tied at

144

the waist. As an outer garment women wore a shawl. Made from a square of colored cloth folded into a triangle, one type of shawl was worn around both the head and the shoulders. In public women wearing this type of shawl often shielded their faces from others by taking the right corner of the shawl and placing it over their left shoulders. Another type of shawl was oblong. On their feet women wore moccasins in the style of the Pueblo peoples or heeless cotton slippers in the style of the Spaniards. Or they went barefoot. If they had jewelry, they wore it. They most commonly wore their hair in long braids. Their cheeks appeared rosy, painted as they were with red juice from *alegría* (coxcomb).

The children, by contrast, wore little or no clothing until about age 8. Then they began to wear clothing like that worn by their parents. Yet even then the boys had to wait years longer before they could wear either shoes or hats. Both shoes and hats were seen as symbols of manhood that had to be earned.

Settlers earn their livings. Most Spanish settlers clearly lived simple lives. They had borrowed many of their ways of living from their Pueblo neighbors. They had also learned to live with what the land of New Mexico had to offer. Most of the villagers were farmers. Next to farming the second most commonly held job among New Mexico villagers in the 1700s was that of day laborer. About one in eight earned a living by working on a daily basis for others. Another one in eight earned a living by working at a job connected with weaving. Among these were people who carded (combed) wool. Others did the spinning or the weaving. There were a lesser number of people—about one in sixteen—who raised livestock. About this same number of people earned their livings as skilled craftsmen. Among these skilled craftsmen were carpenters, shoemakers, blacksmiths, tailors, masons (builders), and silversmiths.

There were still other people whose lives were spent in New Mexico's villages as servants. Most of these were household servants. Not all of them had volunteered to serve others. More than half of the servants were Indians. Another one-third were castes. One in ten was a Spaniard. And the female servants outnumbered the male servants. There were also some people who were owned as slaves.

Wealthy New Mexicans have different ways of living. What you have been reading about are the ways of living that were common to most of the people who lived in New Mexico's Spanish communities. There were, however, some New Mexicans who were wealthy. Some of these wealthy New Mexicans were owners of *haciendas*. The hacienda was a large farm where both crops and livestock were raised. *Hacendados* (hacienda owners) employed workers to farm their land and to care for their livestock. There were also wealthy government officials and military officers. These New Mexicans often tried to

hacienda: large farm where both crops and livestock were raised; found in Spanish Colonial New Mexico

hacendados: hacienda owners; they hired workers to farm their lands and to care for their livestock

copy the ways of living of wealthy Spaniards who lived in New Spain. Their homes were still made of adobe, but they were larger and grander than the homes of most New Mexicans. The wealthy could and did, for example, hire furniture makers to make and carve fine pieces of furniture. In their homes they had tall cupboards, chests of different sizes, tables, and chairs.

In their daily living, wealthy New Mexicans could afford finer things. They had silver knives and forks and sometimes silver plates. They used separate dishes and glasses for their dinner guests. They had copper kettles and iron pots. They, too, ate foods grown in New Mexico. Still, their diet was more varied. So was their clothing. Wealthy men trimmed their fine clothes with silver buttons, silk sashes, and silver buckles. They wore felt hats or beaver sombreros. They wore fine blankets and, when riding horseback, yellow buckskin leggings. The richer they were, the more silver there was on their saddles. Wealthy women trimmed their clothing with ribbons, lace, silk, and velvet. Compared to the clothing common to most women, their skirts were even more colorful. Their wardrobes were larger and contained cotton prints made in New Spain. And, of course, they had more jewelry.

The wealthy New Mexican had finer ways of living than did most of the villagers. Still, no one in New Mexico lived a truly comfortable life. New Mexico was, after all, an isolated area. It was a frontier area. Life was hard for all New Mexicans.

Section Review
1. (a) What did the 1790 census figures show about New Mexico's Spanish-speaking population?
   (b) How did New Mexico's isolation lead to the growth of a native-born population?
   (c) How did the fact that New Mexico was a frontier area help bring about an open society?
   (d) Besides Spaniards, what other groups of people lived in and were accepted into New Mexico's Spanish communities?
2. (a) How was land granted to the people who settled in New Mexico, and what did the settlers have to do before the land formally belonged to them?
   (b) Besides land, what else were settlers given?
   (c) What did the Spanish government say about Indian lands, and how successful was this policy?
3. (a) What crops did New Mexico's farmers grow?
   (b) How did the farmers bring water to their crops?
4. Briefly describe the homes, the furnishings, the food, and the clothing

of most of the people who lived in Spanish communities during the 1700s.

5. In what ways did the people who lived in New Mexico's Spanish communities earn their living?

6. How did the ways of living developed by wealthy New Mexicans differ from those developed by the majority of people who lived in the Spanish communities?

---

2. How did New Mexicans blend their Spanish culture with the land that is New Mexico?

New Mexico's isolation affects its culture. You read in the last section that New Mexico's isolation encouraged the growth of a native-born population. The main reason for this isolation was the distance that separated New Mexico's Spanish communities from the population centers of New Spain. There were other factors that also contributed to this isolation. One was the lack of good roads. What roads there were ran across sandy or packed soil. A second factor was the lack of good methods of transportation. There were only horses and mules or carretas pulled by oxen. A third factor was the lack of trade. A trade fair did take place every year in January in the city of Chihuahua. Caravans that included carretas and pack mules had to leave New Mexico in November in order to arrive in time for the fair. Santa Fe and Chihuahua lay 40 days apart. Even at the fair trade was somewhat limited because New Mexicans had little money with which to buy goods. Having little money, they used a *barter system*. They traded goods for other goods. So traders from New Mexico brought with them Indian blankets, sheep, hides, piñon nuts, and wine from El Paso. They traded these items for iron tools, clothes, shoes, chocolate, sugar, tobacco, liquor, paper, and a few books. The yearly trade fairs at Taos and Abiquiu (page 124) brought the settlers some other goods. Still, neither trade for goods at Chihuahua nor trade for goods with the Indians at Taos and Abiquiu brought many outside goods into New Mexico. A fourth factor in New Mexico's isolation was the lack of communication. Mail service depended on trade caravans, mule trains, and special mail riders.

barter system: system in which people trade goods for other goods

This isolation meant that New Mexicans had little contact with the outside world. They had little contact with Spanish-speaking people who lived elsewhere in New Spain. What happened, then, was that the settlers developed ways of living consistent with the land that is New Mexico. You read about those ways of living in the last section. New Mexicans also developed their own culture. It was a culture that blended the Spanish culture the first settlers had brought to New Mexico with the land in which New Mexicans lived.

147

La Conquistadora

New Mexicans celebrate special occasions. One Spanish tradition brought to New Mexico was the celebration of special occasions. This tradition took root in New Mexico. New Mexicans celebrated Hispanic religious events as well as the birth, death, or marriage of a member of the Spanish royal family. At the same time New Mexicans developed their own local celebrations. These local celebrations became a part of New Mexico's cultural heritage.

One local celebration marked the reconquest of New Mexico by Don Diego de Vargas. When Vargas reentered New Mexico in 1693, he brought with him a statue of Our Lady of the Rosary. He vowed to honor her in a yearly procession once he had retaken Santa Fe. He also vowed to build a chapel to house the statue. Some years after Vargas's successful return to Santa Fe, the tradition of a yearly celebration began. The statue was at the center of that celebration. The town council of Santa Fe then further shaped the celebration in 1712. On September 14 of that year the town council announced that the celebration would thereafter include several parts. There would be a Catholic mass and a sermon. There would be a procession carrying Our Lady of the Rosary, called by some *La Conquistadora,* through the plaza. The people were then to take an oath of loyalty to the Spanish ruler. Finally, the people were to end the celebration with a fiesta. This local celebration still takes place today.

Other celebrations growing out of the Hispanic tradition in New Mexico are observed today as well.

New Mexicans develop their own folk art. Another part of Spanish culture brought to New Mexico was the tradition of displaying images of saints known as *santos.* In Spain and New Spain it was a common practice to display these saints in churches and homes. This tradition also took root in New Mexico. In time it led to the creation of santos by New Mexicans themselves. These religious-image makers, people called *santeros,* began first to emerge as local craftspeople. They made their appearance some time after 1750. In later years the santeros began to travel from place to place to make and sell their santos.

Santeros made two different types of santos. One was a *retablo.* A retablo is a religious painting or carving made on a flat surface. Most commonly retablos are paintings on rectangular wooden tablets or boards. The other type of santo was the *bulto.* Bultos are carved or sculptured representations of a saint. They are wooden figures or statues that santeros have carved in the round from limbs of cottonwood or pine trees. The retablos and bultos of early New Mexican santeros were quite distinctive. Both retablos and bultos were painted to make the images look as real as possible. The Crucifux—the portrayal of Jesus Christ on the cross—was perhaps the most vivid of all New Mexican santos. The santeros showed Christ on the cross. They revealed in Christ's face the feelings

santo: image representing a saint, a divine person, or a religious event

santero: person who makes religious images

retablo: religious painting or carving made on a flat surface

bultos: wooden figures, or statues, carved in the round from limbs of cottonwood or pine trees

A santo

149

A retablo (from *New Spain's Far Northern Frontier,* edited by David J. Weber, UNM Press)

of both pain and forgiveness. New Mexican santos can be seen today in churches, museums, and fine-arts centers. They reflect the Hispanic tradition of displaying holy images.

Some New Mexicans become Penitentes. Other traditions of Spanish culture were brought to New Mexico as well. And in time the people of New Mexico blended these traditions into what became their own cultural heritage. New Mexicans produced unique forms of drama. They made distinctive musical instruments, which they played at social events. They danced special dances. They developed local folk tales. Many of the local traditions that grew up had a religious focus. Spanish culture and the Catholic faith went together. Religion was important to the lives of those who lived in New Mexico's Spanish communities.

As long as the mission received support from the Spanish government and the Franciscans, the Franciscan priests were New Mexico's religious leaders. But in the late 1700s the government withdrew its support from the missions, which had always been costly. The Franciscans could not bear the cost of New Mexico's churches alone. So for New Mexico's churches to survive, the local people had to support and maintain them.

In some northern New Mexico mountain communities in the late 1700s, a brotherhood of villagers began to emerge. The members of this brotherhood, men only, were known as Penitentes. They helped carry out the religious offices of the community. The Penitentes may have been patterned after a group that had been very popular in Europe during the 1400s and the 1500s. The rites of the Penitentes may have been brought to New Mexico by the settlers. Or New Mexicans may have gotten some of the ideas from a book. Whatever the origin of New Mexico's Penitentes, their ritual was accepted in the mountain communities. Men joined the brotherhood to seek forgiveness for their own sins. They joined the brotherhood to ask forgiveness as well for the death of Christ upon the cross.

The Penitentes sought forgiveness by experiencing both spiritual and physical pain. Spiritual pain was the focal point of their meetings. Physical pain was a part of each member's initiation into the brotherhood. It was also very much a part of Holy Week (*Semana Santa*) activities. During Semana Santa the members beat themselves with whips of cactus or yucca. On Good Friday they chose one of their members to play the role of Christ. They made their choice within a private chapel (*morada*), a chapel closed to all but the members of the brotherhood. Inside this morada the Penitentes reenacted the trial of Jesus according to the gospels. After the trial they held a procession to a hill marked as Calvary (*calvario*). The person playing the role of Christ carried a large, man-size cross on his back. At one time the Penitentes tied this person to the cross and then stood the cross on end. They left the person on the cross until he was near death. Some Penitentes even died in this manner. Later in time, the Penitentes tied a large sculpture of Christ rather than a man to the cross. The Penitentes practiced their religion in the way they did because it met their needs. It met the needs of a deeply religious people isolated from other people and from a formal church.

Procession of Penitentes at San Antonito, a small village in the Sandia Mountains, 1880s

151

Another important function of the Penitentes was community service. The services Penitentes provided might be considered early welfare services. The Penitentes aided the sick and the poor. They comforted people whose relative or friend had died. In a way they were also counselors. In addition, this group was politically active. Through their service and political activities the Penitentes contributed to a stronger and more unified community.

Formal education and medicine are limited. New Mexico's isolation, then, led to the development of local traditions. In turn New Mexico's isolation kept its people from sharing the thoughts and practices of the rest of the world. All the time that New Mexico was a Spanish colony, not one public school or college was established in New Mexico. New Mexico had no newspapers. It had no locally printed books. What books there were belonged to just a few people. Educated New Mexicans exchanged books and ideas. Some formal schooling was available in the few private schools that had been set up. Still, most New Mexicans were simply removed from the thoughts of people who lived in the rest of the world.

Isolation also affected medical practices. It meant that little formal medicine was practiced in New Mexico during the entire time New Mexico was a colony of Spain. Doctors were few in number. So the people had to rely on local remedies and medicines made from plants. Herbalists treated many ailments, but life remained uncertain during outbreaks of diseases. Smallpox outbreaks took a very heavy toll. In just a two-month period in 1781, 142 people died from smallpox in Santa Fe. New Mexicans benefited greatly when they could share in outside medical practices. In 1805, 6 years after the development of the cowpox vaccination method, the first vaccine reached New Mexico. What followed was a 10-year vaccination program for New Mexicans. This program reduced the outbreaks of smallpox. It increased the life expectancy of New Mexicans. It contributed to the growth of New Mexico's population during the early 1800s.

New Mexico remained a Spanish colony until 1821. At the end of its history as a colony of Spain, New Mexico had become a distinctive area. Its people had developed their own ways of living. Its people had developed their own cultural traditions.

Section Review

1. List the factors that contributed to the isolation of New Mexico's Spanish communities.

2. **(a)** What were some of the traditions of Spanish culture that were brought to New Mexico?

   (b) What local celebrations, folk art, and other cultural traditions grew up in New Mexico?

3. Why did the Penitentes appear in some communities? What contributions did the Penitentes make to their communities?

4. What was the condition of education and medicine in New Mexico during the time it was a colony of Spain?

Chapter Review

Words You Should Know

Find each word in your reading and explain its meaning.

1. mestizos
2. frontier area
3. castes
4. *genízaros*
5. mulattoes
6. land grants
7. subsistence farming
8. acequias
9. carretas
10. hornos
11. haciendas
12. hacendados
13. barter system
14. santeros
15. santos
16. retablos
17. bultos

Places You Should Be Able to Locate

Be able to locate these places on the maps in your book.

1. Santa Fe
2. Santa Cruz de la Cañada
3. Rio Grande
4. Abiquiu
5. Laguna
6. San Miguel del Vado
7. Chihuahua Trail
8. Taos

Facts You Should Remember

Answer the following questions by recalling information presented in this chapter.

1. What kind of population and society grew up in New Mexico's Spanish communities as a result of New Mexico's isolation and frontier conditions?

2. **(a)** Why was the ownership of land important to New Mexico's settlers, and how could they get land?

(b) How did the people who lived in New Mexico's Spanish communities earn their livings?

3. What ways of living developed in the Spanish communities and showed that the people had adjusted to the land that is New Mexico?

4. Explain what is meant by the following statement: "The culture of New Mexico's Spanish communities was a culture that blended Spanish cultural traditions with local conditions." Then give two examples of local cultural traditions that grew out of this blending process.

153

Eyewitness to New Mexico's History
The Problems of Mexican Rule as Seen by Donaciano Vigil, 1846
From: Janet LeCompte, *Rebellion in Rio Arriba, 1837* (University of New Mexico
Press, 1985), pp. 85–86.

Señor Don Alvino Pérez came to New Mexico [as Governor] in 1835 with the highest recommendation of the Supreme Government [of Mexico], of the governmental periodicals, and of many other newspapers of the interior. Scarcely had he arrived in Santa Fe than he surrounded himself with the best-educated men of the country and also, as he thought, the most patriotic, and he delivered himself entirely to their counsel. With the help of these on various occasions he hoped to establish a government in New Mexico similar to the constitution and laws in force in the Republic [of Mexico], cutting at the root the abuses of the old colonial system and other irregularities that he observed, and the ignorance or lack of zeal of the previous governors. The people of New Mexico did not doubt the good intentions of Señor Pérez; at that time, in spite of later events, most were persuaded that if the happiness of New Mexico could have been dependent on only the good intentions and vigilance of this gentleman, he would have procured it for us. But in spite of his great aptitude, his lack of practical knowledge of the character, interests, and traditional customs of New Mexicans made him commit errors that caused us bitter days matched in our history only by the general rebellion of the Indians in the year 1680.

CHAPTER 7

New Mexico under Mexican Rule, 1821–1848

What you will learn in this chapter—

Today New Mexicans are citizens of the United States. They are reminded of this fact daily. The United States Postal Service delivers their mail. "The Star Spangled Banner" is played at the start of a school day, at sports events, and on other occasions. School children pledge their allegiance to the flag of the United States of America.

New Mexicans are also often reminded that they have not always been United States citizens. There are sometimes even visual reminders of New Mexico's history under the rule of different nations. There may, for example, be flags of these different nations on display in the public squares or plazas of some cities and towns. The number of flags may vary from place to place. Nonetheless, three flags are always included. These are the flags of Spain, Mexico, and the United States. New Mexico belonged to Spain until 1821. In that year it became a part of Mexico, formerly the Viceroyalty of New Spain. New Mexico remained a part of Mexico until 1848. In that year it formally came under the control of the United States.

In this chapter you will learn about New Mexico during the period of Mexican rule. You will also learn about the way in which New Mexico came under the control of the United States. As you read, you will find answers to the following questions:

1. How was New Mexico opened to the outside world during the period of Mexican rule?
2. What happened in New Mexico during the period of Mexican rule?
3. How did New Mexico come to be under the control of the United States?

1. How was New Mexico opened to the outside world during the period of Mexican rule?

New Mexico becomes a part of Mexico. Spain, you will recall, had been the first European nation to expand into the Americas. Through

155

exploration, conquest, and settlement, Spain had established its control over a vast area. This area included the Caribbean Islands and Central and South America. It also included parts of North America. At the heart of Spain's North American lands was New Spain. New Mexico, in turn, was a part of New Spain. Spain's rule over its American colonies went unchallenged for 300 years. Then in the 1810s the people in various parts of Spanish America began to throw off the rule of Spain. Among the first Spanish American people to succeed in overthrowing Spanish rule were the people of New Spain. In September 1821 Mexico became an independent country.

News of Mexican independence did not reach Santa Fe until some weeks later. New Mexicans had taken no part in the revolution against Spain. Still, New Mexicans welcomed the news. The end of Spanish rule meant that the old restrictions on trade outside the Spanish empire might be set aside (page 121). Now, perhaps, New Mexicans could begin to trade legally with outsiders. In an effort to bring about such trade, Mexican officials soon announced the end of the old trade restrictions.

Traders enter New Mexico. The first person to profit under this free-trade policy was Captain William Becknell. Becknell was from Franklin, Missouri. In 1821 he traveled onto the Great Plains. There he hoped to trade with the Indians for horses, mules, and other items. In the course of his travels he met a group from Santa Fe. They invited him to go into New Mexico. Becknell accepted the invitation. Still, he was surprised by the friendly welcome he received in Santa Fe. The people of New Mexico eagerly bought what he had to sell. They paid for these goods with silver coins.

Wagon Mound on the Santa Fe Trail

Becknell then hurried back to Missouri with news of his trading venture.

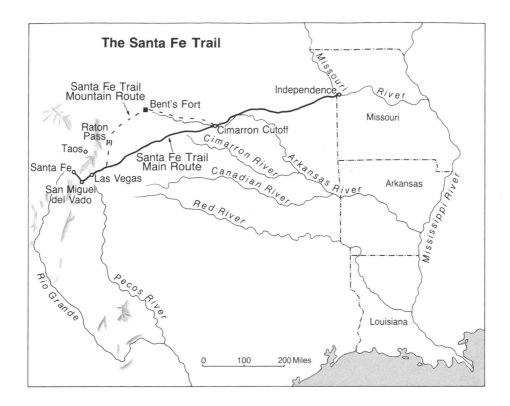

The Santa Fe Trail

Legal trade with Mexico could now take place. Within a year traders from the United States made it clear that they intended to take advantage of this new trade. Beginning in 1822 trade caravans from the United States traveled into New Mexico every year.

The Santa Fe Trail is established. At first the trade caravans were made up of pack animals only. But by 1824 traders were using wagons along with pack animals to carry their goods. Mostly from Missouri, the traders crossed plains and mountains as they traveled on into New Mexico. The village of Taos served as New Mexico's first *port of entry*. It was the first settlement in Mexican territory that foreign traders visited. In time Santa Fe became New Mexico's main port of entry and trading center. Some traders pushed on through New Mexico. They carried their trade from Santa Fe to Chihuahua along the Chihuahua Trail. This route was also known as the Camino Real, or "Royal Road." Everywhere they traded the Missourians found a people starved for outside goods. By the 1840s the yearly caravans that headed for Santa Fe included many wagons. Each carried as much as 5,000 pounds of valuable goods. In 1843 alone goods brought into Santa Fe had a value of about half a million dollars.

The wagons bound for Santa Fe traveled over what came to be known as the Santa Fe Trail. Look at the map on this page. There you can see the two

port of entry: place through which goods enter one country from another; Taos and later Santa Fe were ports of entry, the first settlements in Mexican territory entered by foreign traders

157

routes this trail followed. The mountain branch crossed the plains to Bent's Fort (page 160). It entered New Mexico over Raton Pass. The Cimarron Cutoff crossed the plains into New Mexico through the present-day Oklahoma panhandle. Once in New Mexico both branches of the trail followed along the east side of the Sangre de Cristo Mountains. The two branches came together before the trail cut around the southern end of the mountains and passed through San Miguel del Vado. The trail then entered Santa Fe from the southeast.

The new trade has an effect on New Mexico. Mexican officials had not realized in advance just how great the trade with the outside world would be. They soon realized, however, that the trade would be extensive. They also realized that traders from the United States would control much of this very profitable trade. Once the trade had begun, the Mexican officials were powerless to stop it. They could and did require traders to obey certain regulations and to fill out detailed papers. They could and did tax the goods brought into Mexican territory. Nonetheless, the trade had an effect on New Mexico. It affected both the society and economy of New Mexico.

First, the trade met the needs and wants of the residents of Santa Fe and other Mexican towns. From the traders these people could buy (1) different kinds of cloth and clothing, including hats, gloves, handkerchiefs, and ribbons; (2) building materials, furniture, tools, silverware, glassware, dishes, candles, paints, paper, and ink; (3) foods, spices, medicines, and tobacco; (4) books and almanacs; and (5) wagons with metal-rimmed wheels, wagons the traders sometimes sold before returning to their home bases. From the traders New Mexicans also got their first printing press.

Second, the trade enabled Anglo-Americans to enter New Mexico and to control much of New Mexico's economy. The government of the United States recognized the value of the Mexican trade. It spent money to improve the Santa Fe Trail. The people of the United States realized the largest profits from this trade. Also profiting were the Mexican citizens who actively traded for outside goods. Among the Mexican traders were members of New Mexico's most prominent families. By 1839 these traders were sending their own wagons into the United States for goods that found a ready market in Santa Fe. José Chávez y Castillo and Antonio José Chávez were two of these traders. Other Mexican traders carried the trade south from Santa Fe. They traded goods brought from the United States in Chihuahua, Durango, and other towns in northern Mexico. Among these traders were Governor Manuel Armijo, José and Juan Perea, Ambrosio Armijo, Antonio J. Ortiz, Antonio José Otero, and Santiago Flores.

The mountain men arrive in New Mexico. At the same time as the growth of the new trade, Anglo-Americans showed an interest in New

Covered wagons in front of the Governor's Palace, 1861

Mexico for different reasons. These Anglo-Americans looked at New Mexico as a source of animal furs. Trappers had shown interest in New Mexico as early as 1805. In the 1820s this interest reached its height. Hat makers in Paris, London, New York, and other cities demanded more and more beaver pelts. So into the mountains of northern New Mexico moved a special group of fur trappers, people known as *mountain men.* Many of these mountain men were French Canadians. The rest were citizens of the United States.

In most cases the mountain men were in New Mexico illegally. They had not obtained permission from the Mexican government to enter the area. Under an 1824 Mexican law, only permanent residents of Mexico could trap beaver. To get around this law, the mountain men illegally bought licenses from New Mexico residents who had obtained licenses for themselves. Or they illegally operated as the silent partners of New Mexico residents.

Taos is the headquarters for the fur trade. Taos was the village nearest the mountain waters where the beaver lived. As a result, Taos became the headquarters for the fur trade. Here the mountain men got together what supplies they could. They added these supplies to the equipment they had brought with them from St. Louis. Leaving Taos in the fall, the trappers made

mountain men: special group of fur trappers who moved into New Mexico during the Mexican period; Taos was the center of their activities

159

their way into the mountains nearby. Of greatest danger to the trappers were Indians, who fought to hold on to what had been their hunting grounds. Also a danger to the mountain men were the grizzly bears that roamed the mountain forests in great numbers. Whether alone or as members of small parties, the mountain men feared other trappers as well.

Mountain men spent the winter trapping beaver. One person could get as much as 400 pounds in beaver pelts during a single season. With the end of the season, the trappers moved back into Taos. There they faced a new danger. In Taos the Mexican government had built its northernmost customs (tax) house. Mexican officials had not been interested in the mountain men on their arrival in New Mexico. This was because the mountain men had not brought with them any goods to trade. After a trapping season the mountain men had pelts. Government officials were interested in this fact. Some mountain men were arrested and had their entire catch taken away. They had, after all, violated the law that said foreigners could not trap on Mexican soil. Others bribed government officials or produced illegally obtained licenses. Still others escaped the attention of government officials altogether.

Bent's Fort is built. Beginning in the 1820s the fur trade lured many mountain men to Taos. Indeed, they made up the largest single group of Anglo-Americans in Taos. Some of them became well-known fur traders. Included in their number were the Robidoux brothers, François Le Compte, Antoine Le Roux, Bill Williams, and Thomas Fitzpatrick. And better known than all the others was Christopher (Kit) Carson. Carson had arrived in New Mexico with a wagon train in 1826. He stayed on to become a trapper, hunter, and scout. In 1843 he married Josefa Jaramillo. Through this marriage he became a member of one of Taos's most prominent families. Thereafter he was an accepted member of the Taos community.

Besides attracting the mountain men, the fur trade also attracted businessmen. Chief among them were Charles Bent, William Bent, Ceran St. Vrain, and Marcellin St. Vrain. Together these four men in the late 1820s formed their own company—Bent, St. Vrain and Company. The company soon began work on a fort near present-day La Junta, Colorado. The fort was completed in 1832. Built of adobe bricks made by New Mexican workers from Taos, Bent's Fort was secure against any attack.

By the end of the 1840s, Bent's Fort was the economic center of the southern fur trade. Trappers bought their supplies there. Trappers and Indians alike brought their furs to the fort. Over a period of time Bent, St. Vrain and Company expanded its operations. The company traded Mexican blankets to the Plains Indians. It shipped buffalo hides to St. Louis. It caught and sold wild horses. It owned a store in Taos and a branch store in Santa Fe. A company

Kit Carson

mill in Taos supplied flour to the area's residents. Company agents operated in Chihuahua and Sonora. Other Anglo-American businessmen likewise did business in New Mexico.

So it was that Anglo-Americans began to make an impact on New Mexico in the years following Mexican independence. Anglo-American traders, trappers, and businessmen penetrated New Mexico. They became actively involved in the area's economy. Their arrival began to break down the isolation that had separated New Mexico from the outside world.

Section Review

1. (a) How did New Mexico become a part of Mexico?
    (b) Why did New Mexicans rejoice at the news of Mexican independence from Spain?
2. (a) How did Mexican officials try to bring about trade with the outside world?
    (b) In what ways did this new trade have an effect on New Mexico?
3. (a) Who were the mountain men, and what attracted them to New Mexico?
    (b) What did Mexican law have to say about trapping?
    (c) How did Bent, St. Vrain and Company control the southern fur trade, and what business operations did these and other Anglo-American businessmen carry on in New Mexico?

---

2. What happened in New Mexico during the period of Mexican rule?

New Mexico remains a frontier area. The coming of Mexican rule did not change the basic fact that New Mexico was a frontier area. Time and distance separated the people who lived along the upper Rio Grande from settlements in present-day Mexico. Frontier life remained both hard and dangerous. Navajo raids in particular disrupted life during the early 1820s. And, as always, there were too few soldiers in New Mexico to protect its people. A Mexican law in 1826 increased the number of cavalry companies from one to three. However, the two new companies did not arrive at once.

The distance between New Mexico and the Mexican capital meant several things. First, the central government of Mexico only loosely controlled affairs in New Mexico. New Mexico's government officials were thus able to do pretty much what they pleased. Second, Catholic Church officials in Mexico did little to support the church in New Mexico. As a result, New Mexico's church leaders were left on their own. Mexico's lack of control was repeated in other areas of life in New Mexico as well. Separated as they were from the center of Mexico, New Mexicans did not really think of themselves as citizens of Mexico. Left

161

alone by Mexican state and church officials, New Mexicans developed no deep sense of loyalty toward Mexico.

New Mexico has its own government. During this period New Mexico had a fairly simple government. Yet the form of government underwent several changes in a short time. From 1821 until 1824 New Mexico was a province, just as it had been under Spanish rule. It had a provincial governor who took care of civil matters. Military affairs were handled by the military commander at Chihuahua. Then in 1824 New Mexico was joined with Chihuahua and Durango to form the Internal State of the North. But within six months Mexico had a new constitution. As a result, New Mexico became a territory without ties to either Chihuahua or Durango. It remained a territory from July 1824 until 1837. It was during this period that New Mexico's main official was the *jefe político,* the political chief. This official headed the civil government. An army officer who served under the military commander at Chihuahua was in charge of New Mexico's military affairs. New Mexico also sent a delegate to the national congress of Mexico.

jefe político: political chief of New Mexico during the Mexican period; headed the civil government

The Mexican central government appointed the jefe político to carry out the laws of the country. This official also acted as a court of appeals for cases earlier decided by the local justices of the peace. The jefe político was in effect New Mexico's governor. Indeed, historians have since often referred to these political chiefs as governors. In addition to its political chief, New Mexico had a small legislative body. But this branch of government had no real power and was usually made up of the political chief's close friends. Its only power was to offer advice. At the local level New Mexicans still had their alcaldes (page 97). The alcaldes served as justices of the peace and sometimes as mayors. In each of New Mexico's largest villages and settlements, a special elected official was in charge of the local government.

New Mexico's government worked well some of the time. Other times it broke down. Under Mexican law, for example, there was no trial by jury. Justice depended on the officials themselves. A person could appeal an alcalde's decision to the political chief. That, however, was the one appeal that might bring results. The nearest regular court was in Guadalajara, nearly 1,300 miles from the towns of the upper Rio Grande. Whether the government worked well also depended upon the officeholders. The jefe político especially had a lot of power. Most political chiefs who served during the Mexican period were native New Mexicans. As New Mexicans, they could better control the affairs of the territory. They could count on the support of the people.

The church is in sad shape. No one controlled the affairs of the Catholic Church very effectively. There were several reasons for this. One reason was that the churches in New Mexico had been turned over to local parishes.

This process, you may recall, had begun in the late 1700s (page 150). By the beginning of the Mexican period only a few Franciscans were still present in New Mexico. Another reason was that no high-ranking church official had visited New Mexico's churches for more than 70 years. Indeed, it was not until 1833 that a bishop at last traveled into New Mexico. This bishop came from Durango, a town located more than 500 miles south of El Paso. His visit to New Mexico had two effects. (1) New Mexico's churches now officially came under the direction of a high-ranking religious official. (2) The Franciscan priests were gone from New Mexico forever.

In the absence of the Franciscans, New Mexico's churches were supposed to have become churches headed by priests sent from Durango. These priests were supposed to take charge of the churches in the towns. They were supposed to take charge of the mission churches and mission facilities in the pueblos. But too few priests came. Those priests who did come witnessed the breaking up of New Mexico's churches. The missions, for example, became the property of the Pueblo Indians. For the most part the new caretakers allowed the missions to fall into ruin. Only five pueblos had priests. Churches in the towns were not much better off. Parish priests had to depend upon the people of the parish to support the church. With little support given in most parishes, the priests led hard lives. Their churches fell into disrepair. Still other churches went without parish priests altogether. Whole areas, as a result, had no regular

Sunday mass. They had no one to administer the sacraments (special rites) of the Catholic Church.

The 1830s are a troubled period. New Mexico's residents were deprived in other ways as well. The first public schools appeared during the Mexican period. However, the number of both public and private schools was small. Most of the teachers were not well trained. In 1834 New Mexico got its first printing press. (See Special Interest Feature.) In the same year New Mexico got its first newspaper. However, this newspaper, a weekly named *El Crepúsculo,* meaning "The Dawn," lasted only a month. Also in 1834 the few public schools were closed for lack of funds.

Indeed, the 1830s were a period of money shortages. They were also a period of growing unrest. In 1837 Mexico adopted a new constitution. It placed even more power in the hands of the Mexican central government. And once more the status of New Mexico changed. New Mexico became a department rather than a territory. As a department, it was divided into large units of government called prefects. To head each of the two, and later three, prefects was an official directly responsible to New Mexico's major official. This official, once again given the title of governor, was, in turn, directly responsible to the central government in Mexico. New Mexicans thus lost some control over their own affairs. The timing was bad, for important events were taking place both outside and inside the area.

New Mexico's First Printing Press

New Mexico's first newspaper may have had a brief history, but the press on which it was printed had both a longer and more colorful history. After the demise of *El Crepúsculo,* Father Antonio José Martínez began to use the press. The parish priest of Taos, Martínez was active in local political affairs. He also ran a private school that educated many New Mexican leaders both during the Mexican period and after New Mexico became a territory of the United States. Father Martínez used the press to print both educational and religious materials for his pupils.

During the last years of the Mexican period the printing press again changed hands. It was used once more to publish newspapers. Government officials got the use of the press by either buying it or renting it from Martínez. They printed two government newspapers in 1844 and 1845. Neither the newspaper *La Verdad,* meaning "The Truth," nor the newspaper *El Payo de Nuevo Méjico,* meaning "The Countryman of New Mexico," lasted long.

Father Antonio José Martínez

The printing press became the property of the United States Army when it took over Santa Fe in 1846. On this press United States officials printed the Kearny Code. The Kearny Code provided the basic rules under which New Mexicans first lived as citizens of the United States. You will learn more about the Kearny Code in the chapter that follows.

In 1836, for example, Anglo-Americans in Texas revolted against Mexican rule. They fought for and won their independence. They then formed the Republic of Texas. In New Mexico more and more Anglo-Americans made their presence known. They entered the area as traders. They set up businesses. They also introduced New Mexicans to their own ideas about freedom and the right of people to govern themselves. New Mexicans had no real interest in or reason for attempting to overthrow Mexican rule. Nonetheless, the potential for unrest in New Mexico did exist.

New Mexico gets a new governor. Unrest did, in time, occur. It took the form of a revolt. What set off the revolt was the appointment of Colonel Albino Pérez as New Mexico's governor in 1837. Pérez was unacceptable to some New Mexicans for a number of reasons. First, he was not a native New Mexican. Rather, he was an officer in the Mexican army. Second, Pérez was determined to control the affairs of New Mexico. He did not believe in local government. Third, he announced new taxes under orders from the central government in Mexico. Some of these taxes applied to Anglo-Americans and other foreigners who traded and ran businesses in New Mexico. Other taxes affected the economic well-being of New Mexico's people in general. Pérez taxed woodcutters and sheep that were herded through Santa Fe on their way to market. He taxed dances and other public performances. Pérez also announced that all those who did not have regular jobs would be arrested. And while Pérez reopened the public schools, his new law placed many restrictions on parents. So even the reopening of the schools was unpopular.

As a result of Pérez's actions, people began to resent his government. In time an underground movement was formed to oppose Pérez. People who lived along the Rio Grande from Albuquerque northward joined this movement. So did people who lived in the pueblos and in the Spanish mountain communities. During the Mexican period all of New Mexico's Indians were granted citizenship and land rights. Under this policy the Pueblo Indians continued their traditional ways of living. Many of them also joined other New Mexico settlers in protecting their ways of life. All that was needed to set off a revolt was a single incident. That incident occurred in the summer of 1837.

The revolt of 1837 breaks out. The summer of 1837 found the

Pérez government short of money. There was not enough money to buy the supplies needed to run the government. There was not even enough money to supply the army stationed in Santa Fe. So Pérez appealed for help to the Anglo-American traders who were in Santa Fe for the summer. These traders lent money to the government for needed supplies. However, some officials used their positions when buying supplies to make money for themselves. In other words, they were guilty of a crime called graft. Pérez dismissed those officials known to be corrupt. But the government lost popularity when it punished native New Mexicans. In fact, the punishment of a local official in Taos led to an open revolt against Pérez.

What happened had a simple enough beginning. The Taos official was arrested on charges of graft. He was jailed in La Cañada, a village 25 miles northwest of Santa Fe. Rebels opposed to Pérez soon rallied together in La Cañada. The northern pueblos were especially well represented. The rebels' first action was to march on the jail and free the prisoner. Their second action was to draw up a plan. The plan stated that the rebels would accept for New Mexico nothing less than statehood under Mexico. It further stated that the rebels would not submit to taxation or obey the officials who collected the taxes. The rebels agreed to this on August 3. Once their plan was known, the rebels were quickly joined by others. The so-called Chimayó Rebellion had begun.

Pérez is overthrown. Pérez was in Santa Fe when he received news of the rebellion. Believing that the rebels could not be very strong, he set out for La Cañada with only 150 militiamen. Most were from Santo Domingo Pueblo. Some soldiers from the presidio in Santa Fe went along as well. Pérez and his force left Santa Fe on August 7. They took with them one wheeled cannon. Early the next morning the rebels surrounded Pérez and his men near the black mesa of San Ildefonso. Pérez tried to talk with the rebels, but the time for talking was past. The rebels attacked. Deserted by the Santo Domingo members of the force, Pérez and 23 soldiers retreated to Santa Fe. They left behind the cannon. Six or 7 of their number had died in the fighting.

It was still August 8 when Pérez and some of his followers left Santa Fe and headed southward along the river road. It was late at night. They fled for their lives. The next morning revealed that there was no escape. Indians blocked the road to safety. All of those who had tried to escape now acted on their own. Pérez decided to walk back toward Santa Fe. He hoped he would not be noticed. Such was not the case. Followed by a group of Pueblo people, Pérez was seized shortly after entering a farmhouse at Agua Fría west of Santa Fe. There Pérez lost his head to his captors. The Indians took their prize to Santa Fe, where they joined the rebels who had marched in triumph into the capital. The rebels celebrated their victory by using Pérez's head as a football.

Armijo comes to power. The rebels met on August 10 to choose as governor a native New Mexican. They might have chosen Albuquerque's Manuel Armijo, a former governor. He had helped organize the underground movement that had opposed Pérez. Instead, the rebels chose a northern rebel, José Gonzáles, a native of Ranchos de Taos. Armijo at first stayed in Santa Fe to work with the new governor. Soon tiring of the situation there, he left the capital and returned to Albuquerque. Within a short time Armijo began to gather around him a group to oppose Gonzáles. On September 8 Armijo and his followers announced their formal opposition to the new governor. At the same time they announced their loyalty to Mexico.

Governor Manuel Armijo

Armijo and his followers marched on Santa Fe near the end of September 1837. Having been told by Armijo to stay out of what he called "Mexican affairs," the Pueblo people remained at their homes. Armijo's forces took Santa Fe without a fight. Governor Gonzáles had fled northward. In time Armijo ordered the execution of four rebel leaders. He also ordered the execution of Gonzáles, who was captured at a later date. These executions took place in early 1838. Armijo had finally crushed the rebels. He had, in the process, made for himself a reputation as a Mexican hero. At the same time he had named himself the new governor of New Mexico. The Mexican government rewarded him by allowing him to remain in power. Armijo served as governor during most of the next 8 years. He ruled New Mexico with an iron hand.

The Texas–Santa Fe expedition takes place. The revolt in New Mexico in 1837 troubled the Mexican government. Mexican officials suspected that Anglo-Americans had aided the anti-Pérez rebels. Such was not the case. In fact, Anglo-Americans had provided supplies to Pérez. Some of them had later given financial aid to Armijo in support of his actions against the rebels. They had welcomed the return of order to New Mexico by 1838. Nonetheless, Mexican officials remained suspicious of Anglo-Americans.

In New Mexico, for example, Armijo blamed the Anglo-Americans for all of New Mexico's problems. He took away some of the property that belonged to foreigners. He hurt the Santa Fe trade by taxing each Anglo-American wagon that brought goods into the capital. And he took harsh actions against an expedition sent by the president of the Republic of Texas to New Mexico in the summer of 1841. Made up of about 270 Texans, the expedition appeared to be concerned with both trading and military matters. The expedition's real purpose might have been to take control of New Mexico for Texas.

The Texans never reached Santa Fe. Instead, they got lost on the plains. They lost their horses to roving Indians. They ran short of food and supplies. So when Armijo's representative promised them a general pardon, the Texans surrendered. Armijo promptly broke his promise. He sent the captives on a

Members of the Texas–Santa Fe
expedition are marched to Mexico City
after their capture

2,000-mile march southward to Mexico City. Tied together and given little to eat, the Texans suffered every step of the way. Those who lagged behind during the march were shot. Some were released on their arrival in Mexico. Some escaped. Most captives did not, however, gain their freedom until 1842. Besides the fate of the captives, the Texas expedition had still other results. First, Armijo was once again a hero in the eyes of the Mexican government. He had defended New Mexico against an invading force. Thereafter, his power to rule New Mexico had few if any limits. Second, bad feelings had developed between New Mexicans and Texans. These two groups distrusted and hated one another for a long time thereafter.

Section Review
1. What government officials did New Mexico have during the Mexican period, and how well did the government work?
2. Describe the condition of New Mexico's churches during the Mexican period.
3. **(a)** What conditions existed in New Mexico during the 1830s that created the potential for unrest?
    (b) Why was Pérez unacceptable to many as New Mexico's governor?
    (c) What happened to the Pérez government?
4. **(a)** How did Armijo come to power?
    (b) What was the Texas–Santa Fe expedition, and what were its results?

3. How did New Mexico come under the control of the United States?

Armijo is unpopular. Armijo was a hero to the Mexican government but not to the people of New Mexico. He mostly ruled in a harsh and unfair manner. Indeed, Armijo became an even more hated figure than Pérez had been. But Armijo also had some supporters. These were people whose support the governor bought with land. As governor, Armijo could make land grants. By law, limits were placed on the size of land grants to be awarded. But Armijo ignored the law. He made a number of grants that were larger than 100,000 acres. Three Armijo land grants were particularly large. One, a million acres in size, lay in present-day Colorado north of Taos. A second grant, also in Colorado, was farther east. A third, the land grant that in time became the property of Lucien Maxwell, spread across much of northeastern New Mexico. In making the grants, Armijo kept for himself a share in the land. This was true of two of the three huge land grants mentioned above.

Armijo's support was not, however, either strong or loyal. Nor was support for the Mexican government in New Mexico. One revolt against Mexican rule had occurred in 1837. Discontent against Armijo grew throughout the 1840s. New Mexicans, to be sure, made no move to overthrow Armijo's government. Yet neither Armijo nor the Mexican government could expect much help if either were challenged.

Relations between the United States and Mexico are strained. The challenge to Mexican rule came in 1846. In that year war broke out between the United States and Mexico. War came at a time when relations between the United States and Mexico were at an all-time low. For one thing, the United States annexed (officially added) Texas to its territory in 1845. In so doing, the United States became the defender of Texas. It inherited a war between Texans and Mexicans that had been fought off and on since 1836. The United States also inherited a dispute over the boundary line between Texas and Mexico. Texas and now the United States claimed that Texas's southern boundary was the Rio Grande. Mexico claimed that its territory extended as far north of the Rio Grande as the Nueces River. Another factor in the dispute was the claim by United States citizens that the Mexican government owed them money for property losses suffered inside Mexico. Yet another factor was the mood of the United States that favored expansion westward. This notion, known as *manifest destiny,* had led to the annexation of Texas. Manifest destiny called as well for the addition to the United States of Oregon and California. Oregon was jointly occupied by the United States and Great Britain. California was a Mexican possession.

manifest destiny: belief that the United States should expand across the continent; the mood in the United States that favored westward expansion

Gertrudes Barceló

One of the most fascinating New Mexicans during the Mexican period was Gertrudes Barceló. Having spent much of her youth in Taos and Tomé, she moved in time to Santa Fe. There during the 1840s she set up and ran a gambling house at the corner of San Francisco Street and Burro Alley. The building itself extended all the way through to Palace Avenue on the north. It was as the proprietress of this gambling house that Gertrudes Barceló, better known in the 1840s as Doña Tules, became famous.

Gertrudes Barcelo
(Doña Tules)

To the gambling house of Doña Tules came the high and mighty of New Mexican society. Huge mirrors hung on the walls. Brussels carpets brought from the United States covered the dirt floors. Homemade chandeliers lighted by many candles dangled from the ceiling. In the building's long hall were held New Mexico's grandest dances. High-ranking government and military personnel attended these balls. Admission to the dances was by invitation only.

The favorite game of chance in the 1840s was monte. Here, too, Doña Tules gained fame. She was considered the finest monte dealer in New Mexico if not in all of Mexico. Played with Mexican cards, cards quite different from those we know, monte was played at a table. On top of the table was a red or green cover divided into four squares. The dealer laid a card face-up in each of the squares. The players placed bets on their favorite cards. The dealer or one of the players then drew cards one at a time from the bottom of the deck. As winning or losing cards were drawn, the results were announced. The winners collected their money, and the game began anew.

Doña Tules remained a popular member of New Mexican society even after the conquest of Santa Fe by the United States. She was a favorite of United States army officers. In fact, she warned army officers in December 1846 about the planned rebellion against their authority.

Doña Tules died in 1851. She had during her lifetime amassed quite a fortune. One story told about her is that she had at one point sent much of her money to a bank in St. Louis. The money, however, was stolen and hidden by robbers. The story further says that $150,000 of Doña Tules's fortune still lies buried some 40 miles east of Taos. Whatever the truth of this story, Doña Tules died a wealthy woman. She had a fancy funeral and was buried with the highest honors of the Catholic Church. Up to $1,600 was spent on spiritual services for the burial ceremony alone. In death as in life Doña Tules left her mark on the history of New Mexico.

Indeed, James K. Polk, elected president of the United States in 1844, had run a manifest destiny campaign. He had called for expansion into Texas, Oregon, and California. Texas was, of course, soon annexed. The United States and Great Britain agreed in 1846 to divide Oregon between the two countries along the 49th parallel. The question of California was not, however, so easily settled. Polk tried to buy California from Mexico. That is why Polk sent John Slidell to Mexico in the fall of 1845. For California, the United States was prepared to pay $25 million and to take over debts owed United States citizens by the Mexican government. These debts had been fixed in 1840 at about $2 million. The Mexican government knew it would lose popularity if it sold California. So the Mexican government refused to see Slidell. If the United States wanted California, it would have to find some other way to get it.

The war between the United States and Mexico begins. With problems increasing between the two countries, both sides began to prepare for war. For their part the Mexican people fully expected to defeat the United States. They believed this even though conditions in Mexico were unstable. One government after another rose and fell from power. The army had little equipment, and its morale was low. Conditions in the United States were stable, but not all its citizens supported the idea of war with Mexico. In fact, not all United States citizens favored expansion. Nonetheless, Polk was determined to get California. He therefore ordered General Zachary Taylor to lead about 3,000 troops into the disputed area between Texas and Mexico. Specifically, Taylor was ordered to take his soldiers all the way to the banks of the Rio Grande.

Taylor moved his army to the Rio Grande in late March 1846. On April 12 Taylor received a request from the Mexican general Pedro Ampudia. General Ampudia asked Taylor to move back across the Nueces or face war. Taylor did not move, and on April 25 Ampudia's force crossed the Rio Grande. Mexican troops encountered American soldiers sent out from the fort Taylor had built. The Mexican army soundly defeated Taylor's men. Learning on May 9 of this encounter and of the loss of American lives, President Polk went to Congress. He asked Congress to declare war against Mexico. Congress did just that on May 13, 1846. By waging war against Mexico, the United States hoped to gain the land it wanted.

Kearny conquers New Mexico. The war once begun was notable for several reasons. First, United States armies attacked both present-day Mexico and the northern Mexican borderlands of California, Arizona, and New Mexico. Second, the United States armies were fairly small. The largest army, the one that attacked Mexico City, numbered 10,000. The other armies were much smaller. Third, United States armies marched across vast areas. This was especially true of the army commanded by Stephen W. Kearny.

Kearny's Army of the West set forth on the Santa Fe Trail in June 1846. It totaled 1,700 men. Its objective was to occupy New Mexico and then march on to help take California. Following the mountain branch of the Santa Fe Trail, Kearny's army reached Bent's Fort in early August. There Kearny stayed to plan his entry into New Mexico. He sent a message to Santa Fe urging Governor Armijo to surrender. The two men who carried the message met privately with Armijo. The governor may have received thousands of dollars for his cooperation. Whatever happened in Santa Fe, Kearny went ahead and entered New Mexico. He approached Santa Fe by way of Las Vegas. He did so to avoid a possible confrontation with Indians from Taos Pueblo. Arriving in Las Vegas on August 15, Kearny claimed New Mexico for the United States. Kearny and his army then moved toward Santa Fe. They fully expected to have to fight a battle, perhaps in Apache Canyon to the east of Santa Fe. But no battle took place. In fact, as Kearny entered Santa Fe, Armijo and a few supporters were already on the way to Albuquerque. Their wagons carried all the riches Armijo had been able to gather. As for his retreat from New Mexico, Armijo blamed his soldiers. He told the Mexican government that they and not he were responsible for the loss of New Mexico.

Doniphan arrives in New Mexico. Kearny's conquest of New Mexico was bloodless. He assured the people of Santa Fe just as he had assured the people of Las Vegas that the Anglo-Americans were their friends and protectors.

General Stephen W. Kearny

New Mexico in the War with Mexico, 1846–1847

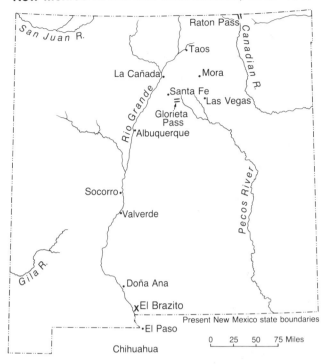

During the more than five weeks that he remained in Santa Fe, Kearny accomplished several things. He received the allegiance of some Pueblo leaders. He issued a code of laws that recognized Spanish civil law and institutions. He appointed Charles Bent of Taos as New Mexico's civil governor. And he helped select the site for a fort near Santa Fe. The building of Fort Marcy began soon thereafter. Kearny then left Santa Fe on September 25. His destination was California. Remaining behind to defend Santa Fe was Colonel Alexander W. Doniphan and his Missouri Volunteers.

Once additional troops arrived in Santa Fe, Doniphan was free to leave. Doniphan and his men headed down the Rio Grande. They reached Doña Ana, a village located just north of present-day Las Cruces, on December 22. There they learned that the Mexican colonel Antonio Ponce and 2,000 soldiers were prepared to fight. The two armies fought for half an hour at El Brazito. Doniphan's men beat back the attacking Mexican soldiers. Seven of Doniphan's men were wounded. Some 43 Mexican soldiers lost their lives. The Battle of El Brazito was the only armed resistance that Doniphan faced within New Mexico. Look at the map on this page. This map shows the places in New Mexico that were involved in the war with Mexico.

The 1847 rebellion breaks out. Doniphan now headed toward Chihuahua. He left New Mexico just as Kearny had, believing that New Mexico

Governor Charles Bent

173

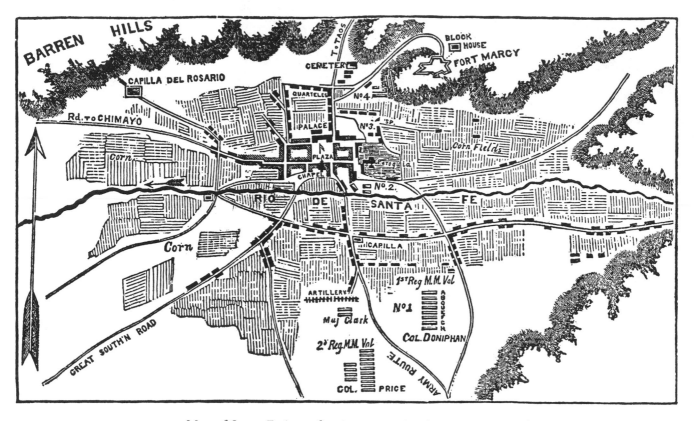

Map of Santa Fe just after its occupation by Kearny in 1846

was securely a possession of the United States. Neither Doniphan nor Kearny had reckoned with Colonel Diego Archuleta. Archuleta had been second in command to Armijo. He had been led to believe that the United States would claim only the land east of the Rio Grande. He would then be free to rule that part of New Mexico that lay west of the Rio Grande. In fact, Kearny had officially claimed only the area east of the Rio Grande. However, Anglo-Americans had soon taken control of the land west of the river as well. Angry at this turn of events, Archuleta began to conspire against the Anglo-Americans. Among other things, he stirred up some of the northern Pueblo peoples.

Colonel Sterling Price was Doniphan's replacement in Santa Fe. Learning of the conspiracy, Price arrested several rebels. Archuleta and another leading conspirator had, however, already left for Mexico. Nonetheless, a rebellion against United States rule was soon underway. A group of Mexicans and Taos Indians rose up on January 19, 1847. They attacked the village of Taos, where they killed a Mexican official, the Anglo-American sheriff, and Governor Bent. They spared the lives of the women and children in the Bent house who tried to escape through a hole in an adobe wall. Josefa Carson, Bent's sister-in-law,

Land Gained from Mexico, 1848

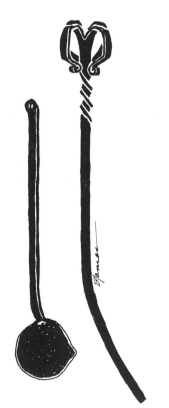

and 2 other women had chipped away at the adobe with kitchen tools. North of Taos at Arroyo Hondo, 8 more Anglo-Americans lost their lives. In early February Colonel Price fought a battle near La Cañada. There he routed the Taos rebels. Price soon caught up with most of these rebels at Taos Pueblo. He and his men killed 150 rebels before the 400 others who had taken cover in the pueblo mission of San Geronimo surrendered. United States officials later hanged 6 of those taken captive.

Other revolts occurred at Mora and Las Vegas. At Mora, a village east of the mountains, rebels killed 5 Anglo-American businessmen. In late February a United States army officer, Captain J. R. Hendley, led a counterattack against the rebels in Mora. Hendley lost his life in the fighting. So, too, did 15 New Mexican rebels. Mora itself was almost destroyed, but the rebellion had been put down. Then in June word of a conspiracy in Las Vegas reached United States officials. Soon thereafter, United States soldiers marched into Las Vegas. There they killed a handful of New Mexicans who resisted. They also took 50 captives back with them to Santa Fe. Of these captives, 30 were later executed.

The Treaty of Guadalupe Hidalgo is signed. So while the initial conquest of New Mexico had been bloodless, bloodshed had followed. Still, New Mexico had been brought under the control of the United States. Elsewhere United States armies had equal successes. They occupied California. They scored

175

important victories at Buena Vista in northern Mexico under Taylor and at Chihuahua under Doniphan. An army under General Winfield Scott captured Mexico City. Scott took control of the Mexican capital in September 1847. Peace talks began soon thereafter.

The peace talks went slowly, dragging on until early 1848. Finally, on February 2, 1848, both sides signed the treaty that ended the war. The United States Senate then ratified (accepted) the treaty on March 10. This was the Treaty of Guadalupe Hidalgo. By the terms of this treaty, the United States had its claims to Texas recognized. The Rio Grande was also recognized as the southern boundary of Texas. In addition, the United States gained from Mexico the northern lands its forces had occupied. Added to the United States were California and most of the present-day American Southwest. In return for this land, the United States gave Mexico $15 million. The United States also agreed to pay up to $3.25 million in money claims American citizens had against the Mexican government. Look at the map on page 175. There you will see the land the United States gained by the Treaty of Guadalupe Hidalgo. Spanish-speaking people who lived on the land transferred to the United States were given a choice. They could move to Mexico or stay where they were. Most stayed and thus became citizens of the United States. Citizenship for the Indians who lived on the land was not decided at this time. Nonetheless, in 1848 New Mexico and all of its people came under the formal rule of the United States.

Section Review

1. **(a)** What was the story of land grants in New Mexico during the time Armijo was in power?

   (b) How did most New Mexicans feel about Armijo?

2. **(a)** List the reasons for the strained relations between the United States and Mexico during the 1840s.

   (b) What events led to the outbreak of war between the United States and Mexico in 1846?

3. **(a)** Briefly describe Kearny's conquest of New Mexico.

   (b) What took place at El Brazito?

4. Describe the events that were part of the rebellion of 1847.

5. What were the terms of the Treaty of Guadalupe Hidalgo?

Chapter Review

Words You Should Know

Find each word in your reading and explain its meaning.

1. port of entry
2. mountain men
3. jefe político
4. manifest destiny

Places You Should Be Able to Locate

Be able to locate these places on the maps in your book.

1. Taos	8. Albuquerque
2. Santa Fe	9. La Cañada
3. Santa Fe Trail	10. Rio Grande
4. Chihuahua	11. Las Vegas
5. San Miguel del Vado	12. Doña Ana
6. El Paso	13. El Brazito
7. Bent's Fort	14. Mora

Facts You Should Remember

Answer the following questions by recalling information presented in this chapter.

1. What major changes took place in New Mexico during the Mexican period?

2. As a result of New Mexico's separation from the population centers in present-day Mexico, how did New Mexico's government function, and what happened to New Mexico's churches?

3. Compare and contrast the Chimayó Rebellion of 1837 and the rebellion of 1847.

4. To what extent did New Mexicans resist conquest by the United States, and why was this so?

5. Who are the following people, and why are they important?
   (a) William Becknell;
   (b) Kit Carson;
   (c) the Bents and the St. Vrains;
   (d) Albino Pérez;
   (e) José Gonzáles;
   (f) Manuel Armijo;
   (g) James K. Polk;
   (h) Stephen W. Kearny;
   (i) Charles Bent;
   (j) Alexander W. Doniphan;
   (k) Sterling Price;
   (l) Diego Archuleta.

Unit Summary

The Spaniards decided to return to New Mexico after the Pueblo Revolt of 1680 for a number of reasons. Chief among these was the desire to establish New Mexico as a buffer zone. New Mexico would protect present-day Mexico from outside forces. The Spaniards also wanted to return

Christianity to New Mexico's Pueblo Indians. So in 1692 and again in 1693, Don Diego de Vargas reconquered New Mexico. It was not until 1696, however, that the Spaniards were able to regain control over the Rio Grande Pueblo Indians.

During the 1700s the Pueblo peoples and the Spaniards lived side by side. Life was not easy for either group, but life was especially hard for the Indians. The Pueblo Indian population declined. So, too, did the number of pueblos. The Spanish-speaking population, on the other hand, grew throughout the 1700s. By 1800 New Mexico had become one of New Spain's most populous outer provinces.

Also in the 1700s, New Mexico was threatened by outside forces. The French offered one such threat. New Mexico, closed under Spanish law to outside trade, attracted French traders. Raiding Indian groups offered a second threat. Apaches, Navajos, Comanches, and Utes disrupted life in both the pueblos and the Spanish communities. A third threat appeared in the early 1800s. This threat came from the United States, a country interested in expanding westward.

In spite of these outside threats, the people who lived in New Mexico's Spanish communities during the 1700s developed their own ways of living. These ways of living reflected the adjustments of the people to the conditions they found present in New Mexico. New Mexico was isolated. It was a frontier area. In part because of these conditions, New Mexico's Spanish-speaking population became a native-born population. It became more and more a mixed population. Most New Mexicans had to work hard to make a living. A majority were farmers. The people lived in the same kinds of houses. They ate the same food. They wore the same clothing. The people likewise developed a culture consistent with their heritage and their homeland. It was a culture that blended Spanish cultural traditions with local conditions. There was, to be sure, an upper class in New Mexico. Yet even the upper class had to live with New Mexico's frontier conditions.

New Mexico remained a Spanish possession until 1821. Then in that year New Mexico became part of a newly independent Mexico. Mexican rule brought changes to New Mexico. United States traders now brought goods into New Mexico over the Santa Fe Trail. Mountain men arrived to trap beaver in the northern mountains. Mexican rule did not, at the same time, produce among New Mexicans any great feeling of belonging to Mexico. Mexican officials were too far away to control either the government or the churches. In the long run this lack of control—added to other events that took place in New Mexico and elsewhere—meant yet another change for New Mexico. A United States wartime victory over Mexico brought about the end of Mexican rule in New Mexico. In 1848 New Mexico became a part of the United States.

Time Line:
New Mexico Is a Territory of the United States

New Mexico Territory formed ——— **1850**

Confederates invade New Mexico ——— **1862**
Navajo Long Walk begins ——— **1864**

Railroads enter New Mexico ——— **1879**

Apache wars end ——— **1886**

Rough Riders fight in war with Spain ——— **1898**

Congress passes statehood bill ——— **1910**

UNIT FOUR

New Mexico Is a Territory of the United States

New Mexico was organized as a territory of the United States in 1850. It remained a territory for more than 60 years. This means that much of New Mexico's history as a part of the United States took place during the territorial period. It was a time when New Mexico was still a frontier. It was a time as well when New Mexico became more like the rest of the nation.

As a territory for so many years, New Mexico was bound to undergo a number of changes. And undergo changes New Mexico did. One of these changes was the marked growth of its population. In 1850 the population of New Mexico was 61,547. This figure climbed to 119,565 in 1880 and 327,301 in 1910. Another change was the coming of the railroads. They broke down New Mexico's isolation from the population centers of the United States. Still another change was the arrival in New Mexico of large numbers of newcomers. Most came from other parts of the United States. Some came from other countries. You will read about these and other things in the chapters that follow. In chapter 8 you will read about a troubled New Mexico during the first half of the territorial period. In chapter 9 you will read about the end of New Mexico's isolation and of the changes that then occurred.

Eyewitness to New Mexico's History
A Pioneer Woman Comes to the Silver City Area, 1877
From: Helen J. Lundwall, ed., *Pioneering in Territorial Silver City: H. B. Ailman's Recollections of Silver City and the Southwest* (University of New Mexico Press, 1983), pp. 109–11.

In 1877 we went to New Mexico by wagon. . . . After crossing the Raton mountains going south, we were too early for the summer rains so had long drives without water; one of sixty miles, one of ninety, and one forty. We could not carry much, so traveled at night and gave our animals only a few swallows of water at a time, first washing their mouths with a cloth just wet. We got along very well, and did not lose any by thirst or fatigue, though the way seemed very long sometimes. We passed through some strange old ruins of a former civilization which we would like to have examined, but the people who were living in them were having smallpox of a malignant type. As we could not help them except with our sympathy, we moved on rapidly, for we feared contagion.

We stopped at last in the shadow of the Santa Rita mountain near the town of Silver City in Grant County, New Mexico. Georgetown, another mining camp, was nearby, and Pinos Altos was twelve miles away. Fort Bayard, four miles away, was a twelve-company post and supposed to protect us from Indian raids, but was really a farce, for they took good care of themselves and let the Indians steal our horses and sometimes children. Sometimes the Indians killed whole families and took what they liked and burned the houses. It seemed we had left one trouble to find another, but there was no turning back.

CHAPTER 8

Troubled Days in Territorial New Mexico

What you will learn in this chapter—

Today more than a hundred and thirty years have passed since Mexican rule ended in our state. When we look back to the middle of the 1800s, we have to remember that people living then did not know what their future might bring. New Mexico was not a state. It was a new territory within the United States. Peace was fragile in territorial New Mexico. Turmoil existed everywhere.

New Mexico's future was not at all certain for many years. New Mexicans endured a struggle for control of their territory during the Civil War. New Mexicans also faced the problem of continuing raids on settlements by Indian groups. Wars between rival groups of New Mexicans caused much violence as well. In this chapter you will learn about these troubles in territorial New Mexico. As you read, you will find answers to the following questions.

1. What did it mean for New Mexico to become a territory of the United States?
2. What problems did the people of New Mexico face during and after the Civil War?
3. What did the lack of law and order mean for territorial New Mexico?

1. What did it mean for New Mexico to become a territory of the United States?

New Mexicans get a new form of government. New Mexico was not officially added to the United States until 1848 and the Treaty of Guadalupe Hidalgo. Yet New Mexico had been under United States rule since Kearny's conquest of the area in 1846. It was Kearny who gave New Mexicans their first new government. He did so by issuing the Kearny Code. Announced in September 1846, the Kearny Code combined Mexican and Anglo-American law. There was a governor, a court system, and a legislature. The legislature had the power to make laws. The code also called for local government. Some

185

offices outlined by the Kearny Code had existed during the Mexican period. Others were new to New Mexico.

Once Kearny had drawn up and printed his code, he began to appoint people to different posts. He appointed a governor, judges, and other officials. Some officeholders were also elected. This was true of members of the legislature. The idea of electing lawmakers was new to New Mexicans. Other ideas were also new. One was the concept of trial by jury.

New Mexicans come under military rule. New Mexicans were not governed by the Kearny Code for long. There were several reasons for this. First, some members of New Mexico's leading families were unhappy with the turn of events. They did not like what they observed. Kearny's appointments to office, for example, favored Anglo-American traders and businessmen. Some native New Mexicans had been part of the power structure during the Mexican period. Only two of them received appointment from Kearny to high office. A number of leading New Mexicans were also unhappy with the very fact of United States rule. Second, the rumors about what would now happen to New Mexicans caused concern. Some rumors predicted that Hispanic and Pueblo people would lose their lands. Other rumors said that land would be taxed. Finally, church leaders were concerned about Anglo-American rule. They feared they would no longer influence the lives of the people. So they expressed distrust in the new government.

In response to United States rule, some New Mexicans rebelled. They did so in 1847 (page 174). This so-called Taos Rebellion resulted in loss of life both among Americans and among the rebels. In addition, it brought down the first United States civil government in New Mexico. After the rebellion, New Mexicans had a military government. For the next four years their lives were controlled by the army. Officials sent to New Mexico as military commanders ruled over the people with an iron hand. They expected appointed officials to do as they were told. Their main concern was to keep peace and order. So they declared martial (military) law. They fought against Indians who raided the settlements.

New Mexico's boundaries are in dispute. United States rule also brought boundary problems for New Mexico. The Treaty of Guadalupe Hidalgo in 1848 stated what parts of the Southwest would go the United States. But an 1849 boundary line survey failed to satisfy either the United States or Mexico. New Mexico's southern boundary remained an issue. Yet its eastern boundary caused even more concern. Texas claimed all land west to the Rio Grande. This claim included Santa Fe. Because of national events, this problem would involve New Mexicans in a debate that concerned all Americans.

The great debate that divided Americans was over slavery. They were

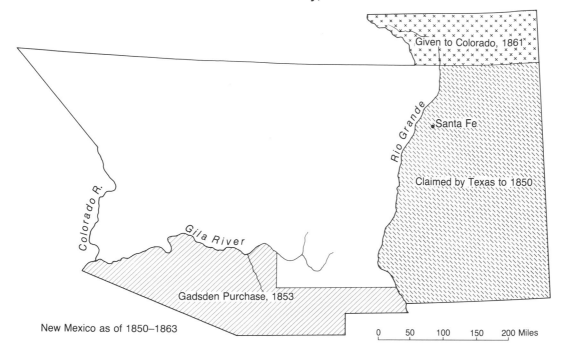

New Mexico Territory, 1850–1863

Given to Colorado, 1861

Rio Grande

•Santa Fe

Claimed by Texas to 1850

Colorado R.

Gila River

Gadsden Purchase, 1853

New Mexico as of 1850–1863

0   50   100   150   200 Miles

divided over the issue of extending slavery into new territories. Some Americans had even opposed statehood for Texas because Texans owned slaves. Others wanted slavery outlawed in the lands gained from Mexico. Upon becoming a territory of the United States, New Mexico found itself involved in national politics. Politics would give New Mexico an eastern boundary. Politics would decide if New Mexico could become a state. And politics would try to decide the future of slavery in New Mexico.

The Compromise of 1850 affects New Mexico. In 1850 these issues were decided. They were part of the Compromise of 1850, which Congress passed after heated debate. This compromise delayed the Civil War until the 1860s. It also settled once and for all the Texas–New Mexico boundary issue. New Mexico's eastern boundary was fixed on paper at 103° west longitude. When finally drawn, the boundary line was in fact one-half mile west of this longitude. (See the map on this page.) In exchange for Texas giving up its claims to eastern New Mexico, the United States gave Texas $10 million. This gave Texas the money needed to pay off its debts.

The Compromise of 1850 did not grant statehood to New Mexico. The statehood question had split New Mexicans into two opposing groups as early as 1848. In the summer of 1850, those favoring statehood drew up a constitution. They applied for admission to the Union as a state. Congress turned down this request. Instead, Congress established New Mexico as a territory on September 9, 1850. New Mexico's bid for statehood failed chiefly because of the slavery issue. Northerners feared New Mexico would enter the Union as a slave state. Many northern citizens opposed slavery in the western territories. Southerners, on the other hand, favored it.

The Compromise of 1850 also tried to decide the future of slavery in New Mexico. It divided the land gained from Mexico, excepting California, into two territories. One was the Utah Territory. The other was the New Mexico Territory. New Mexicans had gone on record in 1848 as opposing slavery. They had taken their stand more from a dislike of Texans than from a dislike of slavery. Now the compromise gave the people in Utah and New Mexico the right to decide their own futures. They could vote to be slave states or free states when they applied for statehood. As events turned out, New Mexicans never voted on this issue. The Civil War came along. It determined that slavery would exist nowhere in the United States.

New Mexicans get a new government. The ten years following the Compromise of 1850 were a time of growing conflict. It was a conflict between the northern and southern sections of the country. Yet for New Mexico the 1850s were mostly a time of development. Now organized as a territory, it once again had a government of appointed and elected officials. It had a government that would remain much the same throughout the territorial period. Heading the government was a governor appointed by the president. The president also named supreme court judges. Each of these judges, in turn, headed one of the district courts in New Mexico. A territorial legislature was made up of persons elected to represent the people who lived in different parts of New Mexico. The people likewise elected a delegate to Congress. The delegate

Santa Fe, the territorial capital, in 1859

did not, however, have the power to vote on bills. Still other officials served New Mexicans on the territorial or the local level. In other words, New Mexico's government was like that of other American territories.

New Mexico gets new land. During the 1850s the United States added land to the New Mexico Territory. The failure in 1849 to agree on a boundary line between the United States and Mexico had left both sides unhappy. So in 1853 the president of the United States sent James Gadsden to Mexico to propose a settlement. The Mexican government accepted. The United States gave Mexico $10 million. In exchange, Mexico gave up a large area of desert land in what is today the southern part of New Mexico and Arizona. (See the map on page 187.)

Known as the Gadsden Purchase, this settlement did two things. (1) It fixed the southern boundary of what was then the New Mexico Territory. The new land became part of Doña Ana County. This county was one of the nine counties into which New Mexico was then divided. (2) The new land provided a possible route for a transcontinental railroad. This route would cross the southern part of the country. Such a route would be mostly on flat land. It would eliminate the need for laying railroad tracks across high mountains.

New Mexico grows. During the 1850s New Mexico grew in population as well as in area. It was a time when Americans were moving westward. California attracted the most new settlers. After all, gold had been discovered there in 1849. Still, New Mexico became home to people caught up in the westward movement. It became a place where many soldiers were stationed. Between 1850 and 1860 the population of New Mexico grew from 61,547 to 93,516. The birth rate accounted for some of this increase. Newcomers from the East made up the rest of it.

Among the people who moved into New Mexico were many with backgrounds in business. They helped change New Mexico's economy. They took the place of the traders and shopkeepers of the Santa Fe and Chihuahua trails. These new businessmen operated on a much larger scale. They built stores in New Mexican towns. They supplied these stores with goods brought from the eastern business centers of the United States. Chief among these businessmen were German-Jewish merchants. The first of these merchants was Jacob Solomon Spiegelberg. Spiegelberg had arrived with Kearny in New Mexico in 1846. Non-Jewish merchants entered the area as well. Franz Huning, born in Germany, settled in Albuquerque in 1857. He built business interests there and later expanded them into Los Lunas.

New Mexico's northern boundary is redrawn. Also in the 1850s New Mexico's settled areas expanded. In southern New Mexico the first real settlement of the area took place. The Mesilla Valley became a farming center.

Forts and Stagecoach Routes in New Mexico

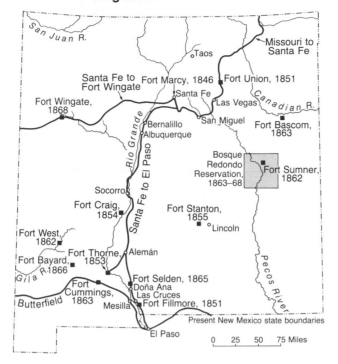

Northern New Mexico had long been settled. But in the 1850s a number of New Mexicans moved even farther north. Some moved into the San Luis Valley. Others moved up the Conejos River into the area where the Spaniards had arrested Zebulon Pike (page 129).

Yet these northern settlers and the land they settled did not long remain a part of New Mexico. Instead, the settlers and the land became a part of the Colorado Territory. The discovery of gold in the Colorado Rockies in 1859 led to a gold rush. It was much like the gold rush in California 10 years earlier. People moved in quickly. The population of the area grew rapidly. The people demanded attention from Congress. California's gold rush had led to statehood for Californians. The gold rush to the Rockies and the approach of the Civil War led to the formation of the Colorado Territory. Congress formed the Colorado Territory in February 1861. Under this act Congress moved New Mexico's northern boundary southward to 37° north latitude. New Mexico lost its settlements in the San Luis Valley and along the Conejos River. At the same time it lost control of the rich coal deposits near Trinidad. These losses were not in New Mexico's best interests. Still, New Mexicans mostly benefited from the changes caused by the growth of the West.

New Mexicans get better protection and transportation. Among

The stagecoach at Hillsboro

the changes was a new interest by the national government in the well-being
of westerners. To help protect New Mexicans, for example, the government
began to build new forts. It built these forts as defensive positions against
Indian raids. It located these forts along the territory's major transportation
and communication routes. Look at the map on page 190. There you can see
the locations of the forts in territorial New Mexico. Note the date of their
construction. On that same map you can also see the main stagecoach routes
in New Mexico. The Butterfield Overland Mail Company was the leading
stagecoach line. By 1858 Butterfield stages ran from St. Louis, Missouri, to
San Francisco, California, twice a week. The route they followed carried them
across southern New Mexico. They helped link New Mexico to the rest of the
country. The Butterfield stages played a major role in the development of New
Mexico during the 1850s.

New Mexico's Catholic churches undergo changes. Soon after
getting a territorial government in 1850, New Mexicans also got a new leader
for the Catholic Church. This church leader was Jean B. Lamy. Born in France,
Lamy had served the church in the United States. A stern person, Lamy arrived
in New Mexico in 1851. Two years later he became the bishop for Santa Fe.
At the same time New Mexico was removed from the Mexican diocese of
Durango.

191

Inscription Rock

Camels in New Mexico

In the summer of 1857, New Mexicans thought the circus had arrived. A camel caravan marched through the villages along the Rio Grande, but it was no circus. The camels belonged to the United States Army, and they were part of an experiment to see how well they worked in the southwestern desert. Desert conditions quickly wore out mules and horses. It was hoped that camels would be stronger animals. Brought from the Middle East in 1855, the first army camels were stationed in Texas.

Lieutenant Edward Beale brought 25 of these camels to New Mexico in 1857. They were part of an army caravan assigned to build a road westward from New Mexico to California. The camels proved their worth quickly by carrying loads of 600 pounds or more. Neither did they, like mules and horses, quickly develop sore feet from the rocky roads. Entering New Mexico near El Paso, Beale's camels traveled northward toward Albuquerque. All along the way excited villagers turned out to stare at the strange animals. Village after village buzzed with excitement, and on August 10 the camel train reached Albuquerque. Moving westward toward California, the caravan camped at Inscription Rock on August 23. There some of the soldiers scratched their names into the rock.

Beale surveyed the new road to California, and the camel proved equal to the American desert. Yet the army did not replace the horse and mule with the camel. Soldiers disliked handling them. The Civil War ended interest in a Camel Corps, and many of the animals were sold or left to run wild. Today the skeleton of one of the New Mexico camel caravan stands in the Smithsonian Institution in Washington, D.C.—the last remains of the camels' visit to New Mexico.

Lamy studied the behavior of New Mexico's church officials. He concluded that they were lacking in discipline. He was, in fact, greatly disturbed by the carefree way in which they lived and conducted the affairs of the church. So Bishop Lamy began a reform program. In trying to change New Mexico's clergy, Lamy met resistance. Some clergymen felt the reforms would change New Mexico's traditional Hispanic Catholicism. Chief among those who resisted were Father Antonio José Martínez in Taos (page 164) and Father José Manuel Gallegos of Albuquerque. Lamy separated both men from the church. Indeed, he brought many changes to New Mexico's long established church. In the years that followed he oversaw the building of 45 new churches. He encouraged the building of St. Michael's, a Catholic college in Santa Fe. He supervised

St. Vrain's flour mill near Mora

the building of many parochial (church-sponsored) schools. New Mexico did not yet have public schools. It would not have free public schools for many years. Parochial schools were therefore important in educating New Mexico's young people. In 1875 Lamy was elevated to archbishop of Santa Fe.

Non-Catholic churches get their start. Soon after coming under United States rule, New Mexico also got its first Protestant churches and schools. Baptist missionaries and ministers began arriving in New Mexico as early as 1849. In 1854 the Baptists built a church in Santa Fe. This church was the first Protestant church built in New Mexico. Presbyterian and Methodist missionaries arrived in New Mexico beginning in the 1850s. New Mexico's first Episcopalian church service was led by a visiting bishop in 1863. The earliest Episcopalian groups did not, however, form until later. Protestant churches in the 1850s and 1860s focused on missionary work among the Indians. In addition, Protestants built church-related schools. Thomas Harwood's arrival at Watrous in 1871 signaled much new activity among New Mexico's Protestants. A Methodist minister, Harwood was a very active church leader until the end of the 1800s. Protestant churches were in New Mexico to stay. Their growth awaited only the coming of the railroads and the arrival in New Mexico of large numbers of Protestant Americans.

Also in New Mexico to stay was the Church of Jesus Christ of Latter-

193

Three bishops (left to right): Salpointe of Santa Fe, Lamy of Santa Fe, and Machebeuf of Denver, with two unidentified men at right

Day Saints. The members of this church, the Mormons, had arrived in the West in the 1840s. Led into Utah by Brigham Young, they had at first settled around the Great Salt Lake. Irrigation projects had enabled the Mormons to prosper. From Utah Mormon families moved to nearby areas. In the 1870s they moved into western New Mexico. They settled at Ramah near Gallup and elsewhere. Still greater numbers of Mormons moved into New Mexico in the years that followed. Today New Mexico has a very active Mormon community.

Section Review

1.   **(a)** Briefly describe what the Kearny Code was and what it did.
      (b) Why did the government set up by this code fail?
      (c) What kind of government did New Mexicans get as a result of the rebellion of 1847?

2.   **(a)** What claim to New Mexican territory did Texas make?
      (b) How was the question of New Mexico's eastern boundary finally settled?

3.   **(a)** Why did New Mexico's bid for statehood in 1850 fail?
      (b) What did the Compromise of 1850 say about the territory of New Mexico and about slavery in New Mexico?

4.   **(a)** Briefly describe New Mexico's territorial government from 1850 on.

(b) Why was the Gadsden Purchase important?

(c) How did the formation of the Colorado Territory affect New Mexico?

(d) Why did the government build new forts in the territory, and where were these forts located?

(e) What route through New Mexico did the Butterfield Overland Mail Company follow?

(f) What changes did Archbishop Lamy and non-Catholic churchmen bring to New Mexico?

---

2. What problems did the people of New Mexico face during and after the Civil War?

The Civil War begins. New Mexico had faced challenges since it became a territory of the United States. Among these had been the transition from Mexican rule to rule by the United States. It was not long, however, before New Mexico faced a more serious challenge. For like the rest of the country, New Mexico soon found itself drawn into the Civil War. After Abraham Lincoln's election as president of the United States in November 1860, seven southern states seceded (withdrew) from the Union. They formed their own country, the Confederate States of America. Their withdrawal was followed by a waiting period. Then on April 12, 1861, southern troops opened fire on Fort Sumter in Charleston harbor, South Carolina. This Confederate action set off the most bitter war in United States history. When the lines were at last drawn, 23 northern states and 11 southern states had chosen opposite sides.

The outbreak of the war had an immediate effect on New Mexico. Many of the army officers stationed in New Mexico resigned from the United States Army. They joined the Confederate armed forces. The outbreak of the war also had a more lasting effect on New Mexico. This was because New Mexico fit into the overall plans of the South. These plans called for the conquest of New Mexico. They had the support of the top Confederate leaders, including Jefferson Davis. Davis was the president of the Confederate States of America. He had long seen the value of the Southwest.

Confederates believe New Mexico is important. The Confederacy wanted to conquer New Mexico for a number of reasons. First, if the Confederacy conquered the New Mexico Territory, it might next take over California. This would mean that the South could draw on California for gold, manpower, and seaports. Second, the control of the Southwest would give the Confederacy a pathway into Mexico. From El Paso and present-day Arizona its troops could move into Chihuahua and Sonora. Finally, if the South controlled the West from New Mexico to California, European nations might take notice.

195

They might recognize the Confederacy as an independent country. They might even help the Confederacy in some way.

At the same time New Mexicans began to think about the future of the territory. They, too, tended to divide along sectional lines. This was because northern and southern New Mexico had grown into two distinct regions. The economic lifeline of northern New Mexico ran along the Santa Fe Trail from Santa Fe to Missouri. Missouri did not secede from the Union. So most northern New Mexicans remained loyal to the Union. They also distrusted the Texans, who had seceded. They remembered the invasion of the Texas expedition of 1841. Many southern New Mexicans, on the other hand, cast their lot with the Confederacy. These were people who were southern in their attitudes. Doña Ana County was a center of secessionist activity. Those who favored secession held an informal convention in Mesilla in March 1861. The delegates to this convention declared that the land south of 34° was Confederate land. They raised the Confederate flag. Fort Fillmore, which was still under Union control, lay less than 3 miles away.

Union forces prepare to defend New Mexico. Military operations began in New Mexico in 1861. During the summer Confederate troops gathered at Fort Bliss in El Paso. From there they advanced on Fort Fillmore. Fort Fillmore was important because it controlled the route westward. The southerners were successful. A battalion of fewer than 300 men under Colonel John R. Baylor captured the fort on July 26, 1861. Union troops at the fort tried to escape to Fort Stanton. Colonel Baylor's forces, however, overtook them at San Agustin Springs and captured 400 Union soldiers.

No other fighting took place in New Mexico during 1861. Nonetheless, it was a time for planning. Making plans for the Union was Colonel Edward R. S. Canby. At first Canby had 2,466 men under his command. Having received permission to raise regiments of volunteers, Canby soon increased his numbers. He organized two volunteer regiments in August 1861. Commanding the regiments were Kit Carson and Miguel Pino. Canby also planned for the defense of New Mexico. He based his defenses on two points. One was Fort Craig located on the Rio Grande 100 miles south of Albuquerque. The other was Fort Union in northeastern New Mexico near Las Vegas. In addition, he strengthened the defenses at Albuquerque and Fort Marcy in Santa Fe. Look at the map on page 198. There you can see the key points in New Mexico during the Civil War.

Confederates plan the invasion of New Mexico. Making plans for the Confederate invasion of New Mexico was Brigadier General Henry H. Sibley. Before the war Sibley had been an army officer in New Mexico. He, like others, had gone over to the Confederacy. By late 1861 he was actively

Colonel Edward R. S. Canby

Fort Marcy officers' quarters (1860s)

preparing to invade New Mexico. He organized and trained his small army at San Antonio, Texas. Most of Sibley's troops were under 25 years of age. Most were experienced frontier fighters.

Sibley planned to invade New Mexico by moving up the Rio Grande Valley. He chose this route for several reasons. (1) His army might live off the food available in the valley. (2) There were military supplies at Albuquerque and Santa Fe. (3) A successful advance would give the Confederacy control of the western end of the Santa Fe Trail. Sibley's small army set off from San Antonio to El Paso in October 1861. Joined in El Paso by some of Baylor's men, Sibley marched northward. Sibley's forces reached Mesilla on January 11, 1862. From there they pushed up the Rio Grande Valley during the first week of February.

The Battle of Valverde takes place. At first Sibley's forces faced little opposition. By February 12 Confederate artillery and a wagon train were only 7 miles south of Fort Craig. By this time Sibley's army numbered about 2,600 men. Opposing the Confederate force from inside Fort Craig were 3,810 Union regulars and New Mexico volunteers under the command of Canby. But no battle occurred at Fort Craig. This was because Sibley decided not to assault the fort but rather to outflank it. In order to do this his forces on February 19 crossed to the east bank of the Rio Grande. They then moved north, screened from Union soldiers by hills that stretched to 7 miles above Fort Craig.

In response to Sibley's movements, some Union troops left the fort. Fighting broke out when men from each side reached a ford (crossing) on the Rio Grande on the morning of February 21, 1862. The ford was at a place

197

The Civil War in New Mexico, 1861–1862

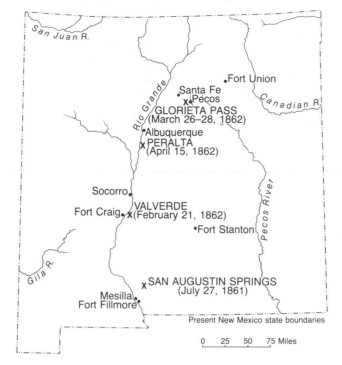

called Valverde. The battle started on a small scale, but both sides soon sent in new troops. Fort Craig was all but abandoned as Union soldiers rushed to Valverde. In time the Union troops formed a battle line at the ford on the east side of the river. The Confederates formed a battle line that faced the Union forces. The two sides fought all day. Then at about 4:30 in the afternoon, Confederate troops attacked the Union left. They captured an artillery battery and turned the guns on the retreating Union forces. Canby retreated across the river and back into Fort Craig. The Union lost 306 officers and enlisted men at Valverde. Confederate losses numbered 185.

Confederate forces advance to Santa Fe. The Confederate soldiers remained at Valverde for a couple of days. On February 24 they broke camp and advanced toward Albuquerque. In doing so they left Canby and his men at their rear. As the troops moved up the valley, they met little resistance. Along the way they received a cool reception from the people they met. These people did not favor the southern cause. They disliked the way in which Confederate troops took their food and other goods without payment. In Albuquerque only a few residents helped the southerners. Nonetheless, the Confederates captured the city on March 2. They laid claim to Albuquerque by raising the Confederate flag in the plaza.

A small Confederate force remained in Albuquerque. The main force marched toward Santa Fe, the capital of the New Mexico Territory. Numbering 500, the main force took Santa Fe. The Confederates ordered the capital city's residents to swear allegiance to the Confederacy. But the capture of Santa Fe did not bring New Mexico under southern control. The Confederacy could not control New Mexico unless it defeated the Union forces in New Mexico, including those at Fort Union.

The Battle of Glorieta Pass takes place. The Confederates now advanced toward but never reached Fort Union. Instead, Union forces engaged them in battle at Glorieta Pass. Located near the Pecos River, Glorieta Pass lies near the southern end of the Sangre de Cristo range. This pass is several miles long and one-fourth mile wide at its center. At either end are steep canyon walls. The west side of the pass is known as Apache Canyon. It was at Glorieta Pass that Union soldiers defended against the Confederate advance toward Fort Union. Among the Union Troops was a regiment of Colorado volunteers.

The Union forces chose Glorieta Pass as the place to halt the Confederate advance, and halt it they did. First they fought the southerners at Apache Canyon on March 26, 1862. The Union forces held their ground. The Confederates retreated. The next day Union troops moved to the eastern end of Glorieta Pass. Reinforcements arrived for both sides, and a second battle took

Battle of Glorieta as portrayed by the Rocky Mountain Civil War Reenactment Association

place on March 28. This was the Battle of Glorieta Pass. The fighting was intense. At last the Confederate forces met defeat. Some of the Colorado volunteers under Major John M. Chivington had made their way behind the Confederate lines. There they destroyed the Confederate ammunition and supply train. They burned 73 wagons and killed between 500 and 600 horses and mules. Believing that Canby had arrived from the south and seeing no hope for new supplies, the Confederates retreated toward Santa Fe. They had lost about 350 men to the Union's 150.

Confederate forces leave New Mexico. The Battle of Glorieta Pass was the beginning of the end of the Confederacy's plans for New Mexico and land farther west. Indeed, historians sometimes refer to the Battle of Glorieta Pass as the "Gettysburg of the West." The Battle of Glorieta Pass was the turning point of the war in the Far West, just as Gettysburg was the turning point in the East. On April 1, 1862, Canby moved from Fort Craig to a position outside Albuquerque. Nine days later he bombarded Confederate positions within the town. On April 12 Sibley ordered a retreat southward. Canby caught and defeated part of Sibley's force at Peralta. From Peralta the southerners retreated down the west bank of the river. Canby's Union troops followed on the east bank as far as Fort Craig. They might have forced a battle but decided against it.

Beyond Fort Craig the Confederate retreat was a disaster. Sibley led his

Confederate cannon in Old Town, Albuquerque

men into the San Mateo Mountains. Exposure and bitter cold caused loss of life. Disease and unfriendly Indians added to their problems. The Apaches even poisoned well water along the route of the retreat. Only 2,000 of Sibley's men returned to San Antonio. Elsewhere in the United States, the Civil War lasted until April 1865. But in New Mexico the fighting ended by August 1862. Nonetheless, the war had an effect on New Mexico even after the fighting ended.

Indian raids take place. One result of the Civil War in the Southwest was the creation of a new territory. In 1863 Congress turned the western half of New Mexico into the Arizona Territory. New Mexicans accepted this action for two basic reasons. (1) New Mexico kept the fertile Mesilla valley. (Under another plan Mesilla would have been lost.) (2) Officials in Santa Fe now had less area to govern. From that time on the people of New Mexico and the people of Arizona went their separate ways.

Another result of the Civil War in the Southwest was a renewal of Indian warfare. The Indians watched as Union and Confederate armies fought each other during the war. They watched forts being abandoned. They watched the withdrawal of Union troops from New Mexico. These troops were needed for battles fought in the eastern half of the United States. So the non-Pueblo Indians stepped up their raids on settlements. They believed they would face little or no opposition. For New Mexicans and other westerners these raids meant horror and hardship.

A new Indian policy goes into effect. Apaches and Navajos raided at will until the arrival of a new commander for the Department of New Mexico. This person was General James Carleton. Carleton arrived in New Mexico with his California Column. He was too late to fight the Confederate forces. Still, Carleton assumed the command formerly held by Canby in September 1862. He then turned his attention to the Indian problem. The new commander reopened existing forts and built new ones. He also announced a new Indian policy. This policy was, moreover, consistent with then current United States Indian policy.

As finally put into force, Carleton's policy had three phases. First, Carleton gave a warning to all Indian leaders. He told them that those who did not respect the peace would be punished. Second, he sent troops against the Indians who continued to raid. Colonel Kit Carson and other field commanders rode off to confront the Mescalero Apaches and then the Navajos. Their orders were to defeat the Indians, not bargain with them. Third, Carleton ordered that the defeated Indians be rounded up and placed on *reservations*. These reservations were areas set aside for the Indian people. They were supposed to become the Indians' permanent homes. On the reservations the Indian people

reservation: area set aside for Indians to live on

201

would learn Christianity and farming. The government would direct their lives.

The Mescalero Apaches were the first Indians in New Mexico to experience life on a reservation. Colonel Carson and his men campaigned against the Mescaleros in southern New Mexico. By the summer of 1863 they completed their campaign. Carson then relocated 400 Mescalero braves and their families to the Bosque Redondo Reservation. It was located on the Pecos River in eastern New Mexico. Nearby stood one of Carleton's new forts, Fort Sumner. (See the map on page 190.)

The Navajos make the Long Walk. Next Colonel Carson set out against the Navajos. Assisting him was Lieutenant Colonel J. Francisco Chaves, commander at Fort Wingate. Carson and Chaves led their troops into western New Mexico, the home of the Navajo. Few Navajos died during the campaign itself. But the Indians did meet defeat. They lost because their very livelihood—their crops and their livestock—were destroyed. Begun in 1863, the campaign against the Navajos lasted two years.

Faced with starvation, one Navajo band after another agreed to resettlement at the Bosque Redondo. Those who surrendered then took part in what is remembered in Navajo history as the "Long Walk." Thousands of Navajos were led away from their homeland. They were marched from western New Mexico to a new home near Fort Sumner. So horrible was this journey that the Navajos often date events by the Long Walk. Some events in Navajo history happened before the Long Walk. Other events happened after the Long Walk.

The Bosque Redondo experiment fails. The removal of the Navajo people to the Fort Sumner area was disastrous. The Navajos and the Mescaleros did not get along. Yet they were settled in the same area. Plains Indians raided the reservation. And the Navajo economy never prospered. Crops failed. The land would not support the population of 9,000 that had been settled on it. Food, fuel, and clothing were in short supply. Finally, the government did not

Navajos at Bosque Redondo

effectively administer the reservation. It found that reservations were costly to operate. For all these reasons the Bosque Redondo Reservation failed. In November 1865 the Mescaleros simply left the reservation. They at first broke up into small bands. In time these bands made their way back to the Fort Stanton area. The government in 1873 established a permanent reservation for the Mescaleros. This reservation was located in the White and Sacramento mountains.

The Navajos stayed at Bosque Redondo until 1868. In May of that year General William Tecumseh Sherman made an offer to the Navajos. He acted in the name of the United States government. If the Navajos promised never again to fight, they could decide where they would call home. They had three choices. (1) They could remain at the Bosque Redondo Reservation. (2) They could move to a reservation that would be set aside for them in the Indian Territory. This reservation would be located in the Arkansas River Valley. It would have fertile soil and a ready water supply. (3) They could return to the land of northwestern New Mexico and northeastern Arizona. On May 29 the Navajo tribe chose option number three. They did so unanimously. They chose to return to the land they had lived on before their removal to the Bosque Redondo.

Sherman may or may not have been surprised by this decision. He advised the president, Andrew Johnson, that the land in option three was of no use whatsoever to the United States. The Navajos, however, saw the land in a different way. To them the land was home. One Navajo clan leader, Barboncito, explained the Navajo's choice in these words:

> I hope to God you will not ask us to go to any
> country but our own. When the Navajos were first
> created, four mountains and four rivers were pointed out
> to us, inside of which we should live, and that was to
> be Dinetah. Changing Woman gave us this land. Our
> God created it specifically for us.

The United States government granted the Navajos' request. It created the Navajo Reservation. The reservation was smaller than the area the Navajos had once lived in. It did not include any of the four mountains Barboncito had mentioned. Nonetheless, the Navajos were happy to return to their homeland. They settled down to life on the reservation. Having learned from their experience, they did not again raid New Mexico's settlements. Rather, the Navajos in 1868 made lasting peace with the United States government. So, too, the Jicarilla Apaches agreed to move onto a permanent reservation in northern New Mexico.

Life in New Mexico is further disrupted. The territorial period

Buffalo soldiers in camp

was a troubled time for most of New Mexico's Indians. The United States government followed a policy of placing non-Pueblo Indians on reservations. At the same time the government largely ignored the Pueblo peoples and their problems. The Pueblo peoples received confirmation of their land grants after 1854, but the government did not actively protect their lands. The Pueblo governors received new Lincoln canes (page 99). These canes were rewards to the Pueblo Indians for remaining neutral during the Civil War. But otherwise, the Pueblo peoples were left to care for themselves. The United States government did not recognize them as full citizens. They had, by contrast, been citizens of Mexico during the Mexican period.

Also during this time Indians who did not even live in the territory became a part of New Mexico's story. Plains Indians disrupted life on the eastern plains in the 1860s. Their raids went unchallenged until the early 1870s. They threatened New Mexico's lifeline to the East. They made it dangerous for anyone to travel to and from New Mexico. Finally, the United States Army struck back in 1874. The Plains Indians were defeated. They were forced onto reservations in the Indian Territory, now part of Oklahoma.

The Buffalo Soldiers help bring peace to New Mexico. Among those fighting the Plains Indians were the Ninth and Tenth Cavalry regiments. The soldiers who made up these units were black. They carried out their work with left-over horses and equipment. They were housed in run-down forts. Nonetheless, they did their work well. They chased various bands of Indians

Chiricahua Apache leader Geronimo

until the Indians surrendered. In the process the black soldiers gained the respect of those they fought. The Indians called them Buffalo Soldiers. They did so because of the soldiers' hair. To the Indians, the soldiers' curly hair resembled that of the buffalo—"God's cattle." The Buffalo Soldiers also gained the respect of their country. Among their number were 11 Medal of Honor winners. The Ninth and Tenth Cavalry had the lowest rate of desertion in the entire army.

The Buffalo Soldiers patrolled the Llano Estacado until after the coming of the railroads. They explored sections of the eastern plains. They thus helped open eastern New Mexico for settlement. But as peace came to the plains region, New Mexico was still left with one place where Indian raids continued. This was southwestern New Mexico. Here Apache bands kept up their raids into the 1880s. The Buffalo Soldiers fought here too.

The Indian wars come to an end. It was the Apaches, then, who wrote the final chapter on Indian wars in New Mexico. Indeed, they were among the last Indians anywhere in the country to resist United States authority. Their story and the story of their leaders—Victorio, Nana, and Geronimo—are well

205

known in fiction and film. In 1879 Victorio led his followers off a reservation. They raided from the Rio Grande into Arizona. They destroyed everything in their path. These raids did not end until Victorio died in 1881.

A band of Apaches resumed the raids under the leadership of Nana, Victorio's son-in-law. Nana fought and won eight battles against United States troops. He was finally confined to the San Carlos Reservation in eastern Arizona. In 1885 Nana and Geronimo escaped from the reservation together. Geronimo was the leader of a small band of Chiricahua Apaches. These Apaches warred against the United States until their surrender in 1886. In that year the United States government sent all 502 Chiricahua Apaches to prison in Florida. Over a period of time they were relocated to Fort Sill in Oklahoma. In 1913 some 187 Chiricahuas received permission to move to New Mexico to live on the reservation with their cousins, the Mescaleros. The Chiricahuas returned in peace.

Section Review
1.   **(a)** Why did the Confederates want to conquer New Mexico?
       (b) Which New Mexicans mostly favored the Union side, and which mostly favored the Confederate side?
       (c) Why did New Mexicans divide in the way they did?
2.   Where did the battles of Valverde and Glorieta Pass take place, and why were they important?
3.   **(a)** What new territory was created as a result of the Civil War?
       (b) How did the war lead to the renewal of Indian raids?
4.   **(a)** Briefly describe Carleton's Indian policy.
       (b) What happened to the Mescaleros and Navajos during the 1860s?
       (c) Why did the Bosque Redondo Reservation experiment fail?
5.   **(a)** How did the Plains Indians affect New Mexico in the 1860s and 1870s, and how were they brought under control?
       (b) Briefly describe New Mexico's final Indian wars and their outcome.

3. What did the lack of law and order mean for territorial New Mexico?

New Mexico is still a frontier. It is understandable that some of the last Indian wars in the United States took place in New Mexico. After all, its people had long been removed from other population centers. Even the settlements within New Mexico had been more or less isolated. In other words, New Mexico was a frontier region for much of its history. It had been a frontier during the period of Spanish rule. It had been a frontier during the Mexican period. It was a frontier long after becoming a part of the United States. This is not to say that life in New Mexico remained unchanged. It did not. You

Old Lincoln County Courthouse (1940s)

read in the last chapter about the Santa Fe trade. You read in this chapter about new ideas being brought into New Mexico by people from the United States. Among these new ideas were trials by jury and the election of lawmakers. In the next chapter you will read about still other changes in territorial New Mexico. The last section in this chapter, however, is about the lawlessness on the New Mexico frontier.

The most celebrated case of lawlessness in New Mexico occurred in Lincoln County during the late 1870s and the early 1880s. At that time Lincoln County covered nearly one-fifth of the entire New Mexico Territory. It was the largest county in the United States. Before the lawlessness in Lincoln County came to an end, two different groups had fought and killed members of the other group. This so-called Lincoln County War began in 1878. It dragged on until 1881.

The people in Lincoln County choose sides. The trouble in Lincoln County had its origins in the aftermath of the Civil War. A man named Lawrence G. Murphy laid the groundwork for it. During the war Murphy served with the New Mexico Volunteers. After the fighting ended, he opened a store in Lincoln and soon controlled the economic life of the county. He owned the area's only store. He farmed and raised cattle. He arranged for most of the wagon trains that traveled to Lincoln. He set the prices for goods, prices that were very high. So powerful was Murphy that he determined who owned land and who could find jobs. He even determined who could stay in the county. Murphy himself was not present in Lincoln County when most of the trouble took place. Poor health forced him to seek treatment in Santa Fe. It forced him in 1876 to sell his business interests in Lincoln. The two men who

207

bought out Murphy were James J. Dolan and John H. Riley. These men were determined to control the economic life of Lincoln just as Murphy had. They would lead one of the two groups that fought in the Lincoln County War.

The other group that fought in the war were newcomers to the area. Their leader was Alexander A. McSween. McSween arrived in Lincoln in 1875. A lawyer, he was soon handling lawsuits, most of them against Murphy. Many of the lawsuits against Murphy were brought by John S. Chisum, a famous cattleman. Chisum disliked Murphy. Indeed, Chisum believed that Murphy was dishonest. Murphy's power in Lincoln County withstood the lawsuits. But then McSween decided to broaden his economic interests. He invested in a cattle ranch. By late August 1877 it became clear that McSween, backed by others, intended to open a bank. He intended to start a new store as well. This new store would challenge the store that Dolan and Riley owned. Some of the money that backed McSween may have come from Chisum. Other money definitely came from John Henry Tunstall. An Englishman from a wealthy family, Tunstall had arrived in Lincoln in November 1876. He formed a partnership with McSween that would go into effect in May 1878. Tunstall's aim was to become a great cattle rancher.

The conflict begins. As it developed, the rivalry in Lincoln was between oldtimers and newcomers. It did not take much to start a war between the two groups. What set off the war was a legal matter. In December 1877 some of McSween's clients appeared in Judge Warren Henry Bristol's court in Mesilla. There they signed a complaint against McSween. The complaint charged McSween with keeping money that he was supposed to have turned over to his clients. Those who signed the complaint had the backing of the local district attorney, William L. Rynerson. With this complaint in hand, Judge Bristol issued a warrant for McSween's arrest. McSween's arrest, in turn, took place in Las Vegas, New Mexico, on December 27. The United States attorney for the territory had sent a telegram to Las Vegas requesting the arrest. This official was none other than Thomas B. Catron. Catron was then and for years to come one of New Mexico's most powerful politicians. Catron, Bristol, and Rynerson were all sympathetic to Dolan and Riley.

From Las Vegas McSween was taken to Mesilla. There he appeared before Judge Bristol. In January 1878 McSween entered a plea of not guilty. Nonetheless, Judge Bristol took court action against McSween on February 7. He told the Lincoln County sheriff to take $8,000 in property from McSween. This was the amount McSween's clients had filed for in their complaint. The sheriff was William Brady. Brady had served with Murphy in the New Mexico Volunteers.

Tunstall is murdered. The legal actions against McSween were part

208

Blazer's Mill, 1939

of a Dolan-Riley campaign to ruin their competitor. But the days of legal actions were soon at an end. For on February 18 Tunstall was shot and killed. A sheriff's posse gunned him down in cold blood on the road to the Tunstall ranch. Sheriff Brady had headed for the Tunstall ranch to enforce a new court order. This order directed the sheriff to take property belonging to Tunstall, McSween's soon-to-be partner. Tunstall had angered the Dolan-Riley group by backing McSween.

Among those who witnessed Tunstall's murder was a young man Tunstall had helped. He was William H. Bonney, alias Billy the Kid. Bonney vowed to seek revenge. And when the territory's legal officers failed to act on Tunstall's murder, revenge became commonplace. Some of McSween's men shot and killed two Dolan-Riley supporters as they rode toward Lincoln. Then on April 1, 1878, some of McSween's men shot and killed Sheriff Brady and one of his deputies. Bonney was involved in this shooting. Three days later Bonney and others shot and killed A. L. "Buckshot" Roberts at Blazer's Mill. This revenge did not, however, really help the McSween side. For taking Brady's place was a new sheriff, who was also a Dolan-Riley sympathizer. The new sheriff received his appointment from the territory's governor, Samuel B. Axtell. Axtell had borrowed money from Murphy.

Billy the Kid

The battle of Lincoln takes place. After Brady's death things went badly for the McSween group. Judge Bristol and District Attorney Rynerson took more legal action against McSween and his men. Finally, in early July, McSween rode out to the Chisum ranch to seek Chisum's advice. The two decided that McSween would return to Lincoln and stand his ground. McSween arrived back in Lincoln on July 15. Forty-one men joined him on the return trip. McSween took 10 of these men into his own house. The others took up positions around the town. Ready to oppose McSween were Sheriff George Peppin and supporters drawn from all over the area. Included in their number were 15 Doña Ana and Grant county gunslingers hired by Dolan. Sheriff Peppin swore all of these men in as deputy sheriffs.

Both the "McSween Crowd" and the "Sheriff's Party" shot at one another for the next three days. But the battle was a stalemate. Then on July 19 the commanding officer at Fort Stanton received word from Peppin that a soldier had been wounded in Lincoln. The army now joined the battle. Soldiers entered Lincoln. Their purpose was to protect women and children. Their presence turned the fight in favor of the sheriff's men. Securing a warrant for McSween's arrest, the sheriff and his men set the McSween house afire on the night of July 19. Still, McSween refused to surrender. In the fighting that followed McSween and 3 of his followers were killed. McSween was shot five times at close range. One of the sheriff's deputies was also killed. Escaping unhurt from the McSween house was Bonney.

New Mexico gets a new governor. The battle of Lincoln was over. The Lincoln County War lingered on. At the same time the lack of law and order was felt in Colfax County as well. Located in northeastern New Mexico, Colfax County had its own rival groups. Land and cattle companies opposed new settlers. They fought over who would control public land in the county. So, too, Colfax County had its murders. Lawlessness in these two counties affected all the people who lived there, even those not involved in the fighting. It caused many people to move elsewhere. Lawlessness in these counties also showed that Governor Axtell was not in control. So in September 1878 President Rutherford B. Hayes removed Axtell from office. Appointed as New Mexico's new governor was Lew Wallace. He was famous for his military roles in both the war with Mexico and the Civil War. A writer, Wallace became most famous for his novel *Ben Hur.* He wrote part of *Ben Hur* while living in the Governor's Palace at Santa Fe.

Wallace was not happy about his appointment as New Mexico's governor. He had hoped for a better office. His wife, Susan Wallace, likewise was not pleased. Indeed, she spent little time in New Mexico. She even suggested, as had a famous general years earlier, that Mexico should be forced to take back

New Mexico. At first Wallace felt that conditions in Lincoln County might well call for strong measures. Such measures might even include martial (military) law. The president, however, did not go this far. Instead, he sent a proclamation to New Mexico. He advised lawbreakers to return to peace. He stressed that armed force might be used in the future to keep the peace. The president's proclamation helped calm Lincoln. As for Wallace, his main act was to offer *amnesty* to those involved in the Lincoln County War. Amnesty meant that those who had broken the law would not be punished unless they had already been charged with or convicted of a crime. Amnesty would be given only to those who would testify about events in Lincoln County and who would remain at peace.

Lincoln County becomes more peaceful. The people of Lincoln were ready for peace. Still, there was to be one more victim of the Lincoln County War. This was Huston Chapman, a lawyer. Chapman wanted Governor Wallace to take action against both sides in the war. He felt that McSween had not been solely to blame for what had happened. In making his feelings known, Chapman made enemies. He was gunned down on February 18, 1879. This was a year to the day after the Tunstall murder. Chapman was standing in front of the Lincoln post office at the time of his killing. Eyewitness to the murder was William H. Bonney. The two killers were well-known gunmen. The person behind the murder was likely James J. Dolan. It was this murder that brought Wallace to Lincoln. Arriving on March 6, Wallace had with him a cavalry escort. He remained in Lincoln about 6 weeks. He talked with most of those who had been involved in the war. He even had a private meeting with Bonney. Wallace hoped that Bonney would testify at the trial of the two men arrested for Chapman's murder. This, however, never came to pass. The two men escaped from jail.

Wallace returned to Santa Fe. Bonney turned to a lawless life. Eighteen months after the meeting between the two, Bonney was arrested in San Miguel County. Moved to Santa Fe for safekeeping, Bonney appealed to the governor for help. Wallace, however, ignored all three of the outlaw's appeals. Transferred to Mesilla, Bonney stood trial on April 8, 1881, for killing Sheriff Brady. The court found Bonney guilty and sentenced him to hang in Lincoln on Friday, May 13, 1881.

Lawlessness continues in New Mexico. Bonney was jailed in Lincoln, but he was never hanged. On April 28 he escaped from the Lincoln County courthouse. In the process he killed his two guards. He shot J. W. Bell with Bell's own pistol. He then grabbed a shotgun and gunned down Robert Olinger, as Olinger ran across the street to the courthouse. To this day, a bullet hole in the wall of the old Lincoln County Courthouse reminds visitors

amnesty: legal term that means that those who have broken the law will not be punished unless they have already been charged with or convicted of a crime

Governor Lew Wallace

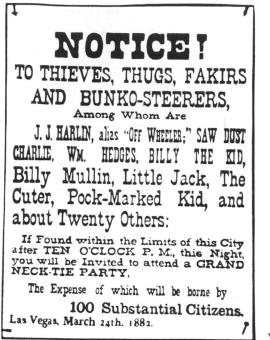

Warning to outlaws, 1882

of this escape. From April 28 on Bonney was a hunted man. Rewards were offered for his capture. Then on July 13, 1881, Bonney entered Fort Sumner, late in the evening. Just after midnight on July 14 he was shot and killed by the then sheriff of Lincoln, Pat Garrett. William H. Bonney was dead. His death ended the Lincoln County War.

The Lincoln and Colfax county wars were the best evidence of lawlessness in frontier New Mexico. There was, however, much other evidence. There was the famous October 1884 gunfight involving Elfego Baca. Baca is said to have held off 80 Texas cowboys for 33 hours at Frisco, now Reserve, New Mexico. There were the gangs in the early 1890s who terrorized San Miguel County in northern New Mexico. The first gang became known as Las Gorras Blancas, the White Caps. Gang members wore white hoods over their heads and faces when they rode on their nighttime raids. They cut the fences on grazing land. They set fire to the houses and barns of those neighbors who did not join them. From Las Gorras Blancas a second gang emerged. This was the gang of Vicente Silva and his 40 bandits. For 3 years the Silva gang robbed, murdered, and set fires throughout San Miguel County. Then there was the disappearance of Colonel Albert Jennings Fountain and his son near Las Cruces in 1896. Three men were tried for the murder of the Fountains. All 3 were found not guilty because the bodies of the Fountains were never found. There were other acts of random violence in frontier New Mexico. The fact that New Mexico long remained a frontier meant that law and order was late in arriving.

"O, Fair New Mexico"

Elizabeth Garrett was the daughter of Pat Garrett, the man who shot and killed Billy the Kid. She was also one of New Mexico's most remarkable citizens. A blind woman and the personal friend of Helen Keller, Elizabeth Garrett was a talented musician. She was a professional concert singer. She performed throughout the United States. Her companion on her concert tours was her seeing-eye dog. Elizabeth Garrett wrote music as well. Her song "O, Fair New Mexico" became New Mexico's official state song in 1917. The words to that song appear below. Read the words to the song. In them you will find the description of a beautiful land. It was a land that Elizabeth Garrett never saw but clearly loved.

O, FAIR NEW MEXICO

Verses

1. Under a sky of azure, Where balmy breezes blow;
   Kissed by the golden sunshine, Is Nuevo Mejico.
   Home of the Montezuma, With fiery heart aglow,
   State of the deeds historic, Is Nuevo Mejico.

2. Rugged and high sierras, With deep cañons below;
   Dotted with fertile valleys, Is Nuevo Mejico.
   Fields full of sweet alfalfa, Richest perfumes bestow,
   State of the apple blossoms, Is Nuevo Mejico.

3. Days that are full of heartdreams, Nights when the moon hangs low;
   Beaming its benediction, O'er Nuevo Mejico.
   Land with its bright mañana, Coming through weal and woe,
   State of our esperanza, Is Nuevo Mejico.

Refrain

O, fair New Mexico, We love, we love you so,
Our hearts with pride o'erflow, no matter where we go,
O, fair New Mexico, We love, we love you so,
The grandest state to know, New Mexico.

Section Review   1.   (a) In the Lincoln County War, who were the oldtimers?

(b) Who were the newcomers?

(c) Who were the rival groups in the Colfax County War?

2.   What was the outcome of the July 1878 battle of Lincoln?

3.   (a) What actions did President Hayes and Governor Wallace take to calm Lincoln County?

(b) What event caused Wallace to travel to Lincoln, and what did Wallace accomplish while in Lincoln?

4.   (a) For what murder was Bonney found guilty?

(b) Briefly describe what happened to Bonney after he was sentenced to die.

Chapter Review

Words You Should Know

Find each word in your reading and explain its meaning.

1. reservation   2. amnesty

Places You Should Be Able to Locate

Be able to locate these places on the maps in your book.

1. Mesilla   7. Glorieta Pass
2. Fort Fillmore   8. Peralta
3. Fort Stanton   9. Bosque Redondo Reservation
4. Fort Craig   10. Fort Sumner
5. Fort Union   11. Lincoln
6. Valverde

Facts You Should Remember

Answer the following questions by recalling information presented in this chapter.

1.   What kind of government did New Mexico have under the Kearny Code, during the period of military rule, and after New Mexico was organized as a territory in 1850?

2.   How were each of New Mexico's boundaries settled?

3.   Why did the Confederacy fail to capture New Mexico during the Civil War?

4.   After the Civil War what happened to the Mescaleros, the Navajos, the Plains Indians, the Chiricahuas, and the Jicarillas?

5.   What events in New Mexico during the late 1800s showed a lack of law and order?

6. Who are the following people, and why are they important?

(a) Jean B. Lamy;

(b) Edward R. S. Canby;

(c) Henry H. Sibley;

(d) James Carleton;

(e) Kit Carson;

(f) Geronimo;

(g) William H. Bonney;

(h) Lew Wallace.

Eyewitness to New Mexico's History
An Automobile Ride to Roswell, 1908

From: Marta Weigle, ed., *New Mexicans in Cameo and Camera* (University of New Mexico Press, 1985).

Good roads bring traffic; traffic brings trade; trade brings people. Good roads are now taken as such a matter of course that perhaps it will be of interest for the present generation to learn what experiences their parents had to undergo to reach the plains from Roswell [in the early twentieth century].

"The Sands" stretching north and south between the Pecos River and the cap rock used to be the nightmare of those crossing east to the Texas line. . . .

An auto ride anywhere then [1908] was an exciting experience but an auto ride across the sands was beyond belief. We descended the caprock through what was then known as Clark's Gap, causing much excitement as we passed the house, the first on the road since leaving the T 2 [Ranch], and approached the sands.

Soon we were in them; there was no doubt of this fact to the one in the back seat, a seat wide enough for three persons. I [Joyce Hunter] tried holding onto the seat, without the least effect; I still bounced. Next I grasped the robe rail with both hands in a deathlike grip. No good; my arms were almost torn from their sockets. Mr. FitzGerald looking back to be sure that I was still there asked how I was making it, and my pride would not let me acknowledge that at each bump I expected to be left behind (lucky for me that the car had a top). Finally I found that the best way to bump was just to bump and trust to luck that if I became limp enough my neck would not be broken and my arms and legs would still be of some use if we ever got across the sands. Those seven miles were the longest I ever passed over but as with all things they were at last behind us and from there on such affairs as chuck holes and other minor irregularities of the road were too insignificant to be noticed.

Roswell was finally reached and I was taken to my home feeling that I had been pounded with a heavy mallet from head to foot. It took several days to unloosen the kinks in my anatomy which had been placed there by my auto trip across the sands.

216

CHAPTER 9

The End of Isolation

What you will learn in this chapter—

In the first eight chapters of this book, you have studied a New Mexico that stood apart from other population centers. New Mexico's shortage of water limited population growth. Transportation was by overland routes only. The Santa Fe Trail and the path from Santa Fe southward to Chihuahua were two well-used routes. Still, overland travel was slow, hard, and sometimes dangerous. It left New Mexico separated in time and distance from other places.

In the 1880s, however, New Mexico's isolation began to break down. The railroad brought New Mexico into regular contact with the rest of the United States. It made possible new economic developments. It brought new settlers into the area. New Mexico's isolation came to an end. In this chapter you will learn about the development of territorial New Mexico. As you read, you will find answers to the following questions:

1. How did New Mexico's economy begin to develop during the territorial period?
2. How did the railroad change the face of New Mexico?
3. What was New Mexico's story during its final years as a territory?

1. How did New Mexico's economy begin to develop during the territorial period?

New Mexicans farm the land. To the people who lived off the land in New Mexico, farming was important. It always had been. The Indians had grown crops on irrigated land for hundreds of years. Spanish and later Mexican people had continued to farm the land. Indeed, most New Mexicans had made their livings as farmers. For family use New Mexico's farmers grew grain, vegetables, and fruit. They raised sheep and cattle. Land was put into cultivation in those areas of New Mexico where the water supply was plentiful. Irrigated farms were most common.

When New Mexico became a territory of the United States in 1850,

Branding cattle

its economy did not change at first. The people continued to farm the land. In 1850 the official number of farms in the territory was 3,750. Ten years later the number of farms had increased to 5,086. (The New Mexico Territory until 1863 included both New Mexico and Arizona.) The 1850s, you may recall, were a decade of some growth for New Mexico's population (page 189). The number of farms increased during these same years. So, too, did farm production. Corn production nearly doubled. Wheat production was much greater in 1860 than it had been in 1850.

But farming in New Mexico did not show similar growth during the 1860s. The Civil War disrupted economic life. Indian unrest further disrupted life after the war. In the 1860s the number of farms in fact decreased. Corn production increased slightly, but wheat production was down. Sheep and cattle production also declined. In addition, farming in New Mexico in the 1860s did not attract many newcomers. Getting crops to market was difficult. Besides, settlers could still get good farm land in parts of Minnesota, the Dakotas, Nebraska, and Kansas.

Cattle raising becomes important. Compared to the rest of the country, New Mexico did not become an important farming area. Cattle raising was another story. In fact, after the Civil War cattle became important to New Mexico's economy. Soldiers and miners in New Mexico wanted beef. So cattle were trailed into the territory to meet the demand. The men who first reached the cattle markets in New Mexico were two Texans. They were Charles Goodnight and Oliver Loving. In 1866 Goodnight and Loving combined their herds

George McJunkin, black cowboy and discoverer of Folsom Man (see page 16)

and drove them into New Mexico. The route they took started just west of Fort Worth. It ran southwestward to the Pecos River. It entered New Mexico just south of present-day Carlsbad. The path followed the river valley toward Fort Sumner and the Bosque Redondo Indian Reservation. This route became known as the Goodnight-Loving Cattle Trail. Within a short time cattle trails criss-crossed New Mexico in all directions. Trails heading north carried cattle into Colorado and Wyoming. Trails westward carried cattle into Arizona.

Also within a short time Texans began to raise cattle in New Mexico. Cattlegrowers moved to the Llano Estacado (page 4) and the western valleys of New Mexico. Their Texas longhorns were tough and needed little care. Turned loose, they grazed on the *open range*. The open range was the unfenced public land that covered the western plains. The cattle were left to graze on their own until it was time to drive them to market. Tending to the cattle were cowboys. These cowboys came from varied backgrounds. Among them were many blacks who had moved west after the Civil War. The cowboys' first act was to herd the cattle together. This was called a *roundup*. Next the cowboys branded any new, unmarked cattle. Finally, they drove the cattle to market.

New Mexicans raise cattle on a large scale. The most famous of New Mexico's early cattlegrowers was John S. Chisum (page 208). He claimed for his cattle range an area extending 150 miles north and south along the

open range: unfenced public land that covered the western plains; land on which cattlemen grazed their cattle

roundup: herding cattle together

219

Windmill and pond near Deming

Pecos River and from the Texas border westward to Fort Sumner. At the height of his power, Chisum is said to have raised 60,000 cattle a year. His fight with Lawrence G. Murphy and others was typical of the days of cattle kingdoms. Cattlegrowers fought one another. They also fought sheepgrowers and farmers who began to move onto land that had once been used by cattlegrowers alone. But the fighting did not save the early cattle kingdoms. Quite simply, the days of the open range were numbered.

The open range came to an end for several reasons. One was the competition for land among cattlegrowers, sheepgrowers, and farmers. Another was the weather. In the mid-1880s drought and freezing temperatures killed off thousands of cattle. Still another was the building of more and more miles of railroad tracks. The railroad made a long cattle drive to market a thing of the past. As a result, cattle raising in New Mexico underwent changes in the late 1800s. The ranchers fenced in their land with barbed wire. They used windmills to pump a steady supply of water to the surface. And they raised cattle that were carefully bred for the meat they produced. Some cattle raising occurred in nearly every part of the territory. In 1890 the cattle in New Mexico totaled 1,340,000.

New Mexicans raise sheep. Like cattle raising, the sheep raising industry was also central to New Mexico's economy. In fact, sheep had long been important to the people of New Mexico. Spanish explorers had brought sheep with them. Spanish and later Mexican settlers raised sheep. Indeed, New Mexico's dry climate and high plains were better suited for sheep raising than for cattle raising. In part this was because sheep need less water than cattle. And sheep get some of their water from the grass and other vegetation they eat. About 15 acres of New Mexico pastureland can support one sheep for one year. On the other hand, some 70 acres of New Mexico pastureland are needed to support one cow for one year. So New Mexico was sheep land long before it was cattle land.

Until recently sheep in New Mexico were raised mainly for meat. Thin and hairy, the wool was of poor quality. Nonetheless, both sheep and woolen goods found ready markets elsewhere. In the period from 1800 to 1850, the mining towns of northern Mexico were the main market places for New Mexico's sheep. In an average year 250,000 sheep made their way to Mexico. In some years as many as 500,000 were sold.

New Mexico's sheep industry expands. After becoming a part of the United States, New Mexico continued to export its sheep. In 1850 it led all western territories and states in sheep production. And in the nation's economic expansion that followed the Civil War, New Mexico played a key role. New Mexico was known as the nation's sheep nursery. Sheep by the thousands left New Mexico. They were trailed to Mexico, California, the Midwest, and the North. By the 1870s sheep bred from New Mexico stock were being raised in the Great Plains states. They were by the same period being raised in the Rocky Mountain area.

The sheep boom also brought an expansion of the sheep raising industry within New Mexico. Sheepgrowers from the Las Vegas area, for example, moved onto the eastern plains. Joining them on the plains were sheepgrowers from Mora, Anton Chico, settlements along the Pecos River, and the lower Rio Grande Valley. Known as the richest of these sheepgrowers in the 1870s was Hilario Gonzales. Settled at San Hilario on the Canadian River, he was said to have run sheep on a thousand hills. Ten miles from San Hilario the town of San Lorenzo was home to Francisco Lopez. Lopez, too, owned thousands of sheep. Others whose flocks on the eastern plains numbered in the thousands included Trinidad and Eugenio Romero and Tomas D. Cabeza de Baca.

These sheepgrowers, in turn, lured still other New Mexico sheepgrowers to the plains not only of New Mexico but also of Texas. Most raised some cattle along with their sheep. Still, their main concern was grasslands for their sheep. Cattlegrowers, on the other hand, wanted grasslands for their cattle. By the

221

Cattle ranch in southwestern New Mexico

late 1800s the desire for grazing land brought the sheepgrowers and the cattlegrowers into sharp competition. Until the coming of the railroad, sheepgrowers had the advantage. Sheep were simply more easily trailed to distant markets than were cattle.

New Mexico's sheep industry declines. The coming of the railroad changed this. It was no longer necessary to trail either cattle or sheep long distances. Cattlegrowers thereafter had the advantage. Trains could carry the cattle needed to supply a market that demanded more and more cattle. In 1884 New Mexico totaled about one million head of cattle and five and a half million sheep. Within five years these figures had changed greatly. The territory had a quarter of a million more cattle in 1889 than it did in 1884. At the same time it had two million fewer sheep.

Some sheepgrowers did try to improve wool production in the 1880s. For example, breeders from northeastern New Mexico crossbred better woolproducing sheep with native sheep. Despite this effort New Mexico's sheep raising industry steadily declined. The sheep industry produced fewer and fewer profits. This decline eventually ended, but not until the 1950s.

New Mexico is an early mining frontier. Another part of the territorial economy was mining. But real growth of New Mexico's mining industry was slower than in most other areas of the West. This was true even though New Mexico was known to have mineral wealth. Indeed, miners had long taken turquoise out of the mines of Cerrillos, an area south of Santa Fe.

Early Mining in New Mexico

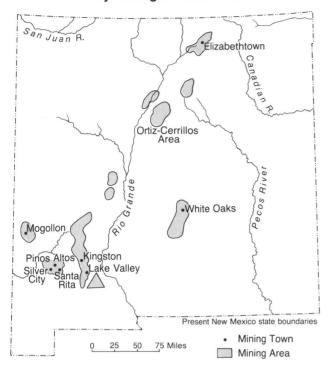

San Juan R.

Elizabethtown

Canadian R.

Ortiz-Cerrillos Area

Rio Grande

Pecos River

White Oaks

Mogollon

Pinos Altos Kingston
Silver   Lake Valley
City   Santa
Rita

Present New Mexico state boundaries

0   25   50   75 Miles

• Mining Town

▨ Mining Area

In fact, Indians had mined this turquoise even before the Spaniards arrived. Spaniards and later settlers continued to mine this turquoise.

In addition, New Mexico revealed the first known gold fields in what is today the western United States. In 1828 gold was discovered in the Ortiz Mountains south of Santa Fe. Another discovery took place in 1839 at the base of the San Pedro Mountains south of Santa Fe as well. Hispanic miners worked these goldfields. In the 1700s and 1800s they also mined the rich copper deposits they discovered at Santa Rita. Santa Rita lies east of present-day Silver City.

Mining continues during the territorial period. Copper mining continued off and on after the United States acquired New Mexico. Gold mining was spurred by the discovery of gold in 1860 at Pinos Altos. Pinos Altos is located north of Santa Rita and Silver City in the Black Range. Finding gold there were miners who had arrived from California. The gold fever in California in 1849 and in Colorado in 1859 had set off a rush of people to those areas. The Pinos Altos find caused much the same sensation. People flocked into what is today southwestern New Mexico. They came from California, Texas, and Missouri. They also came from Chihuahua and Sonora in northern Mexico. However, New Mexico's gold rush did not last long. Apache raids and the

223

onset of the Civil War discouraged mining. By the end of 1861 mining in the Pinos Altos area had stopped.

The war itself further discouraged mining in New Mexico. So, too, did the growing Indian problem that followed the war. In fact, renewed interest in mining occurred only after new discoveries of silver and gold in the late 1860s. Most of these discoveries were in southwestern New Mexico. New towns sprang up as soon as discoveries became known. In some cases only ghost towns remained after the strikes played out. Silver City grew up with the discovery of silver there in 1869. Elsewhere in New Mexico, gold was discovered in 1866 close to Elizabethtown near present-day Eagle Nest. White Oaks, east of White Sands, was founded in 1879 after gold was struck nearby. And still more strikes occurred in southwestern New Mexico in the 1870s and 1880s. Near Pinos Altos gold was discovered at Hillsboro in 1877. Six years later silver was discovered at Kingston. Another silver strike was made at Lake Valley in 1887. Finally, a silver strike occurred at Mogollon in 1889. The map on page 223 shows these mining areas and mining towns.

Conditions limit mining. Despite such discoveries New Mexico's mining was limited. It was limited in large part by conditions miners could not control. Water was in short supply. This fact limited *placer mining.* Placer mining relies on water to separate gold from other, lighter substances found in gold-carrying dirt. Another problem was getting to the ore. Ore veins in New Mexico rock are often hard to trace. This fact limited *lode mining,* the mining of veins of ore. Still another limitation was transportation. Mining

placer mining: mining that relies on the use of water to separate gold from other, lighter substances found in gold-carrying dirt

lode mining: the mining of veins of ore

White Oaks, New Mexico

supplies and equipment were bulky. Before the coming of the railroad, mine owners had to transport such materials into New Mexico by overland routes only.

You can see, then, why mining in New Mexico grew slowly. Some conditions, such as the shortage of water, could not, of course, be changed. What could be changed were some of the frontier conditions that limited all aspects of New Mexico's growth. The end of the Indian problem was one such change. A second change altered the entire face of New Mexico. This was the building of railroads in and through New Mexico.

Section Review

1. Briefly describe farming in New Mexico before the coming of the railroads.
2. **(a)** What first attracted cattlegrowers to New Mexico, and in what parts of New Mexico were cattle raised?
   (b) Why did the open range disappear?
   (c) Briefly describe cattle ranching in New Mexico after the time of the open range.
3. **(a)** How extensive was New Mexico's sheep raising industry in 1850, and how did this industry expand after the Civil War?
   (b) What started the decline of the sheep industry, and how long did the decline continue?
4. **(a)** What mining took place in New Mexico before the Civil War?
   (b) What new mining discoveries were made during the late 1800s, and in what part of the territory did most of these discoveries take place?
   (c) What conditions limited New Mexico's mining industry?

---

2. How did the railroad change the face of New Mexico?

An era of railroad building occurs. Railroad building occurred everywhere in the United States after the Civil War. Much of this building took place west of the Mississippi River. In 1865 there were 3,272 miles of railroad track west of the Mississippi. By 1890 this mileage had increased to 72,473. One reason for this construction boom was the western need for better contact with the East. Another reason was the help given railroads by the United States government. The government gave millions of acres of public land to railroad companies. It advanced millions of dollars in government bonds to these same companies. The government began its railroad assistance program at the end of the Civil War. In 1890 it brought this program to an end. Before the program ended, railroad builders had made vast fortunes. And thousands of new miles of railroad track crossed the country.

The railroad affected the West and its people in a number of ways. For

225

one thing, the isolation of westerners diminished. For another, the railroads aided the growth of the West. The task of laying track provided the first boost. It produced jobs. Among those who worked at building the railroads of the Southwest were many Mexicans and Indians. Newcomers from Europe and Asia, ex–Civil War soldiers, and former prisoners also joined construction crews. Once the tracks were laid, the railroad sparked further growth. This growth was as true for New Mexico as it was for other parts of the West. In fact, the coming of the railroad changed New Mexico in a number of ways. The railroad gave rise to new towns. It changed old towns as well. It allowed for trade on a much larger scale. New Mexico's miners, ranchers, and farmers could send their products to national markets. At the same time the railroad opened up new mining, ranching, and farming opportunities in New Mexico. In turn it brought to New Mexico a steady stream of new residents.

New Mexicans get their first railroad. From late 1878 to early 1881, railroad building in New Mexico was at its peak. Workers laid hundreds of miles of track. They sometimes laid one and a half miles of track in a single day. In fact, of all the track ever laid in New Mexico, almost one-third was laid in slightly more than two years. Tracklaying continued but at a slower rate after that.

The first railroad line constructed in New Mexico was that of the Atchison, Topeka and Santa Fe (A.T.&S.F.). This railroad followed the mountain branch of the Santa Fe Trail westward from Kansas into Colorado. At Trinidad it swung southward. It crossed into New Mexico over Raton Pass. It did so only after winning the right-of-way to the pass from another railroad company, the Denver and Rio Grande. The A.T.&S.F. continued on into New Mexico. As it did, the face of New Mexico that lay along the railroad line changed. The town of Raton sprang up in 1879. Farther south two other towns—Maxwell and Springer—came to life. Farmers had already settled these areas. With the coming of the railroad Maxwell and Springer became major centers for shipping cattle. Wagon Mound, a fourth town along the railroad, lay where the two branches of the Santa Fe Trail met. Called Santa Clara until about 1859, the town had been renamed Wagon Mound because of the covered-wagon-shaped mesa to the east. Still farther south on the A.T.&S.F. route was Watrous. An Old Spanish settlement once known as La Junta, the town had taken the name Watrous just before the Civil War.

The railroad creates new towns in Las Vegas and Albuquerque. Las Vegas was the first major New Mexico town to be affected by the railroad. It welcomed regular train service on April 4, 1879. The people celebrated. The town itself was never again to be the same. Las Vegas had been a thriving town before 1879. It prospered even more as a railroad town. However, it

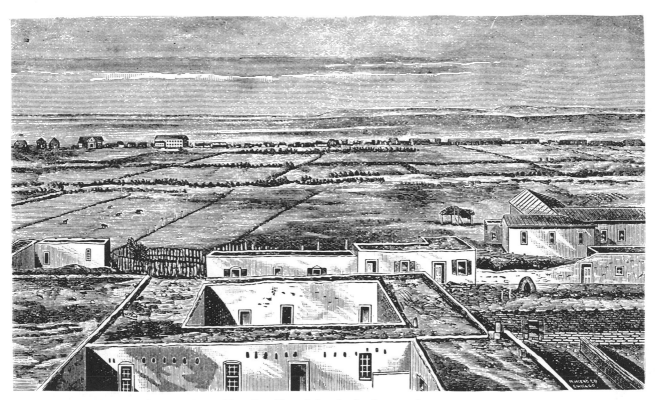

Las Vegas in 1880, with new town (East Las Vegas) in the background

prospered as two towns. This was because the A.T.&S.F. laid its track across the Gallinas River from the old plaza. So along the track grew up a new town. Las Vegas remained for decades a city divided into an old town (West Las Vegas) and a new town (East Las Vegas).

By 1880 the A.T.&S.F. had extended its line far beyond Las Vegas. Santa Fe was bypassed because of its mountainous location. The company laid track through Glorieta Pass and then picked Galisteo Junction as the place to build a depot. Later renamed Lamy, this junction lay some 18 miles from Santa Fe. The company's actions left the Santa Fe residents without a railroad. Most unhappy, they set out to show the A.T.&S.F. that they were going to have a railroad even if they had to pay for it. So they floated a $150,000 bond issue which the voters approved. The sale of the bonds paid for a branch line from Lamy to Santa Fe. The first train reached Santa Fe on February 9, 1880. The days of the Santa Fe Trail were at an end.

In the meantime the A.T.&S.F. had laid track westward to the Rio Grande and southward to Santo Domingo. (See Special Interest Feature.) From there the track ran along the east side of the river. However, it did not run through Old Albuquerque. So like Las Vegas, Albuquerque soon became two

227

A train at Glorieta, 1880

towns. The town that grew up around the railroad became known as New Albuquerque. The first train pulled into New Albuquerque on April 22, 1880. The old part of Albuquerque became known in time as Old Town.

Rails link New Mexico to both coasts. The A.T.&S.F. had entered New Mexico from the north. At about the same time other railroad companies entered New Mexico. One of these was the Southern Pacific Railroad Company. This company built eastward from California. It crossed Arizona and entered New Mexico from the west. Just east of the Arizona–New Mexico border, a new town—Lordsburg—sprang up along the tracks in October 1880. It was settled by people from Shakespeare. An old mining center, Shakespeare had stood 2 miles to the south. From Lordsburg the railroad route continued eastward across New Mexico. At Deming the Southern Pacific and one branch of the A.T.&S.F. met. This union was completed on March 8, 1881. The A.T.&S.F. had reached Deming by laying track from Albuquerque down the Rio Grande Valley. This route ran through Los Lunas, Belen, Socorro, San Marcial, and Rincon. At Rincon, 30 miles north of Las Cruces, the A.T.&S.F.

had followed two branches. One branch continued southward to El Paso. It ran through Las Cruces, where its arrival was welcomed on April 26, 1881. The other branch of the A.T.&S.F. ran westward into Deming.

The meeting of the two railroads at Deming was very important for New Mexico. New Mexicans could now travel by train to both the east and the west coasts. In other words, a railroad route that crossed the continent now ran through New Mexico. This was the country's second such route. The first transcontinental route had been completed in 1869. It ran to the north of New Mexico. The meeting of the two railroads in Deming did not, however, please either railroad company. In fact, the companies became bitter rivals. Each occupied a separate wing in the depot at Deming. Each operated its schedule according to different time zones. The rivalry also encouraged more activity by both companies. The Southern Pacific continued to expand eastward. It took over a railroad line in Texas. It then laid track into New Orleans. This brought San Francisco and New Orleans into line with one another. The route was completed on January 12, 1883. New Mexico was, of course, a part of this route.

The Harvey Girls

A popular stopping-off place along the A.T.&S.F. railroad network was the Harvey House. Harvey Houses served food. And serving this food were the Harvey Girls. Both the houses and the girls were introduced into the Southwest by an enterprising businessman named Fred Harvey. Born in London, Harvey came to the United States at the age of 15. He arrived with only ten dollars in his pocket. Working at different jobs, he in time learned the restaurant business. Then he put his knowledge to work. Wherever the A.T.&S.F. went, Harvey was soon to follow. He built lunchrooms. He built restaurants. At one time more than one hundred Harvey Houses operated along the A.T.&S.F. system.

The food was of good quality. Travelers could count on the meals Harvey Houses served. But it was perhaps the Harvey Girls more than the food that brought weary travelers to Fred Harvey establishments. The Harvey Girls were attractive. They were also, according to Fred Harvey standards, women of good moral character. The Harvey Girls dressed in black dresses with white collars and aprons. They earned $17.50 a month plus tips. In addition, they received free room and board. Their living quarters were dormitories. Harvey's rules required them to be in by ten o'clock. An older woman served as their chaperone.

The Harvey Girls began their jobs by promising that they would not marry for at least a year. Many of them, however, failed to keep this promise. The women and the men they waited on were often attracted to one another. One story is that to the marriages of Harvey Girls were born some 4,000 babies named Fred or Harvey or both.

Besides giving comfort to travelers, Fred Harvey helped promote the Southwest. Indian arts and crafts became familiar sights in many Harvey Houses. This chance to display and sell their works of art encouraged Indian artists. Paintings of southwestern scenes appeared on Fred Harvey menus, placemats, and postcards. Harvey Houses and Harvey Girls were a part of the Southwest for many years. They prospered as long as the railroads prospered. As fewer and fewer people traveled by train, Harvey Houses began to close. Today none remain in New Mexico. Only the Fred Harvey Restaurant in the airport at Albuquerque—under different ownership—even bears the Harvey name.

Track is laid across west-central and into northern New Mexico. For its part, the A.T.&S.F. also kept busy. It laid tracks from Deming to Silver City. This line made the job of hauling goods to and from the mines there easier and less costly. The A.T.&S.F. also encouraged another railroad company to lay track from Albuquerque westward across New Mexico and

Arizona. The tracks reached Needles, California. Gallup—with its nearby mines—became a major point along this railroad route. Then in 1897 this route became the property of the A.T.&S.F. The A.T.&S.F. now had its own line from the Midwest to California.

Besides the railroad routes already mentioned, many other routes crossed the territory. In northern New Mexico the Denver and Rio Grande company was most active. As a narrow-gauge railroad, its tracks were closer together than standard-gauge railroads. The Denver and Rio Grande laid its tracks from Antonito, Colorado, into New Mexico. At first these tracks ran southward to Española. This line was finished in 1880. The railroad was extended in 1887 to Santa Fe. The Denver and Rio Grande also had a second New Mexico line. Built in 1880 and 1881, this line linked Chama, New Mexico, with Durango, Colorado. Today that part of the narrow-gauge that runs between Chama and Antonito, Colorado, operates as the Cumbres and Toltec Scenic Railroad. The states of New Mexico and Colorado jointly operate this line.

Track is laid across northeastern New Mexico and into the Pecos and Estancia valleys. Across northeastern New Mexico workers laid tracks in 1887 and 1888. This activity gave birth to the towns of Folsom, Des Moines, and Clayton. Folsom prospered for a time as the main livestock shipping center between Denver and Fort Worth. Des Moines grew as a small ranching and farming town. Clayton stood at the center of a busy cattle ranching region.

In the 1890s workers laid railroad tracks into the Pecos Valley. This route entered New Mexico along the old Goodnight-Loving Cattle Trail. At the cowboy campsite known as Loving's Bend the railroad arrived in 1891. Here the town of Eddy—now Carlsbad—came into being. In 1894 the railroad reached Roswell. Both Carlsbad and Roswell had been settled before the coming of the railroad. They grew more quickly after the railroad arrived. By 1910 Roswell would be the main city in southeastern New Mexico. To the south of Roswell a new town grew out of a railroad construction camp. This was the town of Artesia. Artesia took its present name in 1903. From Roswell the railroad line left the Pecos Valley. It ran northeastward to Portales and then to Riley's Switch. This point came in 1906 to be Clovis.

A second railroad line ended at the site of Clovis. This was the A.T.&S.F.'s so-called Belen Cutoff. From Belen this route ran eastward to the border of Texas. It traveled south of the Manzano Mountains into the Estancia Valley and the eastern plains. Along this route Mountainair (about 1900), Willard (1903), and Encino (1904) came into being. Farther east the railroad passed through Fort Sumner and the old cattle town of Brownhorn, later Melrose. Finally, the Belen Cutoff Route reached Clovis. As a town located on two railroad lines, Clovis grew quickly. It became a trading center for the eastern plains.

Railroads develop the Tularosa Basin and the town of Tucumcari. Railroad building in the late 1800s and early 1900s further changed the face of New Mexico. Phelps-Dodge, a mining company, began laying track from El Paso into New Mexico. Its goal was to reach the coalfields near Raton. The first stretch of track connected El Paso and Santa Rosa. In the process it helped develop the Tularosa Basin. Alamogordo, laid out in 1899, was the first New Mexico town to grow up along that railroad line. Other towns growing up along this route were Carrizozo, Ancho, Corona, and Torrance. At the point where the Phelps-Dodge line crossed the A.T.&S.F. Belen Cutoff line, Vaughn sprang up. Vaughn became a major shipping center for cattle and sheep. In helping develop the Tularosa Basin the Phelps-Dodge company also built spur lines to special sites. One spur ran from Alamogordo into the Sacramento Mountains. This spur line gave birth to the resort town of Cloudcroft and to lumbering in the nearby forests. A second spur ran from Carrizozo to Capitan. The attraction of Capitan was coal.

In time the Phelps-Dodge company reached its goal. It reached the coalfields of northeastern New Mexico. To meet its goal it leased a railroad line

Stockyards at Clovis

232

New Mexico's Railroads

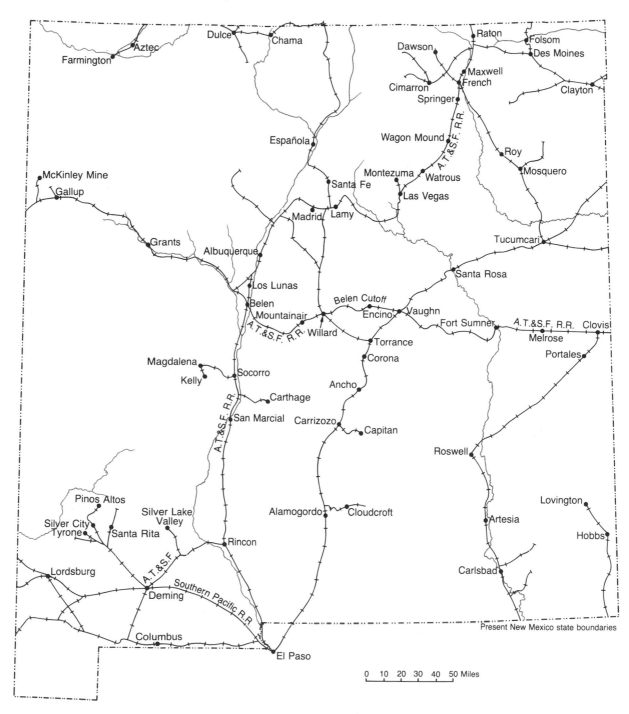

Farmington
Aztec
Dulce
Chama
Raton
Folsom
Des Moines
Dawson
Maxwell
French
Cimarron
Springer
Clayton
Wagon Mound
Roy
Española
Mosquero
Montezuma
Watrous
McKinley Mine
Santa Fe
Las Vegas
Gallup
Madrid
Lamy
Grants
Albuquerque
Tucumcari
Los Lunas
Santa Rosa
Belen Cutoff
Belen
Encino
Vaughn
Mountainair
A.T.&S.F. R.R.
A.T.&S.F. R.R.
Clovis
Willard
Fort Sumner
Magdalena
Torrance
Melrose
Kelly
Socorro
Corona
Portales
Carthage
Ancho
A.T.&S.F. R.R.
San Marcial
Carrizozo
Capitan
Roswell
Pinos Altos
Lovington
Silver Lake
Valley
Alamogordo
Cloudcroft
Silver City
Tyrone
Santa Rita
Artesia
Hobbs
Rincon
Lordsburg
A.T.&S.F
Southern Pacific R.R.
Carlsbad
Deming
Present New Mexico state boundaries
Columbus
El Paso

0 10 20 30 40 50 Miles

that already operated between Santa Rosa and Tucumcari. From Tucumcari Phelps-Dodge then laid track northward to French. Along this stretch of track grew up the towns of Mosquero and Roy. The laying of additional track gave the Phelps-Dodge company access to the rich coal deposits at Dawson near Cimarron. At the same time the Phelps-Dodge line helped Tucumcari grow. Also helping the town grow was a railroad line that reached Tucumcari from the east. Tucumcari had in 1901 been merely a construction camp for a railroad company laying track into New Mexico from the east. At first called Six Shooter Siding, Tucumcari took its present name in 1902. It was formally organized as a town in 1907. Located along two railroad lines, Tucumcari became a major shipping center. Cattle and sheep were shipped from Tucumcari to eastern markets. Coal from the north was also shipped through Tucumcari.

The railroad building era draws to a close. Railroad mileage in New Mexico reached its peak in 1914. This was two years after New Mexico became a state. In 1914 3,124 miles of railroad track criss-crossed the state. Most of this mileage was part of long railroad routes. Some of this mileage lay along railroad routes that were quite short. These short routes ran to special sites. Look at the map on page 233. There you can see where the railroads operated in New Mexico. All these railroads were important to New Mexico. This was because the railroads ended New Mexico's isolation. And with the end of isolation came many changes.

Section Review

1. **(a)** How did the United States government aid the building of railroads?
    (b) In general, what did the railroads mean for western areas?
2. **(a)** Briefly describe how the coming of the railroads changed New Mexico.
    (b) Why was the meeting of the two railroads at Deming in 1881 important for New Mexico?
3. Make a list of the towns and cities in New Mexico that were born or changed as a result of railroad building.

3. What was New Mexico's story during its final years as a territory?

Newcomers are attracted to New Mexico. A great number of newcomers followed the railroads into the territory. These newcomers had reasons for moving into New Mexico. Many sought a new place to live and to make a living. New Mexico's expanding economy offered opportunity. People could, for example, work in mines now linked by the railroads to outside markets. So it was that miners found jobs in the silver mines at Silver City. Others mined silver, lead, and zinc at Kelly. Still others went to work in the coal mines in the Raton and Gallup areas. These were the two largest coal mining regions in New Mexico. Coal mines at Madrid, Carthage, and Capitan also provided jobs.

So some newcomers found jobs in New Mexico's mines. Others found jobs in lumbering, an industry new to New Mexico. Given birth by the railroads, lumbering sprang up wherever mountains offered fine timber. For the most part, however, the lumber industry prospered in such northern New Mexico towns as Cuba and Chama. Other newcomers were attracted by developments in New Mexico's farming. In the Estancia Valley and on the northeastern plains, for example, farmers grew beans on a large scale. The farmers later shipped their crop by train to market. In the Pecos Valley farmers moved onto irrigated land. This irrigated land had been developed and promoted by Charles B. Eddy and James J. Hagerman. From the Pecos Valley farmers shipped their produce to markets in Texas and points farther east. They shipped this produce over the railroad line that Eddy and Hagerman had brought into the Pecos Valley. Still, what newcomers found most attractive about farming in New Mexico was the land open for new settlement. Indeed, farmers in great numbers followed the railroads into New Mexico.

Farmers populate New Mexico. Most of the farmers who came to New Mexico in the late 1800s and early 1900s settled on the eastern plains. For the most part they came seeking sections of public land. Each of these sections came as a *homestead.* A homestead was a 160-acre farm that could be obtained from the national government. Heads of families first applied for a homestead. All they had to pay was a ten-dollar fee. After living on and working the homestead for five years, the land was theirs. Cattle ranchers resented the farmers. They tried to convince the farmers that 160-acre farms in New Mexico were too small to provide a good living. Yet the newly arrived farmers were not to be denied. Roosevelt County in eastern New Mexico is one example of the homestead boom. In 1904 about 3,000 people lived in the county. In 1910 the county's population was more than 12,000. Homesteaders had laid claim to almost all the 160-acre plots of public land in the county. The Roosevelt County story held true for most other counties in eastern New Mexico.

Farmers settled land that seemed suitable for farming elsewhere in the territory as well. It was during the 1880s, for example, that the Farmington region in northwestern New Mexico began to prosper. Major dams had not yet been built along New Mexico's rivers to allow access to irrigation water. So the farmers of the late 1800s and early 1900s had to find other ways to water their crops. The farmers were at first fairly lucky. There was enough rainfall on the eastern plains, for example, for the farmers there to grow crops in much the same way farmers grew crops in the Midwest. But the rainfall did not

homestead: 160-acre farm that heads of families could get from the government for a small fee

235

Farm near Bloomfield
(1880s)

remain steady. So it was that little rain fell in the eastern plain in the years from 1909 to 1912. As a result, many farmers gave up their land. In Roosevelt County about three-fourths of the small farmers lost their farms.

The farmers who remained in eastern New Mexico changed their methods of farming. They had to in order to survive. They still relied on rainfall, but they did so as dry farmers. Dry farming, you may recall, is a method of farming practiced in areas of little rainfall (page 38). Farmers prepare the soil to hold moisture. They then plant crops suited to the growing conditions. New Mexico's dry farmers of the early 1900s began to grow crops that would do well. These included sorghum, corn, and other grains. Dry farmers also began to raise cattle to insure an income even in bad crop-growing years.

Newcomers populate New Mexico's towns. Just as land attracted newcomers, so, too, did New Mexico's growing towns. Some towns in the farming and ranching areas existed to provide services for local farmers and ranchers. And as people moved into these towns, changes occurred. Stores sprang up. New houses, churches, and schools appeared. Other New Mexico towns likewise offered newcomers a chance to make good. Those located along the main railroad lines seemed to offer the most. It was these towns that attracted many newcomers. Las Vegas and Albuquerque were two such towns.

Shortly after the railroad arrived, Las Vegas witnessed much new growth. New Town, or East Las Vegas, soon became the site of three hotels, four restaurants, and two real estate offices. It had three building contractors, three retail merchants, and three doctors. Old Town, or West Las Vegas, also grew. The townspeople built a bridge across the Gallinas River to link the new and the old. The telephone, invented in 1876, even appeared in Las Vegas for a brief time in 1879. This experiment did not last long. Nonetheless, the telephones in Las Vegas introduced this wonder of modern America into New Mexico.

Five miles up the Gallinas Canyon from Las Vegas, the railroad built the Montezuma Hotel. It became a vacation spot. People from all over the country stayed in Montezuma. In time a trolley line carried them to and from Las Vegas. At Montezuma was also the first building in New Mexico to have electric lights.

The town of Las Vegas prospered for 40 years. Mainly a railroad town, it was the major shipping center for the northeastern quarter of New Mexico. The heyday of Las Vegas ended only with the coming of highways and cars.

Albuquerque becomes New Mexico's leading city. Albuquerque's growth took longer to get started than did that of Las Vegas. Still, Albuquerque's growth would be longer lasting. Located in central New Mexico, Albuquerque soon became New Mexico's railroad center and leading city. The railroad reached Albuquerque in the spring of 1880. As in Las Vegas it bypassed the old town. The growth of New Town in Albuquerque began in early 1881. At first New Town grew as a boomtown. Many of the new businesses catered to gamblers, gunfighters, and conmen. These were the drifters who passed through most western boomtowns. They spent their time in the new saloons and gambling halls. Between First and Third streets on Railroad Avenue (now Central Avenue), 14 of these businesses sprang up. They remained open both night and day. Other businesses catered to the newcomers who made Albuquerque their home. Old Town did not grow like New Town. Nonetheless, Albuquerque's old and new towns did have a link. A horse-drawn streetcar connected the plaza in Old Town and the railroad depot in New Town.

As time passed, the city grew in area and population. Albuquerque became home to people who came from other parts of the United States. It

Montezuma Hotel near Las Vegas

237

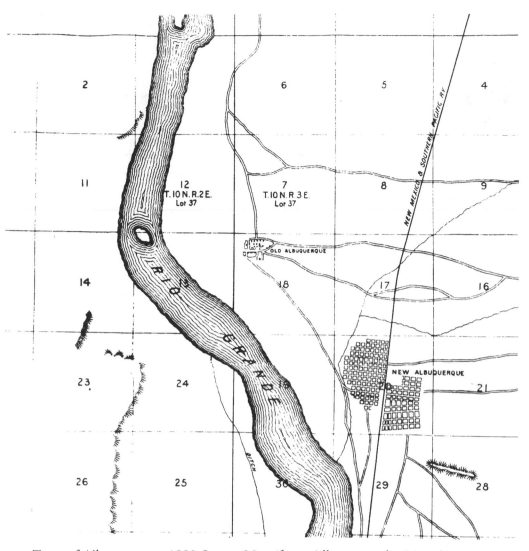

Town of Albuquerque, 1883 Survey Map (from *Albuquerque,* by Marc Simmons, UNM Press)

also became home to immigrants from other countries. Among those attracted to Albuquerque as well as to other parts of New Mexico were health seekers. People with asthma came. So, too, did victims of tuberculosis, a disease that attacks the lungs. These newcomers found relief in New Mexico's clear, dry air. In 1902 the Sisters of Charity founded Albuquerque's first tuberculosis sanitarium. This marked the birth of what was to become St. Joseph Hospital. Other centers for tubercular patients sprang up. Most were built along Central Avenue. As a result, one stretch of Central Avenue was nicknamed "T.B. Avenue." Many of those who came to the city to stay moved into a new housing development. The houses were built on the high land east of the railroad tracks. The person who developed the new neighborhood was Franz Huning (page

189). Thus the new houses were said to be part of Huning's Highlands. They were part of Albuquerque's first suburb.

Newcomers cause New Mexico to grow. All of those who followed the railroad into New Mexico should have their stories told. But this is not really possible. Nonetheless, it is important for you to realize that these people helped shape modern New Mexico. With them came their cultures, which affected the culture of New Mexico. Of the foreign immigrants the Italians were the biggest group. Perhaps the second largest group were those who came from Lebanon. Immigrants came from many different countries in Europe. They came from non-European countries as well. Then there were those who moved into New Mexico from other parts of the United States. Large numbers from Texas, Oklahoma, Missouri, and Arkansas, for example, peopled the eastern plains. Other newcomers came from places in the United States too numerous to mention.

Together they caused New Mexico to grow. In 1870 New Mexico's population was 91,874. It was 119,565 in 1880 and 160,282 in 1890. The population grew to 195,310 in 1900 and to 327,301 in 1910. In the ten years between 1900 and 1910 alone, New Mexico's population grew by 67.6 percent. Most New Mexicans still lived in *rural areas*. This means they lived in the country or in towns of fewer than 2,500. Nonetheless, 10 New Mexico towns in 1910 numbered more than 2,500. The people who lived in these towns lived in *urban areas*. Among these towns the largest were Albuquerque (11,020), Roswell (6,172), Santa Fe (5,072), and Raton (4,539).

rural area: either the country or a town of fewer than 2,500 people

urban area: city or town with a population of more than 2,500 people

Titles to land are a problem. New Mexico felt the presence of its newcomers in a number of ways. One of these was the question of who owned millions of acres of New Mexico land. This question was tied up in the complex issue of land grant titles. Land grants had, of course, been made during the Spanish and Mexican periods. The issue was complex in part because of the land grant titles themselves. The land was not always held by private parties. Grants of land had often been made to a group of people. Also confusing were the boundary lines of Spanish and Mexican grants. Real estate lines were often only marked by such landmarks as trees and arroyos. The Treaty of Guadalupe Hidalgo had confirmed existing titles to land. The United States Congress had in 1854 tried to settle the question of land ownership by setting up the Office of Surveyor General. The office confirmed Pueblo Indian land titles. It did not, however, settle the issue of who owned the Spanish and Mexican land grants. And as time passed, this problem became more and more confused.

Some land grant claims are settled. The arrival of ever more newcomers further confused the land title issue. This growth made land in New Mexico worth more. It led to land speculation. People from as far away as the

239

East Coast and Europe invested in New Mexico land. Some bought land grant titles in the belief that land values would rise. Some speculators were dishonest. Some even succeeded in claiming much more land than had been in the original land grants. The Maxwell Land Grant, for example, had at the outset included 97,000 acres of land. In 1879 the owners of the Maxwell Grant were awarded nearly 2,000,000 acres of land by the United States land commissioner. Further speculation in New Mexico land in the 1880s was so questionable that it became a national concern. Congress reacted in 1891 by setting up the Court of Private Land Claims. The task of this court was to settle land questions once and for all. It heard lawsuits brought by those claiming land. By 1903 the court had ruled on all land grant claims.

Those who gained most from these land cases were often Anglo-American lawyers. Many lawyers collected their legal fees in land. Others who gained were Anglo-American settlers newly arrived in New Mexico. About 80 percent of the Spanish and Mexican land grants ended up in the hands of Anglo-American lawyers and settlers. The one person who most profited was Thomas B. Catron (page 208). As a land grant lawyer, Catron became involved in 75 grants. In time he owned some 2,000,000 acres of land. He shared in the ownership or was a lawyer for another 4,000,000 acres. Those who lost most were Hispanic-Americans. They felt the courts had taken away land that was rightfully theirs. Much of this land was land once held in common for grazing by the whole community. United States courts simply did not recognize the concept of land ownership by a community of people.

New Mexico's culture changes. Among other ways in which New Mexico felt the presence of newcomers were the following. First, more non-Catholic churches appeared. By 1900 all the Protestant groups had churches in New Mexico. Second, the legislature passed a bill in 1889 that set up New Mexico's first public colleges. These were the University of New Mexico in Albuquerque, the School of Mines in Socorro, and the Agricultural College in Las Cruces. Third, free public education became law in 1891. Before this, schooling had been left up to the churches or to private individuals. Public education then got a big boost in 1898. In that year Congress passed a bill that provided for setting aside public lands for the support of New Mexico's public schools and colleges. New Mexico's delegate to Congress, H. B. Fergusson, succeeded in getting this bill passed. Fourth, new building styles began to appear in New Mexico. Newcomers brought with them the building styles with which they were most familiar. Fifth, New Mexico got its first daily newspaper. By 1900 there were five daily newspapers printed in the territory. Sixth, New Mexico got its first public library. The person behind this change was Julia Asplund. She arrived in the territory in 1903 and became active in

Senator Thomas B. Catron

Kingston, New Mexico's daily newspaper (1886)

public affairs. Among other things, she pushed for the right of women to vote.

The presence of newcomers was, of course, felt in other ways. Yet some ways of living in New Mexico changed very little. This was true of life in most of the Hispanic communities in northern New Mexico. The railroads and newcomers did not really touch these places or their ways of living. This was also true of Indian life. What changes did occur were mainly changes in Indian crafts. In the late 1880s the Navajos began to weave the rugs for which they are so famous. Navajo rug making replaced Navajo blanket making. The introduction of machine-made blankets brought this change. At this time as well Navajos and Pueblo Indians began to develop as fine jewelers and silversmiths. The Pueblo peoples continued to make pottery. New Mexico during its final years as a territory was a land of many cultures. The cultures of the newcomers had taken root beside the cultures of the Hispanic and Indian populations.

Most New Mexicans favor statehood. As mentioned earlier, New Mexico remained a territory for a very long time. In fact, New Mexico was a

Cochiti pottery (1880s)

territory for more than 60 years. It was bypassed for statehood no fewer than 15 times before statehood was granted. Efforts in Congress at different times to admit New Mexico as a state failed. So, too, did the many statehood efforts that began in New Mexico. Three of these efforts even led to constitutional conventions. New Mexicans in 1850, 1872, and 1889 met and drew up state constitutions. Each time New Mexico's bid for statehood was turned down by Congress. Some New Mexicans opposed statehood at these and other times. Nonetheless, most New Mexicans favored statehood. The movement for statehood grew stronger as newcomers followed the railroad into New Mexico.

New Mexicans fight in the Spanish-American War. In the late 1890s an event occurred that helped New Mexico gain its statehood. This event was the Spanish-American War. In 1898 Congress declared war against Spain. It was the intent of the United States to help Cuba win its independence from Spain. In a sense the 6-month war became for New Mexicans a test of their loyalty to the United States. Would New Mexicans join in the fight against Spain, New Mexico's first mother country? The answer was a resounding "yes!" New Mexico's governor at the time was Miguel A. Otero, Jr. Otero received his appointment to office from President William McKinley in 1897. He remained in office until 1906. An able governor, Otero holds two distinctions. First, he was New Mexico's first Hispanic governor since 1846. Second, his service as governor was the longest in New Mexico's history as a part of the United States. He also actively pushed for statehood.

Governor Miguel A. Otero, Jr.

As governor in 1898, Otero called for volunteers to fight in the war. The response was immediate. Both Hispanos and Anglo-Americans volunteered in great numbers. In fact, more New Mexicans volunteered than there were places for them in the armed forces. Many New Mexicans who did fight served under the command of Colonel Leonard Wood and Lieutenant Colonel Theodore Roosevelt. They were part of the famous Rough Riders regiment. (See Special Interest Feature.) Indeed, about one-third of the Rough Riders came from New Mexico. Among these was Captain Maximiliano Luna. He served at San Juan Hill in Cuba. Shortly thereafter he served in the Philippines, where he was killed in action. A bronze bust to Luna's memory is located in the capitol building in Santa Fe. In honor of New Mexico's many volunteers Roosevelt held the first Rough Riders reunion in Las Vegas, New Mexico, in 1899. At that time Roosevelt said that he favored statehood for New Mexico.

Congress invites New Mexico to become a state. The wait for statehood was, however, longer than most New Mexicans wanted or expected. In 1900 William McKinley won election to a second term as president. His new vice-president was Theodore Roosevelt. New Mexicans took heart. But when a train carrying the president to California stopped in Deming in May 1901, McKinley would not commit himself on the issue of statehood. Even Roosevelt failed to promote New Mexico for statehood when he became president upon McKinley's assassination in September 1901. A president's support might have speeded up statehood, but such support was not needed. What was needed was an act of Congress making it possible for New Mexico to become a state. The problem was the lack of wholehearted congressional support. This made it easy for congressmen to oppose statehood for New Mexico.

Bust of Maximiliano Luna

So it was not until 1910 that Congress invited New Mexico to become a state. In that year it passed an enabling act. Under this act New Mexicans would be able to draw up a constitution with the assurance that Congress would welcome New Mexico as a state. The constitution would spell out New Mexico's government. It would have to be acceptable to a majority of New Mexico's voters. It would also have to be acceptable to Congress. Once this constitution

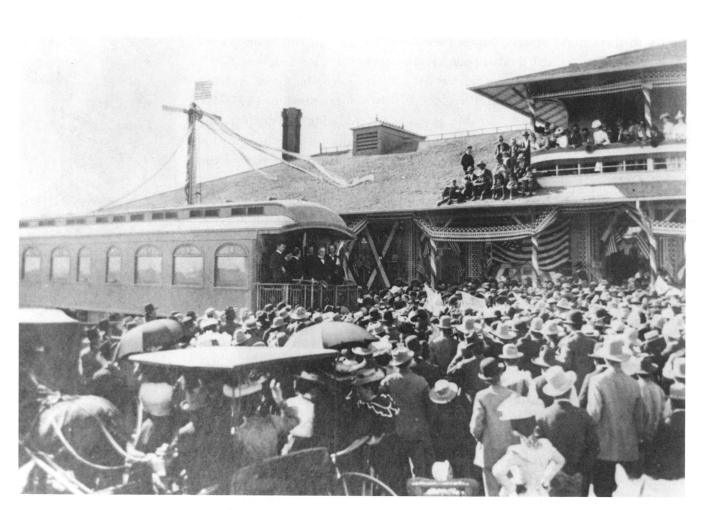

President William McKinley at Deming, 1901

was approved by all concerned, the president would proclaim New Mexico's entry into the Union as a state. You will read about the steps by which New Mexicans achieved this goal of statehood in the next chapter.

New Mexico's Rough Riders

Colonel Teddy Roosevelt believed that cowboys from western states and territories would make the best fighters in Cuba. He called his cavalry unit the Rough Riders. Governor Otero of New Mexico answered Roosevelt's call for fighters by offering to send 340 men. One town that received a call for 30 men was Clayton, a prairie cowtown in the far northeastern corner of New Mexico territory. The volunteers were collected by Albert Thompson of the U.S. Land Office, located next door to the Favorite

Saloon. Thompson went to the saloon to read the governor's request, but few men signed up. The next day a tall cowboy named Jack Robinson, who was roundup boss for the huge Bar T Cross ranch and one of the most respected riders around, enlisted. Then Thompson had no trouble signing up the 30 men needed.

The men and their horses traveled by train to San Antonio, Texas, and then to Florida. The men went on by ship to Cuba, but lack of transport ships forced their horses to remain behind. The cowboys had to fight on foot. As one New Mexico Rough Rider later said: "I was born in a dugout right here in Las Vegas, raised a cowboy, enlisted expecting to do my fighting on horseback as all the boys, but landed in Cuba afoot; marched, sweated, and fought afoot; earned whatever fame afoot." One of the first to die in the famous charge up San Juan Hill in Cuba was Jack Robinson from Clayton. He was shot by a Spanish sharpshooter because he refused to keep down during the charge.

As a result of the bravery and loyalty of the men from New Mexico, however, many people in the United States were convinced that New Mexicans had earned their right to statehood. Indeed, when Governor Otero received the call for volunteers, he personally appealed to leading Hispanic families of the territory to show their patriotism and enlist. A number of Spanish-speaking troopers were recruited in this way.

Section Review

1. **(a)** What opportunities did New Mexico's expanding economy offer newcomers?
   (b) Briefly describe the settlement of New Mexico by homesteaders.
2. **(a)** What function did towns located near homesteads and ranches serve?
   (b) Briefly describe the rapid growth of Las Vegas and Albuquerque.
3. How was the question of land grant titles at last settled, and who were the winners and the losers?
4. **(a)** What changes took place in New Mexico life because of the presence of so many newcomers?
   (b) What ways of living in New Mexico changed very little?
5. **(a)** How did New Mexicans respond to Governor Otero's call for volunteers to fight in the Spanish-American War?
   (b) Why was this response important?
   (c) When did Congress pass a statehood act for New Mexico, and what did New Mexicans then have to do in order to achieve statehood?

Chapter Review

Words You Should Know

Find each word in your reading and explain its meaning.

1. open range
2. roundup
3. placer mining
4. lode mining
5. homestead
6. rural areas
7. urban areas

Places You Should Be Able to Locate

Be able to locate these places on the maps in your book.

1. mining areas
2. mining towns
3. railroad routes
4. railroad towns
5. Farmington

Facts You Should Remember

Answer the following questions by recalling information presented in this chapter.

1. Compare and contrast New Mexico's farming, cattle and sheep raising, and mining industries before and after the coming of the railroads.
2. How did the railroads end New Mexico's isolation and, at the same time, change the face of New Mexico?
3. From where did the people new to New Mexico in the late 1800s and early 1900s come, and why were they attracted to New Mexico?
4. Briefly describe the long struggle of New Mexicans for statehood.
5. Who are the following people, and why are they important?
   (a) Charles Goodnight and Oliver Loving;
   (b) John S. Chisum;
   (c) Charles B. Eddy and James J. Hagerman;
   (d) Franz Huning;
   (e) H. B. Fergusson;
   (f) Julia Asplund;
   (g) Thomas B. Catron;
   (h) Miguel A. Otero, Jr.

Unit Summary

The United States territorial period in New Mexico lasted for more than 60 years. For much of this period New Mexico was a troubled land. At the same time it was a changing land. Some of the changes had to do with government. So it was that New Mexicans got their first American government in 1846 under the Kearny Code. After 1850 New Mexicans had a government like that of other territories of the United States. The president appointed New Mexico's governor and judges. The people elected their lawmakers. Also after 1850 New Mexico had its boundaries set. Congress fixed its eastern boundary by the Compromise of 1850. The Gadsden Purchase of 1853 established its southern boundary. Congress declared its northern boundary when it formed the Colorado Territory in 1861. And Congress set its western boundary when it formed the territory of Arizona in 1863.

These changes were important for New Mexico. However, they were overshadowed by the problems New Mexicans faced. One of these was the Civil War and its effects on New Mexico. The Confederacy wanted New Mexico, and its forces invaded the territory in 1862. In the fight for control of New Mexico Confederate and Union troops fought several battles. The two major battles were fought at Valverde and Glorieta Pass. Indeed, the battle of Glorieta Pass, a Union victory, was the turning point of the war in the Far West. Confederate troops marched out of New Mexico. Nonetheless, New Mexicans found that their problems had not ended. Indeed, the war created new problems. One was Indian warfare. After the Civil War Navajos, Apaches, and Plains Indians attacked settlements in New Mexico. The last of the fighting did not come until 1886. By that time all non-Pueblo Indians in New Mexico had been placed on reservations. A second problem was the lack of law and order. Lawlessness plagued frontier New Mexico. Wars even broke out between rival groups in some areas of the territory. Two such wars occurred in Lincoln and Colfax counties.

Despite these problems there was some economic growth in the territory. The number of farms, for example, increased along with the population during the 1850s. Further growth then occurred after the Civil War. Cattle raising became an important part of New Mexico's economy. Sheep raising expanded. The mining industry grew as more and more minerals were discovered. Still, some conditions inside New Mexico limited economic growth. Chief among these was transportation. Overland transportation was slow and costly. As a result, New Mexico's real growth did not come until after the railroad arrived in 1879. Indeed, the railroad changed the face of New Mexico. Along the railroad lines new towns sprang up and old towns changed. The railroad carried New Mexico's products to national markets. Such changes, in turn, brought many newcomers to New Mexico.

These newcomers came from other parts of the United States and foreign countries. They came to homestead. They came to work in New Mexico's industries. They came to live in New Mexico's towns and cities. They came seeking a healthful climate. These newcomers brought with them their cultures. And because of the territory's new population, New Mexico's culture changed. At the same time some ways of living in New Mexico remained mostly unchanged.

The territorial period at last drew to a close in the early 1900s. Most New Mexicans had long favored statehood. Yet every attempt at statehood had failed. New Mexicans proved their loyalty to the United States by joining the fight against Spain in 1898. Then they waited again. Finally, Congress in 1910 passed a statehood bill for New Mexico. New Mexico had grown and changed so much during the territorial period. It was more than ready to enter the Union as a state.

Time Line:
New Mexico Is a State within the United States

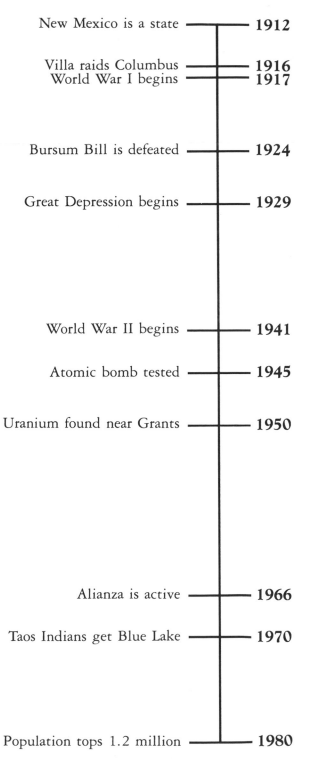

New Mexico is a state ——— **1912**

Villa raids Columbus ——— **1916**
World War I begins ——— **1917**

Bursum Bill is defeated ——— **1924**

Great Depression begins ——— **1929**

World War II begins ——— **1941**

Atomic bomb tested ——— **1945**

Uranium found near Grants ——— **1950**

Alianza is active ——— **1966**

Taos Indians get Blue Lake ——— **1970**

Population tops 1.2 million ——— **1980**

New Mexico Is a State within the United States

New Mexico entered the Union as the 47th state in 1912. It has been a state for more than 70 years. This means that New Mexico's statehood period has been longer than its territorial period. This also means that New Mexico's history as a state has occurred within the twentieth century. And in this century New Mexicans have been caught up in the major events that have affected all Americans.

In the 1900s, for instance, the United States fought in World War I and World War II. New Mexicans felt the effects of both world wars. Between the two wars the country went through the Great Depression. New Mexicans in the 1930s went through the hard times brought on by the depression.

At the same time New Mexico has kept its own unique character. It has remained the Land of Enchantment. You will read about New Mexico's history as a state in the chapters that follow. In chapter 10 you will read about New Mexico's political and economic life between 1910 and 1930. In chapters 11 and 12 you will read about life in New Mexico during the 1930s, the Second World War, and the years that followed.

Eyewitness to New Mexico's History
The United States Has Been Invaded, 1916

From: Oscar J. Martínez, ed., *Fragments of the Mexican Revolution: Personal Accounts from the Border* (University of New Mexico Press, 1983), pp. 177–78.

Many mothers, fathers, and loved ones over the country were anxiously awaiting just such a message as this. There were no ham operators feverishly relaying distressed or calming news. The one telephone line was busy. In fact, the heroic operator had continued at her post amidst chaos and fear, but telephones then were few and seldom used for long distance. The telegram was the accepted bearer of urgent messages, and our short message to El Paso was urgent.

Pancho Villa had raided Columbus! The United States had been invaded! The town was a holocaust, and many were said to have been murdered in their beds—military and civilian alike.

It has been many, many years, and I was a very small child, but there are countless, disjointed impressions indelibly imprinted on my mind.

CHAPTER 10

Politics and Prosperity, 1910–1930

What you will learn in this chapter—

Today you are aware that New Mexico is one of the 50 states. You are further aware that New Mexico has recently grown at a fairly rapid rate. People are attracted to New Mexico because of its climate. They are attracted to the state because of the opportunities it offers.

In 1910, however, New Mexico's future was not at all certain. Invited by Congress to become a state, New Mexico had no statehood constitution. New Mexicans would have to meet in convention to draw up such a document. They would also have to choose the people who would hold office in the new state government. They would then have to move on to the task of developing their new state. They would have to meet the challenges that faced all Americans. In this chapter you will learn about how New Mexicans accomplished these tasks. As you read, you will find answers to the following questions:

1. How did New Mexicans shape their new state government?
2. How was New Mexico affected by international events?
3. What political activities had an effect on New Mexicans during the 1920s?
4. How did New Mexico change during the early statehood period?

1. How did New Mexicans shape their new state government?

A constitutional convention is held. Once Congress had passed the statehood bill for New Mexico, the people of the territory had to take the next step. They first had to draw up a constitution for their state. So it was that a constitutional convention was held in Santa Fe, in 1910. The 100 convention delegates were chosen by the voters. (They were all men, and only men could vote.) The majority reflected the territory's political power structure. At one time such power had belonged to the so-called Santa Fe Ring. The ring had come into being in the early 1870s. Ring members had shared a common interest in land grants. They had thereafter controlled the territory's politics.

Most but not all ring members had been Republicans. The Santa Fe Ring was gone by 1910. Yet New Mexico's politics were still under the control of one group. This group was the Republican party. Its leaders were known as Old Guard Republicans.

These Old Guard Republicans planned to control the constitutional convention. And control the convention they did. Of the 100 delegates chosen, 71 were Republicans. Only 28 were Democrats. One belonged to neither party. Such a large Republican majority insured two outcomes. (1) It meant that leading Republicans ran the convention. Charles A. Spiess, an A.T.&S.F. lawyer from Las Vegas, served as president. Solomon Luna, a large sheepgrower from Valencia County, chaired a very powerful special committee. Luna's committee decided what delegates served on what committees. It even had the final say on the contents of the constitution. Among other influential Republicans at the convention were Thomas B. Catron, Charles Springer, Albert B. Fall, and Holm O. Bursum. (2) The Republican majority meant that delegates would write a constitution that reflected their points of view. Old Guard Republicans were conservative in their outlook. They wanted New Mexico to remain unchanged. They did not want the economy to change. They wanted, of course, to stay in power. Thus they worked to protect their interests. The constitution they wrote favored certain groups. Among the interest groups it favored were railroads and mines. It also favored sheep ranchers and cattle ranchers.

Solomon Luna

The constitution outlines state government. New Mexico's constitution has undergone changes since 1910. Nonetheless, the constitution written in 1910 remains in effect today. This constitution outlines the basic structure of state government for New Mexico. It spells out (1) what officeholders are to have what powers; (2) what qualifications officeholders must meet; (3) how these officeholders are to be chosen; (4) the length of officeholders' terms in office, and (5) the process for amending (changing) the constitution. New Mexicans could meet and draw up a new constitution. A group of citizens did just that in 1969. But the voters turned this constitution down. That is why New Mexicans still live under the constitution of 1910.

Under its constitution New Mexico has three branches of government. The three are the executive, the legislative, and the judicial. The governor and lieutenant governor head the executive branch. The governor sees to it that the laws of the state are carried out. The lieutenant governor acts as governor in the governor's absence. He succeeds to the governorship when a governor does not serve an entire term. For most of the statehood period governors and lieutenant governors have served 2-year terms. Today they serve 4-year terms. They may not, however, hold back-to-back terms. The legislative branch is the law-making body of government. It has a senate and a house of representatives. Senators serve 4-year terms. Representatives serve 2-year terms. Both senators and representatives are elected from districts. Each senate district includes about the same number of people. So does each house district. The judicial branch of government interprets the law. It includes a supreme court and district courts, both of which were written into the 1910 constitution. Voters approved the addition of a court of appeals in 1965. Supreme court and court of appeals judges are elected to 8-year terms. District court judges serve 6-year terms. Judicial candidates run for office as Democrats or Republicans.

Voters approve the constitution. The basic structure of New Mexico's government is much like that of other state governments. There are, however, features written into the constitution of 1910 that are quite unique. These features were included in the constitution at the request of Hispanic leaders. In fact, 35 of the 100 delegates at the constitutional convention were of Hispanic descent. Most of these delegates belonged to the Republican party. So did most other Hispanic New Mexicans in 1910. Convention delegates wanted protection for all the people. Thus the constitution protects voting rights. It states that citizens are not to be denied the right to vote because of "religion, race, language, or color." Nor are citizens to be denied the right to vote because they cannot read or write either English or Spanish. Further, the constitution protects Hispanic rights to education. It states that Hispanic children are not to be denied the "right and privilege" of attending public schools. It also states that Hispanic children are never to be placed in separate schools. They are instead to "enjoy perfect equality with other children in all public schools."

Once written, the constitution had to be approved by the voters. And only men had the right to vote for or against the document. Most New Mexicans favored statehood. They were indeed anxious for statehood and willing to accept any constitution. But some New Mexicans worked against the constitution. They opposed it as being too conservative. Among other things, they believed that the people and not the legislators should choose New Mexico's United States senators. They felt that women should have the right to vote in all elections. They thought the constitution gave too much protection to special interest groups. Those against the constitution explained their opposition to the voters. They urged the people to vote against the constitution. But they had no success. New Mexico's voters had waited too long to turn down a chance at statehood. So on January 19, 1911, voters by a large majority approved the constitution. The vote total for the constitution was 31,742. Only 13,399 men cast their votes against it.

New Mexicans elect their first state officials. New Mexicans now waited for congressional and presidential action. The Congress approved state-

Governor
William C. McDonald

Governor Octaviano Larrazolo

hood on August 19, 1911. Presidential approval followed. On January 6, 1912, President William Howard Taft signed the proclamation making New Mexico the nation's 47th state. New Mexico's male voters had chosen their first state officeholders nearly two months prior to President Taft's signing of the statehood bill. The election on November 7, 1911, had followed a hard campaign fight between Republicans and Democrats. The Republicans had had the advantage of being the majority. Even so the Democrats had done quite well.

In fact, New Mexico's first statehood governor was a Democrat. He was William C. McDonald of Lincoln County. Elected lieutenant governor was Ezequiel C de Baca of San Miguel County. He, too, was a Democrat. The Republicans, on the other hand, won control of the state supreme court. Two of the first three justices were Republicans. The Republicans likewise won control of the state legislature. This was of added importance because legislators would choose New Mexico's first two United States senators. Meeting on March 11, 1912, they selected two Republicans. One was Thomas B. Catron of Santa Fe. Catron was a long-time leader of the Republican party. The other was Albert B. Fall of Otero County. Fall had begun his political career as a Democrat. He had switched parties because the Republican party was stronger. In 1913 the power to select United States senators passed from the state's legislators to the voters. In that year the Seventeenth Amendment became a part of the United States Constitution. It provided for the direct election of senators by the voters.

The state's population entitled New Mexicans to just one representative. But in 1911 the voters elected two because of a mixup in Washington, D.C. This mixup had given the new state two representatives instead of one. The top vote getter in the November 7, 1911, election was a Republican, George Curry. H. B. Fergusson, a Democrat, got the second highest number of votes. Both were seated in the United States House of Representatives. However, starting with the election of 1912, New Mexico was allowed only one representative.

Republicans control state government. New Mexico's first statehood governor, William C. McDonald, served one 4-year term. Governors were thereafter limited to two back-to-back 2-year terms. Ezequiel C de Baca won the first election for a 2-year term in 1916. He was New Mexico's first Hispanic governor during the statehood period. Both McDonald and C de Baca, you may recall, were Democrats. Still, it was not long before a member of the dominant Republican party became governor, for C de Baca died shortly after taking office. The lieutenant governor who succeeded him was Washington E. Lindsey of Roosevelt County. Lindsey was a Republican. So, too, was his successor. Elected governor in 1918 was Octaviano A. Larrazolo. He was a leading member of the Hispanic community and the Republican party.

For the most part Republicans ran New Mexico's government during its early statehood period. They controlled the courts, the legislature, and most state offices. The key to Republican success was Hispanic New Mexicans. This segment of the population was New Mexico's largest in the early 1900s. And most Hispanos supported the Republican party. As long as they continued this support, the Republican party remained the state's dominant political group.

Section Review

1.   **(a)** What group controlled the constitutional convention of 1910?
        (b) How did the constitution reflect the points of view of the Old Guard Republicans?
2.   **(a)** What three branches of government does New Mexico have, and what is the job of each branch?
        (b) What special protections for New Mexicans were written into the constitution?
3.   When was New Mexico at last proclaimed a state?
4.   **(a)** Why did some New Mexicans oppose the 1910 constitution?
        (b) Why did most New Mexicans support this constitution?
5.   **(a)** What offices did Democrats and Republicans control as a result of the first statehood election in 1911?
        (b) What party mostly controlled government during the early statehood period, and why was this party so successful?

2. How was New Mexico affected by international events?

The United States has trouble with Mexico. During the early statehood period New Mexicans felt the impact of events taking place outside the country. The first of these involved Mexico. In 1910 the Mexican people rebelled. They overthrew the dictator who had ruled them for 30 years. After the overthrow, different groups in Mexico fought for power. The leader of one of these groups was Francisco "Pancho" Villa. He and his followers were strongest in northern Mexico. The fight for power in Mexico soon affected the United States. For one thing, a number of United States citizens in Mexico lost their lives. Others lost their property. For another, Pancho Villa became angry with the United States.

Villa's anger stemmed from the fact that the United States had not backed him in his struggle for power. He felt that most of the Mexican people supported him in his effort to head the government. For its part the United States government chose not to get involved in the fight over who would lead Mexico. Officials in this country stood back and watched while Villa's foes took control of the Mexican government. In an attempt to change his fortunes, Villa in 1916 planned a raid into United States territory. He thought this raid would do two things. First, it would embarrass the Mexican government. Mexican officials had not yet been able to control Villa. Second, the raid would likely bring the United States into the fighting in Mexico. Villa hoped that such a turn of events would bring his foes to their knees.

Villa raids into New Mexico. The place Villa chose to raid was Columbus in southern New Mexico. A town of about 400 people, Columbus was not far from the United States–Mexican border. Part of the 13th United States Cavalry was stationed there. Villa made his raid on March 9, 1916. The people of Columbus were taken by surprise. All told, 108 died in the fighting. Among these were 10 civilians and 8 United States soldiers. Villa lost 90 men.

The United States government quickly responded. President Woodrow Wilson sent an armed force into Mexico to punish Villa. Among the more than 6,000 in the force were troopers from the black 10th Cavalry. Under the command of General John J. Pershing, this force never caught up with Villa. The mission failed because Pershing's troops did not know Mexico's terrain. And it failed because the Mexican people resented the intruders. The United States government soon removed its force from Mexico. Nonetheless, the presence of United States troops in Mexico had a lasting effect. It did not, as Villa had hoped, cause a change in Mexican leadership. But it did further damage relations between Mexico and the United States. The people of Mexico had resented the United States since the war between the two countries in 1846 (page 171). Pershing's mission added to this resentment. So, too, had other United States–Mexican conflicts following the Mexican Revolution of 1910.

New Mexicans fight in World War I. Shortly after sending troops into Mexico, United States officials became involved in Europe. The government sent troops to fight on the side of the Allies in World War I. The main Allies

U.S. troops prepare to chase Villa

were Great Britain, France, Russia, and Italy. Chief among the Central Powers—those countries fighting against the Allies—were Germany and Austria-Hungary. World War I had begun in Europe in August 1914. Remaining neutral, the United States had stayed out of the war for nearly three years. In the years between 1914 and 1917 a series of events strained German-American relations. Then in 1917 relations between the two countries reached the breaking point. In January 1917 Germany announced that its submarines would sink all ships sighted in the war zone. Included were the ships of the United States. Two months later Americans learned the contents of a telegram sent by the German foreign minister, Arthur Zimmermann, to the German minister in Mexico. This so-called Zimmermann Telegram invited Mexico to become a German ally. In return, Germany promised to help Mexico recover land it had lost to the United States. The "lost" land included New Mexico, Arizona, and Texas. United States officials learned of Germany's offer to Mexico from British intelligence, who had intercepted the telegram. They published its contents on March 1, 1917. The American people were outraged.

Convinced that Germany was set on war, President Wilson addressed a joint session of Congress on April 2, 1917. He asked for a declaration of war. Four days later Congress declared war on Germany. This action had an immediate effect on New Mexico. Governor Washington E. Lindsey told New Mexicans that: "Good Friday 1917 will long be remembered in New Mexico, for on that day New Mexico was summoned to combat at home and overseas. April 6, 1917 our people passed from a status of profound industrial peace to a status of universal war." On April 21 President Wilson called up the New Mexico National Guard. By June it was at full strength. State officials made sure the National Guard was quickly prepared to act. The state also housed a training camp for soldiers near Deming. This was Camp Cody. It had the capacity to train 30,000 soldiers. Soldiers from New Mexico took part in the fighting in Europe as well. Some of them fought in the crucial battles of 1918 that turned the tide of war in favor of the Allies. All totaled, 17,251 New Mexicans served in all branches of the armed forces. Of these, 501 died in combat or from other causes while in the service. New Mexico's losses were in fact above the average per capita (for each person) losses of the 48 states.

New Mexicans at home aid the war effort. New Mexicans at home served their country well during the war. They did so in a number of ways. First, they helped raise money for the American war effort. This effort involved both the state government and private individuals. The government bought United States Liberty Bonds amounting to $750,000. Private citizens bought government bonds totaling $17,952,000. This was more than the national government expected from New Mexicans. Private groups like the Red Cross,

World War I soldiers march past the Governor's Mansion

the YWCA and the YMCA, the Knights of Columbus, and the Salvation Army raised money. They provided thousands of dollars in added support for the war effort. Second, New Mexicans joined in the spirit of the American war effort. They urged one another, for example, to plant gardens. Known as "victory gardens," these gardens helped ease the demand for food at home.

New Mexico's farmers and ranchers made a third contribution to the war effort. In 1918 farmers in New Mexico produced 3,334,000 bushels of wheat. They produced 1,276,000 bushels of potatoes. This production was up sharply from the 2,104,000 bushels of wheat and the 816,000 bushels of potatoes they had produced in 1916. Greater wartime demand for food allowed farmers to sell more farm produce. At the same time efforts to improve New Mexico farming after 1910 made increased farm production possible. One such effort was the building of Elephant Butte Dam at Hot Springs, now Truth or Consequences. Aid money provided by the national government helped New Mexico build the dam. Work on the dam began in 1911. It was completed five years later. The dam brought relief to many farmers who had been accustomed to dry farming poor land. Wartime demand for food also allowed ranchers to raise and to sell more cattle. Ranchers shipped many more cattle out of state during the war than they had in previous years. Their profits increased as well. This was because cattle prices doubled during the war years.

Wartime benefits New Mexico mining. One other group that

Elephant Butte Dam

contributed greatly to the war effort in New Mexico were the miners. They, in turn, benefited from greater wartime demand for minerals. Coal, for example, was in demand to help fill the fuel needs of World War I. As a result, coal production in mines near Raton and Gallup and at Madrid and Carthage increased. These mines produced more than four million tons of coal. Copper, too, was in demand. Chief among the state's copper producers was the Kennecott Copper Company. Kennecott had bought the Santa Rita copper mines near Silver City in 1910. It had then developed these mines into large open-pit mines. Using open-cut mining methods, Kennecott in time cut mining costs and increased production. The company increased copper production still further to meet the wartime demands. During the war other new copper mines opened in southern New Mexico.

261

Santa Rita Copper Mine

World War I was not, to be sure, the sole reason for New Mexico's economic growth during its early years as a state. Silver mining in the state, for example, peaked in 1916. In that year silver worth more than $1,000,000 was processed. Nonetheless, international events clearly affected New Mexicans. The fight for power in Mexico spilled over into New Mexico with Pancho Villa's raid on Columbus. World War I then brought New Mexicans into the middle of world affairs. New Mexicans lived in one of the younger states. At the same time they were as loyal to the Union as were the residents of any other state.

Section Review

1. **(a)** Why did Pancho Villa plan a raid into United States territory?
   (b) How did the United States government respond to the raid?
   (c) How did the presence of United States troops in Mexico affect relations between the United States and Mexico?

2. **(a)** What actions did Germany take that caused the United States to enter World War I?
   (b) What contributions did New Mexicans make to the actual fighting of the war?

3. What contributions did New Mexicans at home make to the American war effort?

3. What political activities had an effect on New Mexicans during the 1920s?

Political party rivalry is intense. Most Americans in the 1920s wanted to forget about the rest of the world. They wanted to forget that there ever had been a world war. They wanted to return to what their new president, Warren G. Harding, called *normalcy*. By normalcy Harding meant life in the United States as it had been before the war. Returning to normalcy meant going back to the days before America's involvement in world affairs. For New Mexicans it meant a growing concern about life at home.

An interest in local affairs helped spark a renewal of New Mexico's political party rivalry. And new to the state's political scene were women who gained the right to vote in 1920 with the addition of the 19th Amendment to the United States Constitution. In state politics Republicans still had the upper hand. They generally controlled the state legislature. They elected three of five governors between 1920 and 1929. Republican governors were elected in 1920, 1926, and 1928. Richard C. Dillon won in both 1926 and 1928. He was the first governor to be elected to two terms. One New Mexico Republican even became known nationally during the 1920s, but for the wrong reasons. That person was Albert B. Fall.

Governor Richard C. Dillon

You will recall that Fall was one of New Mexico's first two United States senators (page 256). In 1918 the voters returned Fall to the Senate. Three years later Fall left the Senate to become President Harding's Secretary of the Interior. In time the American people became aware of a number of scandals in the Harding administration. One of these centered on Fall. (See Special Interest Feature.) Fall had taken certain oil reserves belonging to the navy and had leased them to private oil companies. In return for these leases, the companies had lent money to Fall. Fall had used this money to develop his ranch in Otero County. When officials learned about the oil leases, they arrested Fall. The loans Fall had received looked suspicious. He went on trial. And in 1929 Fall was found guilty of accepting bribes. He was sentenced to a one-year term. He was allowed to serve his time in the New Mexico state penitentiary rather than in a federal prison. Fall was the first cabinet member in United States history to be sent to prison for wrongdoing while in office.

Bronson Cutting is a powerful figure. Political activity in the 1920s helped rather than hurt the career of another New Mexico politician. This person was Bronson Cutting. During Cutting's youth, his father had been the director of the Southern Pacific Railroad Company. This position had brought the Cutting family into contact with New Mexico. As a result, Bronson Cutting became interested in New Mexico. In 1910 he moved to New Mexico for his health. Soon thereafter, he got involved in politics. At first he was a

Albert B. Fall

Republican. Then in 1912, the year New Mexico became a state, Cutting saw his influence grow. He bought the Santa Fe *New Mexican,* an important daily newspaper. He used the paper to support the candidates he favored. During World War I Cutting served in the army. After the war he founded the American Legion in New Mexico. He even helped finance the legion.

Crusading Journalism and Politics

Among those who helped bring Albert B. Fall down were two New Mexicans. Both were journalists. Both were newcomers to New Mexico in 1917. One—Carl C. Magee—came because his wife was in poor health. The other—Clinton P. Anderson—sought a healthful climate for himself. Anderson had tuberculosis. Yet he quickly regained his health. He did so even though doctors told him the day after he arrived that he would not live out the week.

A lawyer in Oklahoma, Magee started a new career in New Mexico. He first edited a weekly newspaper. Then in 1920 he took control of the *Albuquerque Journal.* The *Journal* was at that time a Republican daily. It had the largest circulation in the state. As editor, Magee called for changes in the state land office. He called for a cleaning up of the powerful Republican party. His remarks angered party leaders. In time they brought a visit from Fall. Fall warned Magee to lay off or be broken. Magee refused, and before the end of 1921 he had lost control of the *Journal.* But Magee soon came back. He did so as editor of the *New Mexico State Tribune.* The masthead of his *Tribune* eventually became that set on all Scripps-Howard newspapers: "Give Light and the People Will Find Their Own Way."

Anderson, by contrast, went to work as a reporter rather than as an editor. His first job was with the *Albuquerque Evening Herald* in 1918. He reported on the New Mexico Legislature. He began to get involved in Democratic politics. As journalists concerned with politics, both Magee and Anderson followed news about Fall. Of course they looked into rumors about his finances. In fact, Magee visited Fall's Three Rivers Ranch in 1923. So did a reporter from the *Denver Post.* The ranch clearly showed off Fall's new wealth. Magee, Anderson, and others told their readers all about Fall's actions. Magee even carried his story to the floor of the United States Senate. There he testified before a committee investigating Fall's leasing of naval oil reserves.

In 1924 Magee tried his own hand at politics. However, he lost

Carl C. McGee

his bid to be the Democratic candidate for United States senator. Three years later he returned to Oklahoma. While there he invented the parking meter. Anderson's later entry into politics met with more success. New Mexicans elected him to 2 terms in the House of Representatives. They elected him to 4 terms in the United States Senate.

Cutting now had two power bases. One was his newspaper. The other was the American Legion. The 17,000 legion members formed the core that Cutting could rely on for political support. Thus Bronson Cutting greatly influenced New Mexico politics. This he did not as a Republican or as a Democrat. Rather, he threw his support from one party to the other. In the process he watched his own political importance grow. So powerful did Cutting become that his support for one or more candidates in major races was usually enough to get them elected. Cutting himself became a United States senator in 1927. In that year Governor Dillon, a Republican, appointed him to the Senate seat left vacant by the death of A. A. Jones. Yet even this appointment did not lock Cutting into the Republican party. He continued to throw his support behind Democrats as well as Republicans. In honor of his memory a bust of Senator Cutting stands on the south side of the Bataan building on the capitol grounds.

Bust of Senator Bronson Cutting

Government actions affect New Mexico's Indians. Also in the 1920s New Mexico's Pueblo peoples became politically active. They united as they had not done since the Pueblo Revolt of 1680 (page 102). What united them was a threat to their land and to their way of life. The Treaty of Guadalupe Hidalgo in 1848 had promised that New Mexico's Indians would retain their land. The Office of Surveyor General had then confirmed Pueblo land titles (page 239). You may recall that the United States government had otherwise ignored the Pueblo peoples. Lincoln's gift of canes to Pueblo governors was the one exception (page 99). Then in 1876 the United States Supreme Court handed down a decision that greatly affected Pueblo Indians. The court said that the Pueblo peoples were not dependents of the national government as were other Indians. This was due, said the court, to the high level of Pueblo culture. The court also said that Pueblo peoples could handle their land as they saw fit. This decision harmed the Pueblo peoples. Individual Indians sold off tribal lands. In time 30 percent or more of Pueblo property in New Mexico had been sold to non-Indians.

In 1913 the United States Supreme Court reversed the 1876 decision. The question before the court was what to do about the 3,000 non-Indians who owned Pueblo land. The court first said that the Pueblo peoples were

Repair of Zia Church (about 1920)

indeed dependents of the national government. It said that they needed the protection of national officials. The court concluded by ruling that all non-Indian claims to Pueblo lands were illegal.

The Bursum Bill addresses the problem of Pueblo land ownership. The 1913 United States Supreme Court ruling was not, however, the last word on Pueblo lands. Many non-Indians continued to live on Pueblo land after 1913. Some non-Indian families had in fact lived on this land for two or more generations. So the problem of Pueblo land ownership remained. As Secretary of the Interior in 1921, Fall thought that the time for solving the problem was at hand. He therefore asked Holm O. Bursum to draw up an Indian land bill. Bursum, a Republican, had replaced Fall as United States senator in 1921.

Bursum's bill had two basic parts. (1) The bill gave non-Indians who held Indian land before 1902 ownership of that land. (2) The bill gave state courts the power to settle all other disputes over Indian land. Had the Bursum

Bill passed, it would have been disastrous for the Pueblo peoples. It would have meant the loss of some of the best irrigated Pueblo land. It would have given state courts a great deal of power over the Pueblos. And these state courts had long been unfriendly to the Indians.

The Bursum Bill is defeated. The Bursum Bill did not, however, become law. A group of friends that the Pueblo peoples never knew they had came to their support. This group included artists and writers who had settled in Taos. Chief among them was John Collier. A young poet, Collier took it upon himself to let the Pueblo peoples know what was happening. He told them about the contents of the Bursum Bill, and the Indians were stunned. They had not been told by any national or state leader that an Indian land bill was being considered. Collier also rallied support for the Indian cause among his artist and writer friends. At the same time the Indians themselves began to unite.

In time support for the Pueblo cause became widespread. Pueblo Indians themselves traveled widely and spoke out in their own behalf. Some Indian leaders even appeared before Congress in Washington, D.C. The immediate result of all these efforts was defeat of the Bursum Bill. Congress simply refused to act on it. The long-range result of this action was a shift in United States Indian policy. Officials in Washington adopted a friendlier attitude toward the Indian population in New Mexico and in the rest of the nation. In 1924 Congress passed the Pueblo Lands Act. This act recognized once and for all the land rights of the Pueblo peoples. In addition, it outlined ways to get non-Indians off Indian lands. Included was a promise that some non-Indians would receive payment for the lands they had given up. In the same year Congress passed a law that granted American citizenship to Indians born within the United States. Arizona and New Mexico, however, did not allow Indians to vote until 1947. In that year a United States court ruled that all states had to give Indian people the right to vote.

---

1.   **(a)** What kind of political party rivalry occurred in New Mexico during the 1920s?   **Section Review**
        (b) To what extent was the Republican party still the dominant party in the state?

2.   **(a)** What actions taken by Albert B. Fall led to his conviction and imprisonment?
        (b) How influential in New Mexico politics was Bronson Cutting, and how did he become so powerful?

3.   **(a)** What did an 1876 Supreme Court decision say about the Pueblo Indians, and how did this decision affect the Indians?

267

(b) What did the Supreme Court say about the Pueblo Indians in 1913, and how did this decision compare to the one handed down in 1876?

4. **(a)** How would ownership of Pueblo lands have been settled had Congress passed the Bursum Bill?

(b) Why did Congress decide not to pass the Bursum Bill?

(c) What actions taken by Congress in 1924 marked a change in United States Indian policy?

(d) How long did Indians in Arizona and New Mexico have to wait for the right to vote?

---

4. How did New Mexico change during the early statehood period?

New Mexico's population grows. Like the rest of the West, New Mexico's population grew during the 1900s. In 1910 its population was 327,300. Ten years later it was 360,350. The population increase during this decade was small, but then these were troubled years. World War I disrupted the lives of Americans across the country. Near the war's end another disruption began as the Spanish flu swept the world. This epidemic killed more than 21 million people worldwide. In the United States 550,000 died from the flu. The flu reached New Mexico in October 1918. In time it claimed the lives of about 5,000 New Mexicans. Those hit hardest were between the ages of 20 and 45. Most flu victims lived in New Mexico's small towns and rural areas. Once the war and the flu epidemic were at an end, New Mexico's population began to grow at a faster pace. By 1930 the state's population climbed to 423,317.

Among those new to New Mexico were people who moved into the state. Some came in search of a new life. (See Special Interest Feature.) Others came in search of a more healthful climate. Most newcomers came from other parts of the United States. Some came from Mexico. Indeed, the number of immigrants from Mexico had begun to grow even before 1920. The Mexican Revolution (page 257) caused some Mexicans to leave the country. Later on Mexicans were attracted by job openings in the United States. As industry in the United States grew during the world war and the 1920s, Mexican workers helped meet the demand for unskilled workers. Mexican immigrants, in other words, were welcomed as a source of cheap labor. They found jobs as laborers for the railroads and as construction workers. Many more found jobs as farm laborers. In 1910 the number of Mexican immigrants in New Mexico was 6,649. This number increased to 20,272 in 1920 and to 59,340 in 1930.

Travel and tourism increase. Besides a changing population, New Mexico underwent other changes as well. One change was the ever-increasing

number of licensed cars in the state. The greater use of cars, in turn, led to the building of more roads. And aiding the building of roads was the Federal Highway Act. Passed by Congress in 1916, this act gave the state's highway engineer more power within the state. This act also meant that the United States government would pay half the cost of building roads. So during the 1920s New Mexicans got many new miles of road. Between 1920 and 1927 more than 1,700 miles of improved road were completed. The money spent on road building was five times greater in 1931 than it had been in 1921. By 1932 the total mileage of improved roads within the state was 5,700. As new roads were built, some towns grew. Others, those bypassed by major highways, lost population or became less important economic centers. At the same time trucks became a major carrier of goods. Trucks challenged the railroads, and some short-run railroad routes were closed.

New Mexico's Black Citizens

New Mexico is a unique land. It is a land that has benefited from many groups of people. And among the people who have helped shape the state are its black citizens. Blacks came to New Mexico quite early. Indeed, the first blacks came as explorers and cowboys. They came as soldiers and miners. They came as former slaves, men and women searching for a better way of life.

Some of the blacks who came settled in New Mexico's cities. Albuquerque was one such city. The first sizable number of blacks in Albuquerque arrived after the completion of the railroad. Few, however, stayed in Albuquerque in the late 1800s. The city had little industry

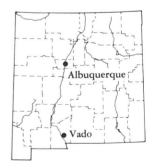

269

and therefore few job openings. In addition, the large numbers of Hispanos and Indians in the city limited opportunities for blacks. Some blacks did stay in Albuquerque, and those who did soon built a community for their people. They had their own church. The Grant Chapel African Methodist Church was founded in 1882. They held jobs as small businessmen and barbers. They worked as porters, cooks, and laborers for the railroads. In 1912, when New Mexico became a state, about 100 blacks lived in Albuquerque. By 1920 the black population had grown to about 300. Many of these people had moved to Albuquerque after World War I.

Other blacks settled in New Mexico's rural areas. One such area lay on the east side of the Rio Grande in Doña Ana County. There blacks settled on land that land companies sold to them under long-term contracts. The land was thought to be worthless, but blacks made it valuable. They washed alkalai out of the soil. They introduced a crop new to the Rio Grande Valley—cotton. In time the blacks in the valley paid off their land contracts. After World War I they established what is today the small town of Vado. Located southeast of Las Cruces and slightly east of Interstate 10, Vado has remained a black community.

Like blacks elsewhere, New Mexico's blacks faced discrimination. In 1907, for example, three black students were not allowed to take part in the graduation ceremonies for Albuquerque High School. They received their diplomas in a separate ceremony. And in 1926 the Doña Ana County schools were segregated. A separate school was built for the children who lived in Vado. Yet New Mexico's black citizens have endured these injustices. They have worked for an end to discrimination. Today blacks live in many different parts of the state. They work at all kinds of jobs. By their presence and their culture they add much to the land that is New Mexico.

More cars and roads resulted in the growth of tourism in New Mexico. (See Special Interest Feature.) In fact, tourism grew steadily during the 1920s. To house tourists along the roads, a new type of lodging emerged—the motel. New Mexico's first motel was the Apache Inn at Valley Ranch on the Pecos River. Tourists came to New Mexico to visit many different attractions. One attraction was the ever-growing number of national and state parks and monuments. The first of these was Bandelier National Monument. It was opened to the public in 1916. Carlsbad Caverns became a National Monument in 1923 and a National Park in 1930. The map on page 271 shows the location of

New Mexico's Parks and Monuments

National Monuments
1. White Sands
2. Gila Cliff Dwellings
3. Salinas
4. El Morro
5. Bandelier
6. Pecos Ruins
7. Chaco Canyon
8. Aztec Ruins
9. Fort Union
10. Capulin Mt.

National Park
1. Carlsbad Caverns

State Parks
1. Navajo Lake
2. Heron Lake
3. El Vado Lake
4. Rio Grande Gorge
5. Kit Carson Memorial
6. Clayton Lake
7. Chicosa Lake
8. Coyote Creek
9. Morphy Lake
10. Hyde Memorial
11. Santa Fe River
12. Coronado
13. Red Rocks
14. Bluewater Lake
15. Indian Petroglyph
16. San Gabriel
17. Villanueva
18. Storrie Lake
19. Conchas Lake
20. Ute Lake
21. Chilili Canyon
22. Belen Valley
23. Manzano Mountains
24. Sumner Lake
25. Oasis
26. Bottomless Lakes
27. Living Desert
28. Smokey Bear
29. Valley of Fires
30. Elephant Butte Lake
31. Caballo Lake
32. Percha Dam
33. Leasburg Dam
34. Rock Hound
35. Pancho Villa
36. City of Rocks

Present New Mexico state boundaries
▲ State Park
△ National Monument
□ National Park

0 25 50 75 Miles

parks and monuments in the state today. Another attraction was a number of special activities. These included the Santa Fe Fiesta, begun in 1919 to celebrate the reconquest of New Mexico by Don Diego de Vargas. They included the Inter-Tribal Indian Ceremonial at Gallup. The first Gallup ceremonial was held in 1922.

Gallup: The Gateway to Points West

In the 1920s Gallup became New Mexico's gateway to the west. Improved roads and cars were putting more and more Americans on wheels. In fact, this was especially true in the West. Between 1919 and 1929 western states built more than 1 million miles of highways. They did so with the help of federal funds. In addition, westerners had already developed their love affair with the car. Car ownership by westerners was twice the national average. Californians alone owned 10 percent of the nation's total. And by 1925 more western tourists traveled by car than by train.

What put Gallup on every tourist's map was Highway 66. It was the country's main east-west highway. From points east it ran all the

way across New Mexico. It entered the state east of Tucumcari. It left the state 17 miles west of Gallup. In between it passed through other New Mexico towns and cities. But it was Gallup that tourists remembered. Many of them remembered the red sandstone cliffs just east of Gallup. Seeming to have pushed themselves out of the ground, these cliffs had long caught the eye of those who traveled by railroad. Indeed, the railroad had used pictures of the red cliffs in their advertisements.

Most tourists stopped in Gallup for gasoline or a meal. Some spent the night. Those who stayed longer found an enchanting town. Gallup was not an old town in the 1920s. Its history dated back only to the arrival of the railroad in 1881. The town's name derived from the railway paymaster. Before that, sheep and cattle growers lived on the land. Only two buildings stood on the site of the future town. One was a saloon. The other was the Blue Goose General Store built in 1880. It served passengers traveling by the Westward Overland Stage. After 1881 additional buildings and new townspeople appeared. In 1891 Gallup became an official town. Further growth gave Gallup its special meaning.

By the 1920s Gallup had become a trade center for the Navajos. Nearby coal mines had brought to the region miners from as far away as Europe. And in 1922 the town had hosted its first Inter-Tribal Indian Ceremonial. Lighting for the after dark Indian dances had come from the carbide headlights of the 1920s cars. For the tourists passing through, Gallup was the gateway to Arizona and points west. For the tourists who stopped over, Gallup had much to offer.

The state's economy undergoes changes. The growth of tourism added dollars to New Mexico's economy. So, too, did a fairly new industry, the petroleum (oil) industry. New Mexicans had known about the presence of oil in their state since the early 1880s. Still, the real development of oil did not begin until the 1920s. One oil-producing region was San Juan County on the Navajo reservation. An oil well at the Hogback field produced oil for the first time in 1922. A well in the Rattlesnake field began producing oil in 1924. Other regions of the state began producing oil shortly thereafter. Big oil fields were discovered near Artesia, Hobbs, and Eunice. Besides oil, discoveries of natural gas boosted the state's economy. In 1922 the first well to produce natural gas for commercial use was brought in. This well was located in the Ute Dome field of San Juan County. Companies leased the rights to oil and natural gas from the state. This meant that oil and gas production added revenue

New Mexico oil fields

to the state's treasury. As time passed, oil and gas also began to replace coal as a fuel.

Farmers and ranchers were not as fortunate as oil and gas producers. Making up over 40 percent of New Mexico's population, these people faced difficult times in the 1920s. There was simply less demand for either food crops or livestock after the war. The result was low farm and ranch income and a drop in the value of farms and ranches. Overproduction of farm goods caused prices to drop still lower. Indeed, the depressed condition of farming was common to most parts of the United States during the 1920s. Still, when the weather cooperated, New Mexico's farmers could produce banner crops. In 1926, for example, the state's winter wheat crop totaled 4,876,000 bushels. Yet bad weather could always add to the farmers' woes. A drought caused the

Farming in eastern New Mexico

state's winter wheat crop to drop to a mere 150,000 bushels in 1927. In general, farmers had little hope of improving their lot. Most New Mexico farms were simply too small to provide steady income year after year. Nearly 30 percent of the farms were less than 50 acres in size. New Mexico's ranches were generally too small as well. As a result, the state's ranches tended to become larger as the less successful ranchers were forced to sell out. Farms, too, tended to become larger.

The state undergoes cultural changes. The 1920s, then, were a time of varied economic fortunes for New Mexicans. They were also a time of varied cultural developments. In the field of architecture there were few new building styles introduced. Still, the 1920s were a time when New Mexico's architecture stressed the building styles already familiar to New Mexicans. The Pueblo style was very popular in the 1920s. One of the chief supporters of this building style was John Gaw Meem. Opening an architecture firm in 1924, Meem served for many years as the architect of the University of New Mexico. Today one can see the Pueblo style buildings Meem designed by visiting the university's campus in Albuquerque.

In the field of literature a brother and sister whose ancestors had entered New Mexico over the Santa Fe Trail began to make their mark. From his new home in the East, Harvey Fergusson wrote novels about New Mexico and the West. His *Blood of the Conquerors* was published in 1921. Fergusson then wrote four regional novels, including *Wolf Song. Wolf Song* told the story of Hispanic

274

The University of New Mexico Library

and Anglo-American life in Taos at the time of Kit Carson. Erna Fergusson, unlike her brother, remained in New Mexico. One of her earliest works was *Dancing Gods.* It detailed New Mexico and Arizona Indian ceremonials.

A new cultural development for New Mexico was the growth of colonies of writers and artists at Santa Fe and Taos. Some of the people who settled in these centers came seeking a simpler way of life. Alice Corbin Henderson, who came to New Mexico in 1916, was one of the first writers to settle in Santa Fe. She wrote several books. She also edited *The Turquoise Trail,* an outstanding collection of southwestern poetry. Another newcomer and founder of the Santa Fe writers' colony was Mary Austin. She arrived in 1918. Her *Land of Journey's Ending,* published in 1924, contrasted Pueblo Indian culture with the culture found elsewhere in the United States. To Austin, Pueblo culture was superior. Joining Henderson and Austin in Santa Fe through the years were a number of other distinguished writers. One was Willa Cather, who first visited New Mexico in 1916. It was during a visit to Mary Austin's Santa Fe home that Willa Cather wrote most of her famous novel *Death Comes for the Archbishop.* Published in 1927, this novel is based on the life of Archbishop Lamy (page 191) and the French priests. Another writer attracted to New Mexico was Witter Bynner. Bynner had a home in Santa Fe and wrote books about Indian life. Still another writer attracted by the Southwest region was Oliver La Farge. A New Englander, La Farge won a Pulitzer Prize for his *Laughing Boy,* a 1929 novel about Indian life.

Mary Austin

275

The Taos Society of Artists, 1932: (lower) J. H. Sharp, E. L. Blumenschein; (middle) E. Martin Hennings, Bert G. Phillips, E. Irving Couse, O. E. Berninghaus; (upper) Walter Ufer, W. Herbert Dunton, Victor Higgins, Kenneth Adams

Besides writers, artists came to Santa Fe to create their works. One of the first to come was Robert Henri. Henri stayed but a short time. Nonetheless, he persuaded John Sloan to come to Santa Fe. Arriving in 1921, Sloan spent his summers at a house on Delgado Street. There he painted pictures of pueblos and Indians. Other artists who later came to Santa Fe were Marsden Hartley and Andrew Dasburg. John Marin and Russell Cheney spent time in Santa Fe as well. Still, the most famous of the artists attracted to New Mexico did not gather in Santa Fe. Rather, they gathered in Taos.

The Taos Society of Artists is founded. The founders of the artists' colony at Taos were Bert G. Phillips and Ernest L. Blumenschein. Both men had studied painting in Paris. They had then returned to the United States. Together they arrived at Taos in 1898 with a wagon and a team of horses they had bought in Denver. Having been in Taos only a moment, Blumenschein felt the impact of the different New Mexico cultures. He said to Phillips, "This is what we are looking for. Let's go no farther." Blumenschein and Phillips saw in the land of northern New Mexico "one great naked anatomy of majestic landscape, once tortured, now calm." These two artists—joined by other painters—founded the Taos Art Colony in 1898. Sending paintings to the East required the artists to travel 35 miles by road across the Rio Grande Gorge to Tres Piedras. There the artists loaded their paintings aboard the narrow gauge railroad that joined the A.T.&S.F. line near Lamy.

Then in 1915 the Taos artists formed the Taos Society of Artists. Blumenschein and Phillips were members of the society. So, too, were J. H. Sharp, Oscar Berninghaus, E. Irving Couse, Victor Higgins, Walter Ufer, and Kenneth Adams. Some of these artists painted New Mexico's landscape. Others tried to capture on canvas the Indian and Hispanic cultures. The Taos Society of Artists at first exhibited the paintings of its members anywhere on request. They charged only the price of transporting and insuring the paintings. After a dozen years, though, the society had outlived its usefulness. So in 1927 the members of the society agreed to end their organization. Each artist was free to arrange for the showing of his own paintings.

Also showing her own work was the great twentieth-century painter Georgia O'Keeffe. She arrived in New Mexico shortly after World War I with the photographer Paul Strand and his wife, Becky. From her home in Abiquiu, O'Keeffe painted canvases of her new homeland. Her New Mexico paintings were displayed in New York by Alfred Stieglitz, a famous photographer and O'Keeffe's husband. These paintings established O'Keeffe's reputation as one of America's greatest modern-day painters.

A writers' colony grows up in Taos. Alongside the art colony in Taos grew up a colony of writers. It got its start later than did the art colony. Nonetheless, the colony of writers grew quickly once underway. Its founder was Mabel Dodge Luhan, a wealthy New Yorker. Arriving at Taos in 1916, Mabel Dodge was married for a time to Maurice Sterne, a painter. She later married Tony Luhan, a Taos Indian. To her roomy adobe house in Taos she invited writers from all over. John Collier, a young New York poet, came. He helped lead the fight against the Bursum Bill (page 267). D. H. Lawrence also came. A famous English writer, Lawrence spent the fall and winter of 1922–23 in New Mexico. He then returned to New Mexico in the spring of 1924 for a brief stay. His home in New Mexico was a ranch located in the mountains about 20 miles north of Taos.

Lawrence's presence in Taos attracted other writers and artists to the area. The Luhan home in Taos opened its doors to many well-known artistic figures. Writers and artists alike developed a feeling of kinship with New Mexico's Indians. Together the various writers and artists at Taos and Santa Fe established New Mexico as a major American cultural center. By doing this they changed New Mexico. At the same time they were changed by New Mexico. Writing about his New Mexico experience, D. H. Lawrence stated:

Maria and Julian Martinez of San Ildefonso

> I think New Mexico was the greatest experience from
> the outside world that I have ever had. It certainly
> changed me forever. . . . In the magnificent fierce
> morning of New Mexico one sprang awake, a new part
> of the soul woke up suddenly, and the old world gave
> way to a new.

Indian arts and crafts gain new appreciation. Recognition of New Mexico as a cultural center not only meant that artistic figures moved to or visited New Mexico. It also meant that New Mexico's Indian artists reached larger audiences. In the process Indian artists gained new respect. The building of the Art Museum in Santa Fe in 1917 gave artists a place to display their creations. Among those whose works were displayed were Indian painters. Encouraging Indian artists as well was the Indian Tribal Arts Association. This group encouraged Indian craftspeople to produce high quality work. It worked to inform the public about the quality of Indian crafts. Some Indian artists even showed their paintings in New York City and London during the 1920s.

Included among the Pueblo Indian painters of this period were Awa Tsireh, Cresencio Martinez, Velino Shije, Ma-Pe-We, Tonita Peña, and Alfonso Roybal. Fred Kabotie, a Hopi painter, made his mark in the art world as well.

Indian painters were not the only Indian artists to gain appreciation during the 1920s. Indeed, the 1920s witnessed the revival of superb pottery making. Pueblo Indians in particular made fine pottery. Most notable of the potters was Maria Martinez of San Ildefonso. She rediscovered the forgotten, thousand-year-old technique of black-on-black pottery. Maria shaped and fired the pots. Painting the designs on her pots were her husband, Julian Martinez, and other San Ildefonso men. In time Maria's pottery was sold in elegant shops along Fifth Avenue in New York City. The 1920s also witnessed better-quality Navajo rugs. After 1890 Navajo weavers had concentrated on rugs rather than blankets (page 241). The result had been a decline in the quality of weaving and the near disappearance of native designs. Low-quality Navajo weaving lasted until 1920. Then Navajo weaving began to improve. This was mainly because of encouragement from traders and collectors. After 1920 native designs began to reappear on rugs. So, too, Navajo weavers began again to use dyes made from native plants, fruits, and berries. The 1920s were a time as well when Navajo and Pueblo Indian silversmiths continued their high-quality work. Until its export was stopped by the Mexican government in 1930, the Mexican peso was the main source of the Indian silversmiths' silver supply.

Hispanic arts and crafts gain new respect. Another group—Hispanic craftspeople—also gained new appreciation at this time. Hispanic folk art had flourished as long as New Mexico was isolated. Once outside arts and crafts reached New Mexico, local folk art was in less demand. Lithographs from Europe and Currier and Ives prints from the United States found a market in New Mexico after 1850. So, too, did manufactured crafts brought in by the railroads in the late 1800s. As a result, local folk art was in danger of disappearing. Determined to keep this from happening, some New Mexicans acted. During the early 1920s the artist Frank Applegate and the writer Mary Austin organized the Spanish-Colonial Art Society. This society became active in preserving older objects. The New Mexico State Department of Vocational Education actively promoted a revival of local folk art.

As a result, the carvings and paintings of santeros gained new respect. This encouraged whole families to revive the almost lost art of woodcarving. One such family was the Jose Dolores Lopez family of Cordova, a small village between Chimayó and Truchas. At Chimayó weavers learned to turn out lovely Rio Grande blankets on the looms of their ancestors.

Weaving and embroidery are revived. Weaving as a highly developed Hispanic art form dated back to the early 1800s. At that time master

279

weavers from Mexico had moved into the area to teach their skill to New Mexicans. Two of these Mexican weavers were Ricardo and Juan Bazan. The Bazan brothers turned Chimayó into the center of the weaving industry. Using homespun wool and vegetable dyes, New Mexico weavers made their finest blankets about 1850. The patterns of the blankets were varied. The zig-zag pattern, likely borrowed from Indian pottery designs, was one of the most popular.

After New Mexico became a territory of the United States, the weaving craft declined. The only demand for Chimayó blankets was the tourist trade. By the 1880s these blankets were made with machine-spun wool and commercial dyes. Weaving skills had all but disappeared. And because so little was known about earlier weaving practices, the revival of weaving in the 1920s was slow. Hispanic weavers revived the use of vegetable dyes. Still, the new blankets were less colorful and durable than the older blankets. Weaving again became an art, but only when the demand for quality Chimayó blankets was great. Then village weavers began producing handspun, vegetable-dyed blankets equal to those of 1850.

Another craft revived during the 1920s was the wool embroideries of Hispanic women. This art had always been a part of a wealthy Hispanic woman's education. Now it became valued as an art worthy of preservation. Fashioned with long stitches, the embroideries featured plant and animal forms. The most popular embroideries were *colchas* (bedspreads) and *sabanillas* (altar cloths).

Other folk art survives. Tincrafting had survived the arrival of arts and crafts from outside New Mexico. Indeed, prints from Europe and the United States after 1850 had been framed by New Mexico tinsmiths. They made the frames in the form of birds, stars, and leaves. To decorate the frames they twisted thinly cut tin strips into spiral ropes. Through the years Hispanic tinsmiths made many items. These items were both practical and decorative. Tinsmiths made lanterns, candle holders, and candelabra. They designed flower pots, crosses, pitchers, and mirror frames. Some of their most finely crafted items were tin boxes whose glass sides bore designs created by swirling wet paint into waves.

The revival of Hispanic arts and crafts during the 1920s fostered appreciation for other local art forms as well. One of these art forms was folk drama. In the 1920s one popular Hispanic play was presented for the first time in 25 years. Hispanic folk music as an art form had developed from early music in the first quarter of the nineteenth century. One type of music common to every community was the *canciones populares,* the popular songs. The rhythm and lyrics of the popular songs made them quite singable. In the 1930s teachers at the University of New Mexico undertook the formal study of Hispanic folk songs.

The early statehood period was, then, a time of many changes. New Mexicans found themselves drawn into national and international events. They saw their state grow in population. They helped expand its economy. And they watched their state gain recognition as one of this nation's major cultural centers.

1. **(a)** Why did New Mexico's population grow slowly during the period from 1910 to 1920?
    (b) Why did the number of Mexican immigrants in New Mexico increase sharply during the 1920s?
2. **(a)** When were many of New Mexico's first roads built, and what effects did these roads have on towns, railroads, and tourism?
    (b) What attracted tourists to New Mexico?
    (c) Where and when did oil and gas production begin in New Mexico?
3. Briefly describe each of these people, places, or terms:
    (a) Pueblo style architecture;
    (b) the Santa Fe writers' colony;
    (c) the Santa Fe artists' colony;
    (d) the Taos Society of Artists;
    (e) the Taos writers' colony.
5. **(a)** What Indian arts and crafts gained new appreciation during the 1920s?
    (b) What Hispanic arts and crafts were revived during the 1920s?

Chapter Review

Words You Should Know

Find each word in your reading and explain its meaning.

1. normalcy

Places You Should Be Able to Locate

Be able to locate these places on the maps in your book.

1. Columbus
2. Deming
3. Raton
4. Gallup
5. Santa Rita
6. Artesia

Facts You Should Remember

Answer the following questions by recalling information presented in this chapter.

1. **(a)** Why was the Republican party able to control the constitutional convention of 1910, and what kind of constitution did New Mexico have as a result of this control?

   (b) Why did this constitution receive the overwhelming support of the voters?

2. Briefly explain how events in Mexico and a world war that began in Europe affected the people of New Mexico.

3. **(a)** From the first state election in 1911 until the election of 1930, how successful were the Republicans at controlling the executive, legislative, and judicial branches of government?

   (b) Why was the Republican party New Mexico's dominant political party?

4. **(a)** Why did the Bursum Bill cause such a storm of protest?

   (b) What effect did protest against the bill have on United States Indian policy?

5. **(a)** What economic changes took place in New Mexico during the early statehood period?

   (b) What cultural changes took place during this same period?

6. Who are the following people, and why are they important?

   (a) Solomon Luna;

   (b) William C. McDonald;

   (c) Richard C. Dillon;

   (d) Albert B. Fall;

   (e) Bronson Cutting;

   (f) Alice Corbin Henderson and Mary Austin;

   (g) Bert G. Phillips and Ernest L. Blumenschein;

   (h) Georgia O'Keeffe;

   (i) Mabel Dodge Luhan;

   (j) Maria Martinez.

Eyewitness to New Mexico's History
Changing Times

From: Marc Simmons, *People of the Sun: Some Out-of-Fashion Southwesterners* (University of New Mexico Press, 1979), pp. 7, 9.

The construction of military installations during the Second World War followed by development of the atomic industry brought a new wave of outsiders to insular New Mexico. For the first time, Hispanos and Indians (that is, the traditionalists) found themselves in the minority. . . .

The difficulty of straddling the fence—with one leg hanging into yesterday and the other swinging toward tomorrow—confronts not only the Hispano and Indian. It also affects one diminishing category of Anglos—the American cowboy. "The Hired Man on Horseback," as New Mexican writer Eugene Manlove Rhodes so aptly called him, is the single representative of the Anglo past who outlasted his time. As a lineal descendant of the Hispanic vaquero and the heir to a rich tradition that flowered on our western cattle ranges, he feels even yet a deep commitment to his own history. And he is loath to give it up.

Around the image of the cowboy, a romantic glow has gathered—perhaps because more than any other figure in our history he personifies the lost ideal of the self-sufficient, responsible, free, and moral man. It is no accident that American athletes at the Tokyo Olympics [in 1964] marched in the opening parade wearing cowboy hats.

CHAPTER 11

New Mexico in a Changing World, 1930 to the Present

What you will learn in this chapter—

New Mexicans throughout the twentieth century have witnessed many changes in their lives. They have witnessed many changes in the land that is New Mexico. You read about some of these changes in the last chapter. You will read about other changes in this chapter.

Some of the changes that occurred were the result of major events. These events affected people outside as well as inside New Mexico. During the 1930s, for example, New Mexicans like other Americans felt the effects of hard times. The coming of the Second World War and the war itself likewise involved people from all walks of life across the country. How New Mexicans reacted to and were affected by these major events is the subject of this chapter. So, too, is the way in which New Mexico was changed as the result of these and other events. As you read, you will find answers to the following questions:

1. What effects did the Great Depression of the 1930s have on New Mexico?
2. What role did New Mexico and its citizens play in World War II?
3. How has New Mexico's economy developed since the end of World War II?
4. Who are the people of New Mexico today?

1. What effects did the Great Depression of the 1930s have on New Mexico?

The Great Depression begins. In the last chapter you read about New Mexico in the 1920s. You may recall that, for the most part, New Mexico and its people prospered during that decade. Farmers and ranchers sold less during the period after World War I. Yet most other New Mexicans did quite well. In other parts of the country the story was much the same. Indeed, the 1920s were one of the most prosperous decades in American history. All that, however, began to change in 1929. For in that year the stock market crashed.

The stock market did not by itself cause the hard times that followed. There had in the 1920s been trouble spots in the nation's economy. Farming had been one such trouble spot. Others had been overproduction of consumer goods and stock market speculation. Worldwide, economies had suffered from the aftereffects of the world war. What the stock market crash did was to set off a chain of events. These events led the United States deeper and deeper into depression.

Depression is a term used to describe a very troubled economy. A depression is a time of falling business. It is a time of great unemployment. This unemployment, in turn, leads to less demand for goods. Less demand for goods, in turn, leads to lower prices. The spiral downward into depression then continues. It leads to still more unemployment and still less demand for goods. The depression of the 1930s is called the Great Depression. It was named the Great Depression for two reasons. (1) It was the most severe depression in our nation's history. Millions of people could not find jobs. At the depth of the depression nearly 25 percent of the workers were out of work. Some Americans even starved to death. (2) The depression was a long, drawn-out problem. It lasted throughout the 1930s. It did not end until the United States began to get involved in World War II.

New Mexico's farmers and ranchers are hard hit. One of the hardest hit segments of the economy in New Mexico and elsewhere was farming. By 1931 the state's most important crops were worth about half their 1929 value. Dry farmers were hardest hit. They suffered from the high costs of running a farm. They also suffered from lack of rainfall. Lack of moisture brought some of New Mexico's land into what was called the *Dust Bowl*. From Oklahoma to eastern New Mexico the winds picked up the dry land. They blew away great clouds of topsoil. So thick was the dust that it filled the air. People could not see more than a foot or two in any direction. In Des Moines a farmer remembers a dust storm that suffocated his turkey. The turkey hen, which had roosted in an old barrel, was found buried up to her neck in dust. In the Estancia Valley the people remember the dust storms just as well. Dust clouds killed entire crops of pinto beans. They transformed the once productive valley into "the valley of broken hearts."

In all parts of New Mexico farm land dropped in value. It bottomed out at an average of $4.95 an acre. This was the lowest value for an acre of land in the whole country. Nationwide the average value of an acre of farm land was $31.16. Many farmers in New Mexico had few or no crops to sell. As a result, they fell behind in their taxes. They could not meet their mortgage payments. In time some farmers were forced to sell their land. This forced selling helped cause the overall decline in farmland values. Having been forced

depression: term used to describe a very troubled economy; time of falling business and of great unemployment

Dust Bowl: area during the Great Depression that stretched from Oklahoma to eastern New Mexico; clouds of topsoil were lifted up into the air and blown away

286

A dust cloud rolls over Clayton (May 28, 1937)

off their land, some farmers became *tenant farmers.* They lived on and farmed land that was owned by someone else. Tenant farmers paid rent in crops or money to the person or company that owned the land. Other farmers who lost their land became *migrant workers.* They traveled from place to place to help harvest crops grown by someone else. Still other farmers who were forced off their land could find no work at all.

New Mexico's cattle ranchers were also hard hit by the depression. They, too, suffered from drought. They, too, suffered from conditions present both inside and outside the Dust Bowl area. Grass lands dried up. Ranchers raised fewer cattle. They watched the value of livestock decline. Many ranchers fell behind in their taxes and in other payments. They were like so many of the

tenant farmer: farmer who lives on and farms land that is owned by someone else; a tenant farmer paid rent in crops or money to the person or company that owned the land

migrant workers: workers who travel from place to place to help harvest crops grown by someone else

287

Coal mines at Madrid, with part of famous Christmas display in background, 1940

region's farmers. They were forced to sell their land. This land was, in turn, bought by large ranchers. As a result, cattle ranches in New Mexico tended to become larger.

Other parts of the economy are hurt. The depressed condition of farming and ranching had a harsh effect on New Mexico's economy. New Mexico was, after all, still largely a rural state. Most of its people in the 1930s made their livings by raising crops or livestock. At the same time the depression had harsh effects on other parts of the state's economy. An overall decline in mining had begun during the 1920s. It continued during the 1930s. Coal production, for example, was just 1.7 million tons in 1936. In 1919, shortly after the end of World War I, coal production had peaked. It had in that year been two and one-half times greater than the 1936 figure. In addition, many mines became the property of large companies during the 1930s.

Besides mining, state and local governments felt the effects of depression. Governments had too little money to provide all the needed services. By early 1933 8,000 school-age children in New Mexico were not able to attend schools. Some school districts simply had no money to keep their doors open. Even successful businesses felt the effects of the depression. One of New Mexico's oldest business families, for example, lost profits during the depression. In 1928 the Charles Ilfeld Company enjoyed a profit margin of 14.7 percent. Company profits dropped to 2.2 percent in 1931. In 1932 the company lost money.

New Mexico's northern villages suffered as well. Before 1930 many of the villagers had earned wages by working outside their villages during part of each year. After 1930 most villagers could not find outside work. Families did raise sheep and farm in northern New Mexico. Still, they were not able to support themselves. So in the 1930s many northern New Mexicans sought help.

Needy New Mexicans find help. During the early years of the depression help for those in need came from several sources. At the local level charity was mainly the work of churches, the Salvation Army, and the community chests. Local offices for the needy also provided some help. However, as the depression grew worse, local efforts were not enough. And state and local governments either could not or would not take up the slack. In part this was because they, too, were suffering from the depressed economy.

As a result, major efforts to help those in need shifted in 1933 to the national government. Formal *relief*—the government's caring for people in need—was part of the New Deal. The New Deal was the name given to the programs of President Franklin D. Roosevelt. Roosevelt first won election to the presidency in 1932. Taking office in March 1933, he soon sent a number of New Deal relief measures to Congress. Congress quickly passed most of the acts that Roosevelt wanted.

New Deal relief programs of all kinds were welcomed by New Mexicans. In fact, in some parts of New Mexico more than half the people were enrolled in relief programs by 1935. This was most common in counties where drought and dust storms made dry farming impossible. In Harding County, for example, 72.8 percent of the people were on relief. (See the map on page 291.) In Torrance County the percentage on relief was 61.4. Catron County, hit by drought but not by severe dust storms, had a relief percentage of 58.7. All in all, 14 counties in northeastern and east-central New Mexico suffered from drought. The percentage of the people in these counties who were on relief varied. It ranged from a low of 24.3 to a high of 72.8.

Relief programs make jobs available. Some New Deal relief programs put people to work. One such program was the Works Progress Administration (WPA). The WPA employed people in many kinds of jobs. Writers, artists, and musicians practiced their trades as employees of the WPA. Others who worked for the WPA built schools and other public buildings. The library and the administration building at the University of New Mexico in Albuquerque were built with WPA monies. So was the high school in Clayton. By 1936 more than 13,000 New Mexicans had found jobs through the WPA.

Two other New Deal programs produced jobs for New Mexicans as well. The first was the Civilian Conservation Corps (CCC). The second was the National Youth Administration (NYA). Both programs were designed to help

relief: caring for people in need; relief programs were sponsored by the national government during the Great Depression

289

young people. The CCC employed young men between the ages of 18 and 25. These young men worked in soil conservation projects. They worked in forest improvement projects. They lived in camps. Part of what they earned each month was sent directly to their families. A CCC branch for Indians employed young Indian men in flood control and irrigation projects. This CCC branch helped increase farm production on Pueblo lands. The NYA, the second program, emphasized job training. Those who got training under the NYA were paid for the training they received. In Clayton, for example, young people learned such skills as woodworking, metal work, adobe work, and weaving. In turn the youth of Clayton helped build their school. In the long run the NYA trained many people. The country would need such skilled workers when the Second World War began.

Politics are affected by the depression. New Deal programs brought relief to many thousands of New Mexicans. The New Deal did not, however, bring an end to the depression. The 1930s remained a hard time for many New Mexicans. They were also a time of shifting political fortunes. The Republican party had long dominated New Mexico politics. In the 1930s it began to lose its power. This mainly occurred because the party lost the support of Hispanic New Mexicans. Hispanic New Mexicans began to join the Democratic party in the early 1930s. They liked the New Deal programs of President Roosevelt, a Democrat. They also liked the 1935 appointment of a Hispanic

A CCC project

New Mexico Counties

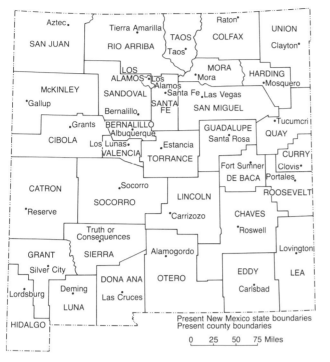

Present New Mexico state boundaries
Present county boundaries

0   25   50   75 Miles

New Mexican to the United States Senate. The new senator was Democrat Dennis Chavez. After 1935 the Hispanic bloc of voters supported the Democratic party. This support began a long period of Democratic control of New Mexico politics.

There are some bright spots in the 1930s. New Mexicans had little to cheer about during the 1930s. At the same time there were some bright spots. The population, for example, continued to grow. In fact, New Mexico was second in the region in the number of families new to one state. By 1940 the population grew to 531,818. Oil production grew as well. This increased oil production provided needed tax money for the state. Tourism did all right during the 1930s. And the number of state parks grew. The increase in parks occurred because the state wanted to make use of money from the national government. The government helped pay for the development of new state parks. New Mexico did, then, enjoy some growth during the 1930s. But this growth was not great. Real growth awaited the end of the Great Depression.

Senator Dennis Chavez

1.　(a) Describe the downward spiral of the economy into depression.

　　(b) Explain why the depression of the 1930s is called the Great Depression.

2.　(a) What was the Dust Bowl?

Section Review

291

(b) What changes occurred in the value of farm products and farm land in New Mexico, and what caused these changes?

(c) What became of New Mexico farmers who were forced off their land?

(d) How did the depression affect cattle raising in New Mexico?

3. (a) What effect did the depression have on mining?

(b) What effect did the depression have on state and local governments and on private businesses?

4. (a) Why were the northern New Mexico communities so hard hit by the depression?

(b) To whom did a majority of these New Mexicans turn for help during the 1930s?

5. (a) What were the purposes of the Works Progress Administration, the Civilian Conservation Corps, and the National Youth Administration?

(b) How did each of these programs operate in New Mexico?

6. How and why did New Mexico politics change during the 1930s?

7. What bright spots were there in New Mexico during the 1930s?

---

2. What role did New Mexico and its citizens play in World War II?

World War II begins. World War II began formally on September 3, 1939. This was two days after German armies invaded Poland. As the war continued, more and more countries were drawn into the fighting. The aggressor nations were the Axis powers. These nations were Germany and Italy. Allied with Germany and Italy was Japan. In Europe the Axis powers overran one country after another. After the fall of France in June 1940, Great Britain stood alone. It was the only country in western Europe that remained to fight against the Axis powers. The Soviet Union was then drawn into the war in June 1941. In that month German troops invaded Russia.

Dr. Robert H. Goddard

The rocket age came to New Mexico in 1930. In that year Dr. Robert H. Goddard moved to Mescalero Ranch near Roswell to build and test liquid-fueled rockets. His earlier flight tests in Massachusetts had alarmed officials there. However, Goddard's work caught the attention of Charles A. Lindbergh, who had made the first solo airplane flight of the Atlantic Ocean in 1927. Lindbergh arranged private funding for Goddard's tests, and Goddard moved to Roswell where open spaces and good weather allowed for bigger test flights.

Goddard's work with liquid-fueled rockets made rapid progress in New Mexico. In the first Roswell test in December 1930, Goddard's rocket flew 2,000 feet into the air. Goddard continued building rockets until October 1941. A later model reached an altitude of 9,000 feet. Goddard's research led to 214 patents for designing, powering, and guiding rockets. Yet the United States armed forces saw little of value in Goddard's ideas. As World War II neared, they moved him East to develop airplane engines.

German scientists, on the other hand, read his research reports and used Goddard's concepts to make rockets of their own. The deadly V-2 rockets, which bombed London, England, in 1944, followed Goddard's design. After the war American soldiers captured Werner von Braun, Germany's leading rocket scientist. When asked to explain how the V-2 worked, von Braun answered, "Why don't you ask Goddard how they work?" Goddard, however, had died on August 10, 1945, before he could return to the Roswell test site. America finally honored Goddard in 1959. In that year he was given the Congressional Gold Medal, our highest civilian award. Today Goddard High School in Roswell bears his name.

The United States did not enter World War II until late 1941. President Roosevelt and the Congress in the meantime lent aid to Great Britain and other countries who opposed the Axis powers and Japan. They also took steps that helped this country prepare for war. The war itself came to the United States on December 7, 1941. On that day the Japanese made a sneak attack on the United States naval base at Pearl Harbor in Hawaii. (See Special Interest Feature.) On December 8 President Roosevelt asked Congress to declare war on Japan. The Congress honored this request the same day. Germany and Italy then declared war on the United States. Thus the United States armed forces fought against Japan and against Japan's allies as well.

New Mexicans fight in the war. New Mexico servicemen were among the first Americans to see action in World War II. New Mexico National Guardsmen had fought in the Pacific even before the formal declaration of war. They had been members of the National Guard 111th Cavalry. In 1940 the 111th became part of the 200th Coast Artillery, Anti-Aircraft Regiment. The troops of the 200th were deployed to the Philippines in September 1941. These islands belonged at that time to the United States. The regiment was to defend Clark Field and Ft. Stotsenberg, which lay 75 miles north of Manila. Thus hundreds of New Mexicans were at Clark Field when the Japanese attacked the Philippines. The attack occurred some 10 hours after the strike on Pearl Harbor. The 200th regiment destroyed some low-flying Japanese fighter planes. The bombers, however, flew above the range of the antiaircraft guns.

In January 1942 Japanese ground forces launched an attack on the Philippines. Some New Mexico servicemen fought the Japanese as members of the 200th regiment. Others had become members of a newly formed unit. This was the 515th Coast Artillery Regiment. In time the United States troops were ordered to withdraw to the Bataan Peninsula. The peninsula was 30 miles long, and the fighting was fierce. During the fighting American and Filipino forces were reduced from 78,000 to 68,000 men. Then on April 9, 1942, the badly outnumbered Americans surrendered to the Japanese.

New Mexicans are war heroes. What followed has come to be called the Bataan Death March. American prisoners were forced to march 65 miles to trains waiting to carry them to a Japanese prison camp. The march took six days. Eleven thousand Americans, including many New Mexicans, died on the march. Those who reached the camp remained prisoners until the end of the war. Within the camps thousands more died, again including many New Mexicans. Of the 1,800 New Mexicans who served in the Philippines, only 900 returned home. A Bataan Memorial was built at Fort Bliss, Texas. Later moved to Santa Fe, the memorial includes our state's eternal flame. It honors the brave New Mexicans who fought and died in the Philippines.

Bell of the battleship
New Mexico

The U.S.S. *New Mexico*

The U.S.S. *New Mexico* was a battleship that saw much action during World War II. The ship had got its start as Battleship 40 in October 1915. All told, the ship took about one and a half years to build. It was finally launched on April 23, 1917. On hand for the christening of the new battleship were a number of special guests. The daughter of New Mexico's late governor, Margarita C de Baca, was present. Miss C de Baca christened the *New Mexico* by breaking a bottle of champagne and water from the Rio Grande across its hull. Also present was the then Assistant Secretary of the Navy, Franklin D. Roosevelt. He would later serve his nation as president.

The *New Mexico* did not see action during World War I. Still, she was a grand ship. She measured 624 feet in length and 106 feet 3 inches in width. Her big guns had a range of nearly 10 miles. She carried a crew of 1,323 men.

Between the two world wars the *New Mexico* came to be known as the queen of the Pacific Fleet. She was stationed in the Pacific until 1941. Then she was transferred to the Atlantic Ocean and missed the attack on Pearl Harbor. After the attack the *New Mexico* returned to the Pacific, where she remained for the rest of the war. She was awarded six battle stars for her outstanding battle record. At the same time she suffered great damage. In January 1945 she received a hit on her bridge. Twenty-nine men and the commanding officers were killed. Then in May 1945 the ship received two hits. This time 54 men were lost.

The *New Mexico* stayed in action despite the damage suffered. She was present at the surrender of the Japanese. But in 1946 she was sold for scrap. Her two bells, her helm, and other mementos were given to New Mexico. One of her bells hangs in the mall at the University of New Mexico in Albuquerque. Her helm hangs on the wall at the university's naval ROTC building. Her silver service has been on display at the Palace of the Governors in Santa Fe. All are proud reminders of the brave ship and crew that served their country well.

The war lasted nearly four years. New Mexicans saw action wherever there was fighting. In fact, New Mexico had the highest casualty rate (dead and wounded) in the Union. One group of New Mexicans even played a special role in the war effort. These were the Navajos. The United States government used Navajos as code talkers. The code talkers translated secret military messages into the Navajo language. Upon reaching their destinations, the messages were decoded by other Navajos. This way of sending messages confused the Japanese. The Japanese never solved the code. Thus the Navajos made a major contribution to the American war effort.

New Mexico's resources are thrown into the war effort. The Navajos were joined by many other New Mexicans in helping win the war. Thousands served in the armed forces. In all, 49,579 New Mexicans were inducted into the armed forces between late 1940 and the end of the war. Congress had passed a Selective Service Act in October 1940. The draft was then in effect until the end of the war. Some New Mexicans who served in the armed forces were volunteers. Indeed, New Mexico had the highest volunteer rate of any state. Thousands of New Mexicans helped the war effort in other ways. The state provided training programs for the army and navy. These programs were offered through the state's colleges. They covered weather forecasting, preflight training, and other types of training.

In some parts of the state the national government built special camps.

An appeal for war bonds and stamps

The camp at Santa Fe housed Japanese-Americans. These Japanese-Americans had been removed from the West Coast under orders from President Roosevelt. The president had reacted to the outbreak of anti-Japanese feelings on the West Coast following the attack on Pearl Harbor. He believed that national security required the relocation of 112,000 Japanese-Americans. Nearly two-thirds of these had been born in the United States. Sent to camps in New Mexico and other states, the Japanese-Americans remained in the camps until war's end. Camps at Roswell and Lordsburg mainly housed German and Italian prisoners of war. New Mexico's prisoner-of-war camps were among the largest in the nation.

The state receives military installations. In some parts of the state the national government built army air force bases. Some of these bases remain in place today. Thus it was during World War II that New Mexico became an important defensive center for the United States. In 1941, for example, Kirtland Air Force Base in Albuquerque got its start. The next year a second base—later named Sandia Base—was opened in Albuquerque. Also in 1942 bases were built in Clovis, Alamogordo, and Roswell. These bases in time were named Cannon, Holloman, and Walker air force bases. In addition, temporary wartime air bases existed at Hobbs, Deming, and Fort Sumner. And in 1945 the White Sands Proving Ground came into being in south-central New Mexico. It is today called White Sands Missile Range.

What happened at Albuquerque's bases during the war is just one example of New Mexico's importance as a military center. Shortly after the attack on Pearl Harbor, the Albuquerque Army Air Base became the site of an air forces advanced flying school. This school was a bombardier school. It was as a bombardier school that the air base—renamed Kirtland Field in early 1942—served its most vital wartime function. By 1945 Kirtland had trained 1,750 B-24 pilots and crew members. On a smaller scale Kirtland had also trained aviation mechanics and navigators. And in 1942 and 1943 it had doubled as a ground school for glider pilots. Its final wartime role was to train combat crews for the B-29.

East of Kirtland the army began construction on the Albuquerque Air Depot Training Station in May 1942. By June the station was open and training crews to service, repair, and maintain aircraft. No longer needed as a training station after 1943, the base became an army air field. Next it became an army air force convalescent center. The center treated wounded pilots and crew members. In addition, it served as a rest and recreation facility. The base again became an army air field in 1945 and was in that year officially named Sandia Base.

During the 1940s New Mexico developed as one of the country's military

The monument at Trinity Site, Ground Zero (from *The Day the Sun Rose Twice*, by Ferenc Szasz, UNM Press)

headquarters. It provided military training for the whole nation. It also helped lead the way in military research. At Los Alamos, research furthered the development of the atomic bomb. The site of a boys' ranch school until 1942, Los Alamos lies 20 miles northwest of Santa Fe. J. Robert Oppenheimer had attended the boys' school there. It was he who suggested that the United States government buy the school and surrounding land for atomic research. The government did so and later established the Manhattan Project there. Oppenheimer helped head this project. The government sealed off the area in 1943. It brought in top scientists, many of whom were Jewish refugees from Hitler's Germany. Research facilities were soon built, and some 7,000 people lived at the project site. The town of Los Alamos had been born. Yet no one outside the site was told what was happening. All aspects of the Manhattan Project were top secret. Numbers were even used rather than names for the drivers' licenses of those who lived and worked at the project site. The address for Los Alamos was P.O. Box 1539, Santa Fe.

The atomic age begins. What went on inside the project was, of course, work on the atomic bomb. The bomb and the idea behind it were new. Not even those who built the bomb knew whether or not it would work. The bomb first had to be tested. This test took place at the Trinity Site on the

White Sands Proving Ground. The date was July 16, 1945. The test was a success. In fact, the blast was heard or the flash was seen all over the state. Still, the new bomb remained a secret for three more weeks. Only after an atomic bomb was dropped on Hiroshima, Japan, on August 6, 1945, did the people of the United States and the world learn of the new weapon. President Harry S. Truman had decided to use the bomb. He believed that its use would save hundreds of thousands of American lives. He believed its use would force the Japanese to surrender. Japan did surrender to the United States, but not until after a second atomic bomb was used. This bomb was dropped on Nagasaki, Japan, on August 9.

With the surrender of the Japanese, World War II came to an end. New Mexico and its people had played a major role in the war effort. Among other things, New Mexico was the birthplace of the atomic age. It has remained a center of atomic research ever since. Los Alamos Scientific Laboratory, directed by the University of California, carries on research for the Department of Energy. So does Sandia National Laboratories. Today Sandia is a private corporation, but it began as a subgroup of the Los Alamos Laboratory during the later stages of the war. Since that time Sandia's main job has been the research and development of nuclear weapons. Its main nonweapons function is to develop new and improved sources of energy. Sandia National Laboratories is located on the military reservation in Albuquerque. It shares space with Kirtland Air Force Base. In the 1950s the Sandia-Kirtland complex led the way in planning nuclear tests. Since 1963 Kirtland has been the site of the Air Force Weapons Laboratory. As such, Kirtland is engaged in weapons research and development. New Mexico's long-term role as a research center has helped the flow of money into the state. Military and defense activity has had other effects as well. During the war it brought people into the state. Many families stayed, and after the war New Mexico continued to grow.

Section Review

1.   (a) When and for what reason did the United States enter World War II?
    (b) Briefly describe the role of New Mexico servicemen in the battle for control of the Philippines.
2.   (a) Who were the Navajo code talkers, and how did they help the war effort?
    (b) How did New Mexico's casualty and volunteer rates during the war compare to those of other states?
3.   (a) How did New Mexico's colleges aid the war effort?
    (b) Where and for what purposes did the national government build special camps in New Mexico?

299

(c) What military bases did the government establish in New Mexico during the war?

4. (a) What was the Manhattan Project, and where was it located?

(b) In what ways has New Mexico become a center of military and defense activities?

3. How has New Mexico's economy developed since the end of World War II?

Mining is important. World War II affected New Mexico in a number of ways. For one thing, it spurred the state's economy, including the mining industry. You may recall that this mining industry had suffered during the Great Depression (page 288). It began to recover during World War II. Its recovery and growth continued after the war. Indeed, New Mexico has become one of the nation's leaders in the value of mineral products mined. The United States Bureau of Mines lists 91 minerals as vital minerals. Of these 91 minerals, New Mexico's mines produce 30.

Two of these minerals are uranium and potash. Uranium was first found in the hills north of Grants in 1950. Its discoverer was Paddy Martinez, a Navajo sheepherder. This discovery set off a major boom for the Grants area. Uranium was also discovered near Gallup. In 1977 the state produced 44 percent of the nation's uranium supply. Uranium is, of course, a source of atomic energy. The uranium boom lasted until about 1980. Potash was found much earlier than uranium. Discovered near Carlsbad in 1925, mining operations began six years later. In 1978 New Mexico supplied 84 percent of the nation's potash. Mainly used in fertilizer, potash has been a key product for the state. It has long been a mainstay of Carlsbad's economy.

Coal becomes important once more. Coal mining is also important to the state's economy. The use of coal has greatly increased in recent years. Yet its production did not begin to grow until well after the end of World War II. In 1958, for example, New Mexico's mines produced only 117,000 tons of coal. Coal production in fact had declined steadily since World War I. New Mexico coal was simply not in high demand.

Then in the 1960s the state's coal production began to increase. There were several reasons for this. First, there was a need for low-sulfur western coal. This coal burns cleaner than other coal. It helps with air quality control. Second, mining companies can extract New Mexico's coal through surface mining techniques. Surface mining costs less than underground mining. Third, the state's public service company built power plants in the Four Corners area. These coal-burning plants generate electricity. Coal production grew at an even faster rate during the 1970s. This expansion occurred for two basic reasons.

A potash mine near Carlsbad

(1) Coal is very important in generating electricity. Nearly 90 percent of New Mexico's coal is used for this purpose. (2) New Mexico has coal reserves that will last for many years. About 550 million tons of coal lie within New Mexico. Today the state's mines produce 20 million tons of coal each year. This figure is expected to remain constant during the 1980s.

Oil, gas, and other minerals are mined. Still other minerals have been important to the state's economy. In 1977, for example, oil production made up 69 percent of the value of the state's total mineral production. In fact, New Mexico was at that time the nation's seventh leading oil producing state. More than 90 percent of the state's oil has in recent years come from the southeastern part of the state. This oil lies in the Permian Basin, an oil-rich basin that extends across parts of Texas and New Mexico. At the same time that older oil fields begin to produce less, oil companies explore for new oil. Oil production does, of course, benefit all of New Mexico. It benefits the places that produce oil as well. It means that such cities as Hobbs prosper because of nearby oil fields.

Also important to the state's economy is natural gas. In the late 1970s New Mexico was the fourth leading gas-producing state. This gas comes from two main areas. One is northwestern New Mexico. The other is southeastern

New Mexico. Like oil, natural gas benefits the whole state and nearby towns and cities. So, too, exploration for new gas fields goes on. All told, about 20,000 New Mexicans work in some area of mineral production. Of these, nearly half work in the production of oil and gas. Others, of course, mine uranium, potash, and coal. Still others mine copper or some other mineral. Copper mines in southwestern New Mexico remain important. Also in operation are mines that produce lead, zinc, molybdenum, gold, and silver. Mining, then, has been a vital part of the state's economy in recent years.

Agriculture remains important. Another vital part of the state's economy has been agriculture. Farms and ranches have over the years become fewer in number. They have, at the same time, become larger in size. The trend toward fewer but larger farms and ranches began in the 1920s. It continued during the 1930s and in the years after World War II. In 1940, for example, there were 32,830 farms and ranches in the state. By the 1970s this number had shrunk to fewer than 12,000. And the average size of farms had grown to more than 4,000 acres. Alongside changes in the number and size of farms and ranches occurred a shift in the state's population. This latter trend—a trend common to New Mexico since the end of the war—is *urbanization*. In other words, people have moved in ever-greater numbers into towns and cities. Urbanization has left fewer people in rural areas. Fewer people still have actively grown food or raised livestock. In fact, today only about 2 percent of the state's population works directly in agriculture.

urbanization: movement of people in great numbers into cities and towns

Two-thirds of the state's agricultural products come from two areas. One is the eastern and southern plains. The other area is along the lower Rio Grande Valley. Of all the 33 counties, Chaves leads the state in farm production. Curry County ranks second. The state's leading products are cattle, sheep, dairy items, and wool. The state produces such other items as cotton lint, hay, sorghum, and grain. It also produces poultry, peanuts, pecans, and chili.

Tourism remains important. Vital as well to New Mexico has been tourism. A big reason for this is that the state offers year-round recreation. New Mexico has 11 ski resorts. It is the home of many lodges and guest ranches. Its many Indian ceremonies attract visitors. So, too, do its parks and monuments. Carlsbad Caverns, a national park, draws thousands upon thousands of tourists yearly. The national monuments of White Sands and Bandelier attract many visitors as well.

Besides national parks and monuments, the state has its own parks and recreational sites. Out-of-state visitors come to camp. They come to hunt and fish. They come to see the state's scenery. The number of out-of-state cars on the state's highways peaks during the summer months. Tourists swarm over the state's recreational sites. They tour its national and state parks and mon-

302

uments. They also share in New Mexico's history by visiting its Indian pueblos. They visit its towns and cities. Tourists spend millions of dollars within the state. Tourism to New Mexico continues to grow. Only in 1974 did tourism decline briefly. This was due to a shortage of gasoline in that year.

Since the end of World War II, then, New Mexico has undergone a number of economic developments. Its economy has grown during this period. It is likely to continue to grow in the years ahead.

Section Review

1. Briefly describe the development of each of these types of mining within New Mexico in recent years:
   (a) uranium;
   (b) potash;
   (c) coal;
   (d) oil;
   (e) natural gas.
2. (a) What trends have occurred in New Mexico's agriculture in recent years?
   (b) Where are the state's leading agricultural areas, and what are the state's main agricultural products?
3. What draws tourists to New Mexico, and why is tourism important?

---

4. Who are the people of New Mexico today?

The population grows. New Mexico began to grow at a rapid rate with the coming of World War II. The population growth continued in the years after the war. Highest during the 1950s, the rate of growth slowed in the 1960s but picked up again in the 1970s. By 1980 New Mexico had a population of 1,299,968. The state's population in that year was 207 percent greater than it had been in 1940.

Population growth has been a factor in shaping modern-day New Mexico and its people. It has in fact meant several things. (1) The movement of people from elsewhere into the state has changed the nature of New Mexico's population. In 1940 Hispanos were a majority of the state's people. The population increase after 1940 changed this. Hispanos were no longer in the majority. (2) More New Mexicans moved into the state's towns and cities. This has meant that the state is becoming more urban and less rural. (3) New Mexico has become the home of many Americans who have moved to the *sunbelt*. The sunbelt is the region that stretches across the United States from North Carolina to southern California. Great numbers of Americans have moved into this region in recent years. In part they have sought a milder climate. New Mexico has thus received newcomers from the north.

sunbelt: region that stretches across the United States from North Carolina to southern California; area into which many Americans have moved in recent years

303

Governor Edwin Mechem

Senator Joseph Montoya

Democrats control state politics. Population growth helped bring about a growth in the state's economy. You read about this economic growth in the last section. In time the changes in population also brought changes in New Mexico politics. The changes in politics did not, however, begin to occur until the 1960s. This meant that from the 1930s to the 1960s state politics remained largely under Democratic party control (page 291). During this period the Democrats controlled the state legislature. They elected most of the governors. In fact, the only two Republicans to win the governorship during this period were Edwin L. Mechem and David Cargo. Mechem won election to four 2-year terms; Cargo, to two 2-year terms. During this same period the Democrats carried every state supreme court race. In addition, they won almost every other race for an office at the state level. They won most of the races for New Mexico's seats in the United States Senate and House of Representatives.

While controlling New Mexico politics, the Democrats produced the state's leading politicians. Chief among these political leaders were Dennis Chavez and Clinton P. Anderson. Chavez served as a United States senator from 1935 to 1962. He did much to insure the development of New Mexico during World War II. He ran hard each time he was up for reelection. He won two very close elections in 1946 and 1952. Chavez served as chairman of the Senate's public works committee. He became the second ranking member of the Senate's appropriations committee.

Clinton P. Anderson also represented New Mexico in Washington, D.C. From 1941 to 1945 he was one of the state's two United States representatives. He served from 1945 to 1948 in President Truman's Cabinet. He was Secretary of Agriculture. New Mexicans in 1948 elected him their United States senator. Reelected in 1954, 1960, and 1966, he remained in that office until he retired in 1972. Anderson became chairperson of Congress's joint committee on atomic energy. As a result of his committee work, New Mexico remained a center of atomic and military research.

Political changes begin to occur. Neither Chavez nor Anderson ever lost a reelection try for a Senate seat. Democratic party strength in New Mexico was simply too great. When Chavez died in 1962, a Republican— Edwin L. Mechem—replaced him. Governor at the time of Chavez's death, Mechem resigned his office. Mechem's successor, Tom Bolack, then appointed Mechem to the vacant Senate seat. But in 1964 the Democrats regained Chavez's seat. The voters sent Joseph M. Montoya to the United States Senate. Reelected in 1970, Montoya, too, became a powerful senator. He used his influence to help New Mexico. However, in 1976 Montoya lost his bid for a third term. This loss showed that politics in New Mexico had undergone changes. Politics changed in part because of the newcomers who arrived in New Mexico during the 1970s. For the most part these newcomers added strength to the Republican party. This party also grew stronger as many people in the West became more conservative in their views. It benefited at times from the votes of registered Democrats who crossed party lines to support Republican candidates.

This shift in state politics showed up at election time. Republicans began to win more elections. Pete V. Domenici was one such winner. He first won a seat in the United States Senate in 1972. He succeeded Anderson, who had retired. Domenici worked hard. In time he became the chairperson of the Senate's powerful budget committee. Other Republicans have served New Mexico in Congress in the 1970s and the 1980s. Yet Democrats have remained the state's majority party. They have continued to win most state offices. One such Democrat was Bruce King. King was the first governor to serve two 4-year terms. The voters elected him to that office in 1970 and again in 1978. Today, then, New Mexico politics show some balance. Both parties can win elections. Neither party controls politics to the extent that one party or the other controlled state politics in the past. Hispanics are more represented in public office in New Mexico than in any other state. They are found at all levels of elected positions, including two recent governors—Jerry Apodaca (1974–1978) and Toney Anaya (1982–1986).

Senator Pete V. Domenici

New Mexico continues to change. A growing population has helped change the political scene. It has, at the same time, given New Mexico a third United States representative. In 1982 New Mexicans for the first time sent three people to serve in the House of Representatives. One other political note deserves mention here. This is the fact that New Mexico has had a special record in presidential elections. This record stretched from statehood in 1912 until the election of 1976. During that period New Mexicans voted for every presidential winner. Then in 1976 New Mexico's electoral votes for the first time went to the candidate not elected president—Gerald Ford.

A growing population and changing times have altered the face of the state. And among those whose life-styles have undergone changes in the last 50 years are New Mexico's oldest residents—the state's Indians and Hispanos.

Governor Bruce King

Changes occur in Indian ways of living. Some of the changes in Indian ways of living have resulted from the actions of the national government. You read, for example, about the laws Congress passed in 1924 (page 267). In 1934 Congress again acted. In that year it passed the Indian Reorganization Act (IRA). The IRA (1) ended the allotment of Indian lands in individual ownership and the sale of unallotted lands to non-Indians; (2) provided for adding to reservation lands; (3) restored a limited degree of self-government to Indian tribes; (4) allowed tribes, if they wished, to incorporate under terms

305

Governor Jerry Apodaca

of the act and to elect tribal governments that had some legal powers; (5) created a $10 million revolving loan fund for incorporated tribal councils to use in promoting economic growth; (6) provided a yearly scholarship fund of up to $250,000 for vocational education; and (7) stated that Indians should receive preference for civil service jobs within the Bureau of Indian Affairs.

Most Indians saw the above mentioned terms as an improvement over previous government policy. Still, the IRA had serious shortcomings. For one thing, it excluded some Indian tribes—although none in New Mexico—from the terms of the act. For another, it granted extreme power to the Secretary of the Interior. The secretary was given the power to (1) set the rules for tribal elections; (2) approve tribal constitutions; (3) veto the choice of tribal lawyers; and (4) make rules for forest and grazing land use. Still other shortcomings included (1) the express provision that the Navajos could not enlarge their reservation; (2) funds that were inadequate for the purchase of additional land or for significant economic development; and (3) too little scholarship aid. In addition to the already inadequate scholarship sum of $250,000, only $50,000, or one-fifth of the total aid, could go to high school or college attendance.

The IRA affects Indians in New Mexico. For New Mexico's Indians, the Indian Reorganization Act meant different things to different people. First, only a few groups in the state chose to adopt constitutional governments under the IRA. These groups drew up constitutions that provided for government like that of the United States. Second, the IRA harmed some groups while helping others. The Navajos, for example, were one group badly affected by the act. Besides being denied the chance to expand their reservation, the Navajos also had their livestock herds greatly reduced. This occurred when the Secretary of the Interior restricted the number of livestock Navajos could graze on their range units. On the other hand, both the Mescalero and Jicarilla Apaches benefited from the IRA. Each tribe—the Mescaleros in 1936 and the Jicarillas in 1937—adopted constitutions under the IRA. Each borrowed money under the terms of the act and experienced dramatic economic growth. At first most of this growth was in the value of livestock and livestock products.

To New Mexico, then, the Indian Reorganization Act brought mixed blessings. And at the same time that it was affecting ways of living for some Indian groups, so, too, were other events. During World War II, for example, some Indian families left their homes. They moved off the reservations and found jobs elsewhere. Some served in the armed forces. Others worked in wartime industries. Still others worked in agriculture. After the war changing times meant new ways of living as well as more formal education for New Mexico's Indians. More and more Indian children began attending school. This trend began in the 1950s. It has continued in the decades since. As a result, more Indians now have a college education. And more have prepared for professions in law and medicine. In 1967 the University of New Mexico Law School established a scholarship program for Indians. Two years later the university opened the American Indian Law Center. One of its purposes has been to continue the scholarship program for Indian and Alaska Native lawyers. In 1966 there were only 11 Indian lawyers in the entire country. Today the number of Indian lawyers is much higher.

There are also a number of Indians active in state politics. Some have sought and won election to state office. For example, Thomas E. Atcitty, Leo Watchman, and Monroe Jymm have all served in the state legislature. A Navajo and a Democrat, Atcitty has been a long-time state representative. He is well known to the Navajo people.

Indian economic life changes. New Mexico's Indians still earn their living in traditional ways. They farm and raise livestock. In addition, the tribes have developed their own businesses. Chief among these is tourism. The Mescalero Apaches, for example, own and operate the Sierra Blanca Ski Area. This ski area is in the Sacramento Mountains in the south-central part of the state. In addition, the Mescaleros own and operate a resort hotel. Their hotel is located 3 miles south of Ruidoso. The tribe has also set up campgrounds for tourists in their forest land. The Jicarilla Apaches, too, have developed tourist sites on their land. These sites are in northwestern New Mexico. They include a lodge at Stone Lake and campgrounds at Dulce and Mundo lakes.

The Navajos, too, have attracted tourists to their reservation. Besides, they have begun a large-scale irrigation project. (See Special Interest Feature.) And they have profited from minerals found on their land. Large companies have leased Navajo land so as to develop the area's coal, oil, and uranium resources. The Jicarillas have profited from minerals found on their land as well.

Indians retain their special identity. Some Indian ways of living, then, have changed in the modern age. Still, some of their traditions have not changed. Most Indians—both Pueblo and non-Pueblo—continue to live at home. They live on the same land where their ancestors lived. Occupation of Pueblo lands, for example, has continued for more than 400 years. While there are fewer pueblos today than there were 400 years ago, the Pueblo Indian population has increased.

Besides living at home, New Mexico's Indians have retained their special ceremonies. There have even been times when they have fought to protect their traditions and ancient ways of living.

Taos Indians fight for the Blue Lake. One example of this fight occurred in the 1960s. The fight involved the Taos Indians and the United

States Forest Service. It centered around the pueblo's claim to Blue Lake. Blue Lake lies in the mountains above the pueblo itself. It is surrounded by national forest land. For the Taos Indians, Blue Lake has always been a sacred place. It has been a place where the Taos people have worshipped. In the 1930s the national government took action to protect Taos Indian access to the lake. It granted them a permit to use Blue Lake as their religious shrine. The government also promised to protect the land around the lake from damage.

Farmington

The Navajo Indian Irrigation Project

The San Juan River Basin in the four corners region has new life. Today this basin contains one of the largest farming units in the country. It is the site of the Navajo Indian Irrigation Project (NIIP) southeast of Farmington. The NIIP, in turn, is the largest economic enterprise ever for an Indian tribe. It is also the Navajo Nation's main hope for future economic growth. The NIIP may in time produce a Navajo economy based on renewable resources. This would be better than an economy based on mineral resources that cannot be replaced.

Irrigation farming is by no means new to the region. Indeed, the Anasazi irrigated crops there until a thirteenth-century drought forced them to move. The Navajos later moved into the region. They, too, practiced irrigation. They did so especially after their return home from the Bosque Redondo in 1868. For the Navajos, crop raising was important. However, it was less important than raising sheep. The Navajos planted their crops in irrigated fields near grazing lands. As late as 1936 livestock and farming made up more than half the Navajo income. Wages made up less than a third. Times changed, and by 1958 wages accounted for two-thirds of the Navajo income. And by the early 1960s only 25 to 30 percent of the Navajo families did any farming at all. The income from the sale of Navajo farm products was almost zero.

It was at that time that action was taken to restore farming to the Navajo economy. The Navajo Indian Irrigation Project was that action. In 1962 a federal act outlined the NIIP. The act set aside 110,630 acres of land to be irrigated as part of the project. It also said that 508,000 acre-feet of water from the Navajo Reservoir would be used each year for irrigation. To run the project, the Navajo Nation set up the Navajo Agricultural Products Industry.

The project is moving ahead, although slowly at times. The building of the project itself began in 1964. It goes on today. And so do the problems. The project has lacked for proper funding. It is such a large project that planning has been hard. Other problems include soil type and water supply. They include the need for trained workers. Still, the NIIP holds great promise for success. The project shows the foresight of the Navajo Nation in working to develop a healthy tribal economy.

The permit worked well until the 1960s. Then heavy public use of the national forest damaged the land near Blue Lake. Public use threatened the lake itself. The Taos people asked the national government to protect their rights. As in the 1920s the fight for Indian rights led them to speak out. It led to widespread attention at a time when people across the nation were made aware of the struggle for minority rights. Under much pressure, Congress at last acted. In late 1970 Congress set aside Blue Lake and 48,000 acres of the Carson National Forest for the sole use of the Taos Indians. As in the case of their fight against the Bursum Bill (page 267), New Mexico's Indians had won a great victory.

Hispanic New Mexicans experience changes. Also among those whose lives have changed since the end of World War II are Hispanic New Mexicans. During the war a large number of Hispanos left their homes. Many of these Hispanos had lived in remote northern mountain villages. After the war large numbers of Hispanic veterans continued their education. Under the G. I. Bill they enrolled in colleges and universities as well as in trade schools. Some gained job skills. Others entered professional fields. A number of Hispanos after the war started their own businesses. Still others ran for and won election to state offices. Indeed, New Mexico was a special land for Hispanic candidates. It was the only state in the Southwest where Hispanic politicians had real power before the late 1960s. Dennis Chavez and Antonio Fernandez, members of Congress, were two such politicians.

In the period since the late 1960s, Hispanos have continued to enjoy successful careers both in and out of politics. Among these is Manuel Lujan, a long-time United States representative from the state's first congressional district. Another has been Jerry Apodaca, who won the governorship in 1974. Yet another has been Toney Anaya. Anaya won the race for governor in 1982.

Northern New Mexicans have problems. The period since World War II has not, however, brought good times to all New Mexicans. The villages in northern New Mexico had been troubled during the Great Depression. The people who lived in these villages continued to have problems after World War II. First, the villages lost population. Indeed, the northern counties were unique among places in the United States with a large concentration of Spanish-speaking people. They were the only such places in the modern period to lose population.

Second, the villagers of northern New Mexico lost land. Third, the small farmers and ranchers had problems with the use of forest land. This land was controlled by the United States Forest Service. So it was in northern New Mexico that many of the people rallied behind a new leader. The time was the mid 1960s. The leader was Reies Lopez Tijerina.

A newcomer to New Mexico, Tijerina was a preacher. He soon began to speak out about what he believed to be the problems of his new home. He talked about the loss of land by Hispanic New Mexicans. He talked about a loss of community spirit in the northern counties. To solve these problems, Tijerina argued that Hispanos ought to join together to work for equal rights.

The Alianza is formed. In his fight for equal rights for Hispanos, Tijerina formed a new group. This was the Alianza Federal de Mercedes. It was, in other words, the Federal Alliance of Land Grants. Known best as the Alianza, the group grew quickly. It had at its peak perhaps as many as 5,000 members. Tijerina claimed that Alianza members were the rightful owners of millions of acres of land. This land, he said, belonged to Alianza members because of their land grant titles. The land was at that time controlled by the forest service and Anglo-American ranchers. The Alianza and its leader got a great deal of national attention in the 1960s. Again there was a public awareness of the struggle for minority rights. This attention grew in the fall of 1966. In October Tijerina and 350 Alianza members moved into the national forest northwest of Abiquiu. They seized control of the Echo Amphitheater, a natural formation within the forest reserve. They then announced the birth of a new country. This country was located on what Tijerina claimed was part of a Spanish land grant.

Forest rangers went to the occupied land. When they arrived, Tijerina and his followers announced the arrest of the forest rangers for trespassing. This move brought the Alianza much news coverage. A raid on the town and courthouse of Tierra Amarilla gained the group even more publicity. The raid occurred in June 1967. It involved a shootout. As a result, two officers of the law were wounded. This time state officials responded. Acting in the absence of the governor, the lieutenant governor sent the state's national guard into Rio Arriba County. Equipped with tanks, the guardsmen arrested some of the area's residents. However, most of those who had taken part in the raid escaped. As for Tijerina, he stood trial for his part in the Tierra Amarilla raid. He chose to defend himself in court, which he did in grand style. The jury ruled in his favor. Tijerina later stood trial in federal court for his role in occupying national forest land. He was charged with destroying government property. This time the jury found him guilty. Tijerina spent more than two years in a federal prison in El Paso.

Tijerina did not bring about the return of any land grants to the villagers of northern New Mexico. He also lost support after the raid on Tierra Amarilla. Still, Tijerina had caught the attention of young Hispanos. He and his followers had voiced the hopes of many New Mexicans.

New Mexico and its people have, then, changed since the end of World War II. Yet despite these changes, New Mexico is still a land apart. It has kept its special identity. It has remained, as you will read in the next chapter, a true land of enchantment.

1. **(a)** What population growth has New Mexico experienced since 1940?
    (b) What has the growth of the state's population meant?
2. **(a)** To what extent did Democrats control New Mexico politics from the 1930s to the 1960s?
    (b) How have New Mexico politics changed in recent years, and what caused these changes?
    (c) What is true about party politics in New Mexico today?
3. **(a)** What were the major provisions of the Indian Reorganization Act of 1934?
    (b) How have the Indian economy and ways of living changed?
    (c) Why did the Taos Indians fight for Blue Lake, and what was the outcome of that fight?
4. **(a)** What opportunities have been available to Hispanic New Mexicans in the modern period?
    (b) What have been some of the problems facing many northern New Mexico villagers?
    (c) What was the Alianza, and what actions did Alianza members take in the 1960s?
    (d) What were the outcomes of these actions?

Words You Should Know

Chapter Review

Find each word in your reading and explain its meaning.

1. depression
2. Dust Bowl
3. tenant farmers
4. migrant workers
5. relief
6. urbanization
7. sunbelt

Places You Should Be Able to Locate

Be able to locate these places on the maps in your book.

1. Harding County
2. Torrance County

3. Catron County	11. Grants
4. Clayton	12. Gallup
5. Roswell	13. Four Corners Area
6. Lordsburg	14. Grant County
7. Clovis	15. Chaves County
8. Alamogordo	16. Curry County
9. White Sands	17. Taos Pueblo
10. Los Alamos	18. Tierra Amarilla

Facts You Should Remember

Answer the following questions by recalling information presented in this chapter.

1. Briefly explain the effects of the depression in New Mexico on each of the following:
    (a) farming and cattle raising;
    (b) mining;
    (c) state and local government;
    (d) the villages of northern New Mexico;
    (e) state politics.

2. In what ways were New Mexicans and their state involved in World War II?

3. How has New Mexico changed in each of these areas since the end of World War II?
    (a) mining;   (d) population;
    (b) agriculture;   (e) politics.
    (c) tourism;

4. Briefly identify the major ways in which Indian and Hispanic ways of living have changed.

5. Who are the following people, and why are they important?
    (a) J. Robert Oppenheimer;   (g) Pete Domenici;
    (b) Edwin L. Mechem;   (h) Bruce King;
    (c) David Cargo;   (i) Thomas E. Atcitty;
    (d) Dennis Chavez;   (j) Manuel Lujan;
    (e) Clinton P. Anderson;   (k) Jerry Apodaca;
    (f) Joseph M. Montoya;   (l) Reies Lopez Tijerina.

Jemez Pueblo

Eyewitness to New Mexico's History
The Land of Enchantment

From: N. Scott Momaday, *The Way to Rainy Mountain* (University of New Mexico Press, 1969), p. 67.

In New Mexico the land is made of many colors. When I was a boy I rode out over the red and yellow and purple earth to the west of Jemez Pueblo. My horse was a small red roan, fast and easy-riding. I rode among the dunes, along the bases of mesas and cliffs, into canyons and arroyos. I came to know that country, not in the way a traveler knows the landmarks he sees in the distance, but more truly and intimately, in every season, from a thousand points of view. I know the living motion of a horse and the sound of hooves. I know what it is, on a hot day in August or September, to ride into a bank of cold, fresh rain.

CHAPTER 12

A Land of Enchantment

In this book you have studied New Mexico's past. It is a history of a land and of the people who have lived on that land. It is a history of varied cultures.

The land that is New Mexico has not provided people an easy life. Its shortage of water has limited where and how people have lived. Its vast area and distance from population centers have also shaped ways of living. For most of its history, New Mexico has been a land apart. It was a frontier region during both the Spanish and Mexican periods. It remained a frontier region for 30 years after becoming a territory of the United States. In fact, this separation from population centers did not begin to break down until the railroad arrived in 1879.

As a land apart, New Mexico grew into a unique place. It became a land of distinct cultures. New Mexico's Pueblo, Navajo, and Apache peoples developed ways of living that were in harmony with the land. They followed many of these same ways for hundreds of years. Alongside these Indian cultures grew up other cultures. Hispanic settlers brought their traditions and customs to New Mexico. They developed other traditions that grew out of their adjustment to the land and to their isolation. Still later settlers brought their ways of living to New Mexico. After 1848 these newcomers helped New Mexico grow as a part of the United States. They helped break down New Mexico's existence as a land apart.

A land with a long and colorful past, New Mexico also has a present and a future. This history of New Mexico cannot tell us for certain what present-day events mean within the context of the past and the future. It cannot look into the future and tell us what will happen at some later time. Still, New Mexico's history has taught us some lessons. It has taught us that New Mexico is a dry land. Its surface and ground water is limited. Some scientists believe that the ground water supply is being exhausted. In some parts of the state it may run out within the next 20 years. The absence of ground water would affect current ways of living. It would mean the loss to farmers of some land

315

Santa Fe Plaza

now under cultivation. The topsoil would become dry and loose. As a result, parts of New Mexico might be subject to the type of dust storms that occurred in the 1930s. Some scientists also question the continued availability of the ground water supply that underlies New Mexico's largest cities. Water has been important to people throughout New Mexico's long history. It remains important.

New Mexico's history has further taught us that it is a land attractive to newcomers. New Mexico's population has increased greatly since 1940. It has grown most recently as a part of the sunbelt. It has grown as well as people have moved into New Mexico from Mexico. As New Mexico has grown, it has changed. Indian and Hispanic cultures have kept their special identities. In addition, other cultures are present in New Mexico. All these cultures exist side by side. The people of these varied cultures must meet the challenge of living in harmony. All of New Mexico's people must have an equal chance to enjoy the fruits of their labor. They must welcome the people who will continue to move into the state.

New Mexico's history has taught us still further that the state is a haven for gifted artists. Today as in the past these artists have drawn inspiration from their surroundings. Some have had lengthy careers. Their talent has provided a link between past and present. Georgia O'Keeffe, for example, fits into the modern period. She also fit into the New Mexico of the 1920s. It was then that she moved here and began her career as a painter (page 277). Joining her as one of New Mexico's best-known painters was Peter Hurd. A native of Roswell, Hurd left New Mexico to study with N. C. Wyeth. Hurd later married Wyeth's daughter and returned to his native state where he remained until his

Georgia O'Keeffe (photo 1929)

death in 1984. New Mexico landscapes are among his most famous paintings. Ruidoso Canyon was a favorite subject. Other well-known painters have joined the artist colonies in Taos and Santa Fe. One of these is R. C. Gorman. Born on the Navajo reservation, Gorman, like his father Carl, has become a famous painter. His paintings hang in art galleries and in private homes around the world.

Other New Mexico artists have in recent years been accomplished writers. Included in their number is Erna Fergusson, whose career spanned several decades (page 275). At the time of her death in 1964, she was recognized as the first lady of New Mexico letters. Another writer, Paul Horgan, knew the Fergusson family as a young child growing up in Albuquerque. Moving to Roswell and then out of state, Horgan includes New Mexico themes in many of his books. He won a Pulitzer Prize in 1955 for his *Great River: The Rio Grande in North American History.* This book relates the history of the people who have lived along the Rio Grande. In 1976 Horgan won a second Pulitzer Prize for his *Lamy of Santa Fe.* Still another well-known writer who has lived

Erna Fergusson

in New Mexico is Frank Waters. A Coloradan by birth, Waters wrote *The Man Who Killed the Deer*. Among his other books is a novel set in the Mora Valley in northern New Mexico. This novel is *People of the Valley*.

In the 1970s and 1980s still other writers have appeared on the New Mexico scene. Included among their number are Rudolfo Anaya, John Nichols, and Mark Medoff. Born in Pastura near Santa Rosa, Rudolfo Anaya has written novels, plays, and screenplays. Two of his best-known works are *Bless Me Ultima* and *Heart of Aztlán*. Both are set in and around Guadalupe County. John Nichols, author of numerous novels and screenplays, has lived in New Mexico since 1969. Three of his novels depict life in New Mexico's northern mountain communities. *The Milagro Beanfield War* is the first and best known of the three. The other two are *The Magic Journey* and *The Nirvana Blues*. Mark Medoff, a member of the drama department faculty at New Mexico State University, is a playwright. His *Children of a Lesser God* won a Tony Award. Tonys are awarded for outstanding Broadway productions. The theme of Medoff's award-winning play is communication between people who can and cannot hear.

The list of painters and writers goes on. So, too, does the list of other artists. Patrocinio Barela and George Lopez are modern santeros. Barela's santos first caught the public eye during the 1930s. George Lopez began crafting santos more recently. He has carried on the tradition of the Lopez family of woodcarvers in Cordova. Pueblo Indian potters have continued their tradition of excellence. Indian silversmiths have continued to craft beautiful items. Tal-

Peter Hurd

George Lopez

ented performers entertain delighted audiences from stages across the state. The Santa Fe Opera began its twenty-fifth season in July 1981. It has won a much deserved reputation for excellence. The Albuquerque Opera Theatre and the Albuquerque Civic Light Opera Association put on productions throughout the year.

New Mexico audiences also delight to performances of classical music. The New Mexico Symphony Orchestra, based in Albuquerque, represents the state as a whole. Local or regional orchestras include the Orchestra of Santa Fe, the Roswell Symphony Orchestra, and the Symphony Orchestra in Las Cruces. Making their home in Albuquerque are the Chamber Orchestra of Albuquerque and the Youth Symphony and Orchestra. Community concert associations sponsor concerts in San Juan County, Carlsbad, and Artesia. Taos hosts the New Mexico Music Festival during the summer months. Music of all kinds is performed at this festival. The state capital hosts the Santa Fe Chamber Music Festival during the summer.

New Mexico audiences can also attend a wide variety of theatrical

The Santa Fe Opera

productions. Community theater groups perform for their friends and neighbors. The theater arts departments at the state's universities also produce plays for the people in their communities. Indeed, state universities—located throughout New Mexico—serve New Mexicans in a number of ways. They offer courses that lead to the granting of college degrees. They also offer courses designed for those interested in continuing their education in many different fields. In addition, the state's universities serve the cultural needs of area residents.

It can be said, then, that New Mexico is and has long been a major cultural area. It is also true that New Mexico's history is a living history. It lives on through the activities of its people. New Mexico's Indians, for example, hold annual ceremonials that have not changed in hundreds of years. During the summer months the Pueblo peoples celebrate annual feast days. They perform dances, most commonly the corn dance. Each pueblo celebrates its feast days and its dances according to its own history and traditions. The Mescalero Apaches hold their Maidens' Puberty Rites and Mountain Spirit Dance in July. In September the Navajos hold the Navajo Nation Fair at Window Rock, Arizona. Also in September the Jicarilla Apaches celebrate their annual feast at Stone Lake.

On different days in the fall pueblos celebrate other feast days. In late November or early December the Zunis celebrate Shalako. Shalako rites are performed to bless new houses built in honor of the Shalako (messengers of the rain gods). During the winter pueblo celebrations vary. At Christmas some

Christmas in New Mexico

Pueblo peoples perform the Matachines, a special Christmas dance. Some perform the Deer dance, the Buffalo dance, or a wide variety of dances. Most winter dances focus on the people's need for abundant game.

Hispanic folk plays also recapture New Mexico's Hispanic heritage. At Christmas some communities stage the Hispanic folk drama *Las Posadas*. It tells the story of Mary and Joseph seeking shelter for the birth of the Christ Child. Another Hispanic folk drama, *Los Pastores,* tells the story of the shepherds seeking the Christ Child. Still another Hispanic folk tradition has found new life through the revival of *zarzuelas,* musical plays, in some communities. (See Special Interest Feature.)

New Mexico's history, past and present, is recaptured in still other ways. Town residents hold annual founders'-day and old timers' celebrations to remind themselves of their town's origins. They hold other celebrations to remember specific historical events and to attract visitors to their communities. Every year, for example, the people of Lincoln stage an Old Lincoln Days celebration. As part of their pageant they reenact the last escape of Billy the Kid. Deming residents recall Butterfield Trail Days every year. In Roswell residents hold an annual John Chisum Trail Ride. And in the state capital the Santa Fe Fiesta celebrates Vargas's reconquest of New Mexico.

The Zarzuela

The zarzuela is an operetta form native to Spain. It is spoken dialogue and set songs and dances, much like a Broadway musical. The term zarzuela is derived from blackberry bushes (*zarzas*). These bushes surrounded the palace of the first Spanish king to support *fiestas de zarzuelas*. The fiestas were the seventeenth-century forerunner of the modern zarzuela. The larger form is called the *zarzuela grande*. It consists of up to four acts. The smaller form is the *género chico,* which is a one-act work. The nineteenth-century zarzuela reflects the spirit of Spain in its lively, rhythmic music. Its patriotic and sentimental songs praise the country and her people. It is also a showcase for the many and varied folk dances of Spain.

Zarzuelas became popular in the New World as Spanish companies organized summer tours. They toured Cuba, Mexico, and South America in the mid–nineteenth century. Though theaters were active in northern Mexico, Mexican companies could not tour the southwestern United States. This was because of the American Civil War and poor road conditions. In later years small circus and puppeteer groups regularly performed in corrals, hotels, and converted bars in the Southwest. And in time the zarzuela itself caught on with American audiences.

In 1884 the Aguilar-Cuello Zarzuela Company performed before enthusiastic Hispanic and Anglo-American audiences for three weeks in Tucson. The Companía Hermanos Areu arrived in El Paso in 1914, where they presented zarzuelas before moving on to Arizona. There may also have been zarzuela activity in New Mexico.

Today zarzuelas continue to be performed in most Latin American countries and in Spain. There has been an increased interest in them among Spain's young people. Zarzuelas have also been performed in recent years before New Mexico audiences. They reflect an interest in reviving Hispanic culture.

Fourth of July celebrations around the state also have a distinctive New Mexico flavor. Rodeos are a part of many communities' Fourth of July festivities. Fiddlers' contests and county fairs are other distinctively New Mexican activities. So are local events like the Hatch Chili Festival, the Hillsboro Apple Festival, the Duck Race in Deming, and the Peanut Valley Festival in Portales. County and regional fairs, in turn, point the way to the New Mexico State Fair held each September in Albuquerque.

Rodeos are popular

Through annual arts-and-crafts shows, New Mexicans find reminders of both their past and present. Each year Indian craftspeople display their wares at the Santa Fe Indian Market. The Feria Artesana, an annual event held in Albuquerque, celebrates New Mexico's Hispanic artists. The annual New Mexico Arts and Crafts Fair gives still other craftspeople a chance to show their work. It, too, is held in Albuquerque.

In their daily lives New Mexicans find their state enjoyable for its present as well as its past. A vast state with varied geographical features, it offers many activities. Summer sports include camping, hiking, and backpacking. Also popular are mountain climbing, horseback riding, and other warm-weather sports. Winter sports benefit from the state's many mountains. Ski areas, especially in the northern New Mexico, cater to skiers from throughout the region. Hunting and fishing choices are many and vary with the season. Fishing New Mexico's streams, rivers, and lakes is popular with people from far and wide.

New Mexico today is a state whose people remember the past and live in the present. New Mexico's history lives on in the museums located throughout the state. It lives on in annual celebrations and in day-to-day ways of living. But New Mexico is very much a part of the United States. The people of New Mexico have been and will continue to be affected by the events that touch the lives of all Americans. In the twentieth century New Mexico has become one of the nation's leading centers of atomic and weapons research. It will likely remain a research center. New Mexico has also become an energy-producing state. Its mineral wealth means that New Mexico will continue to produce

The white sands of New Mexico

energy. To what degree other industries might develop in the state, no one knows. To what extent New Mexico can escape its history as a poor state, no one knows. History provides no crystal ball that allows us to see into the future.

What we do know is that New Mexico is a product of its past. Its history is the story of its land and its people. Its history is the story of a true "land of enchantment."

Unit Summary

The statehood period for New Mexico began in 1912. In that year New Mexico entered the Union as the 47th state. Its constitution, drawn up in 1910, was much like that of the other states. It outlined state government. It separated the powers of government among three branches. At the same time the constitution differed from those of other western states. The constitution was quite conservative. It also contained features designed to protect the rights of all New Mexicans.

Most New Mexicans favored statehood. And a majority of the voters (men only) approved the constitution. They then elected their first state officeholders. The Republicans and Democrats both won offices in the first election. Still, the Republicans controlled New Mexico politics for years thereafter. They had written the constitution. They won most early statehood election contests.

Once it had become a state, New Mexico and its people got caught up in international events. The first of these involved United States relations with Mexico. A struggle for power in Mexico spilled over into New Mexico in 1916. It was then that Pancho Villa's men raided Columbus in southern New Mexico. The United States responded by sending troops into New Mexico. The second event that involved New Mexicans was World War I. New Mexicans fought in the war. They also aided the war effort at home. In part as a result of the war, New Mexico's economy began to grow. It grew for other reasons as well.

After the war, Americans became concerned once more with events at home. So did New Mexicans. The 1920s, for example, were a time of intense political party rivalry in New Mexico. The state's women played a part, for they could now vote. The Republicans still had the upper hand. Yet the struggle for political power in the state continued. The 1920s were, in addition, a time of political activity by the state's Indian peoples. The question of Pueblo land ownership led to the Bursum Bill. This bill caused the Pueblo Indians to unite. They opposed the Bursum Bill and succeeded in defeating it.

As a young state, New Mexico underwent a number of changes. Its population grew as did its economy. One area of growth was tourism. A second area of growth was mining. The oil and natural gas industries prospered. At the same time the state underwent cultural changes. Indeed, art colonies grew up at both Santa Fe and Taos. At each place both writers and painters gathered. Also creating artistic works were Indian and Hispanic New Mexicans. Because of its many artists, New Mexico became one of the nation's leading cultural areas.

The early statehood period was a prosperous time for most New Mexicans. Not all New Mexicans, however, prospered to the same degree. Farmers and ranchers, for example, faced hard times in the 1920s. Then in the 1930s New Mexicans like other Americans suffered through the Great Depression. Part of the state lay within the Dust Bowl. The farmers and ranchers were hard hit. So were the villagers of northern New Mexico.

Many New Mexicans went to work for some of the New Deal relief programs. The hard times continued for years. The depression did not end until the United States got involved in World War II.

During World War II New Mexicans contributed greatly to the war effort. Indeed, New Mexicans were among the first to see action. This was true of the young men stationed with the 200th and 515th coast artillery regiments in the Philippines. The Navajo code talkers likewise helped the war effort. So did other New Mexicans, in many different ways. In New Mexico were located special camps, training centers, and bases. The state was the birthplace of the atomic age. It became one of our country's major centers for military research.

Since the end of the war, New Mexico has undergone much economic development. Mining has become more and more important. Agriculture has remained important. So has tourism. Also since the war's end, New Mexico's people have changed. The population has grown. People have moved into the state in great numbers. As a consequence, the nature of New Mexico's population has changed. This change has brought changes to state politics. The balance between the two parties is much more even today than in the past. The change in population has brought changes to the state's oldest residents as well. Indian and Hispanic ways of living have become more modern. Still, Indians and Hispanos have cherished their traditions and their heritages.

After more than 400 years of recorded history, New Mexico is still a special land. It has developed into one of the nation's leading cultural areas. It is a land where different cultures have thrived side by side. It is a land of unique beauty. It has been and remains a true "land of enchantment."

Acknowledgments

After a five-year labor of love that has at last been completed with the publication of *A History of New Mexico,* we wish to acknowledge the assistance we received in making this book so much better than it might have been. Guiding us with the material in the early chapters and being there to answer the many questions that arose over certain aspects of our state's cultural history was Ele Baker—teacher, archaeologist, neighbor, and friend. Reading and commenting on the manuscript while so many important projects of his own awaited was Marc Simmons, New Mexico's premier historian and a neighbor at Cerrillos. Critiquing the entire manuscript line for line and offering invaluable suggestions concerning content was Joe Baca, Social Studies Specialist with the State Department of Education. And pinpointing needed changes in the final stages of readying the material for publication was Stan Hordes, State Historian with the State Records Center and Archives. The efforts of these people greatly improved the original manuscript.

Others helped us as well. David Holtby, editor for the University of New Mexico Press, deserves credit for having initially approached us with the idea of writing a New Mexico history textbook and for having given us unwavering support throughout the duration of the project. Barbara Jellow, a valued member of the University of New Mexico Press's production department, also deserves recognition for making *A History of New Mexico* such an attractive book through her thoughtful arrangement of text, illustrations, maps, and special interest features. And Betsy James, a talented illustrator, deserves recognition for the marvelous drawings she created for the book. The University of New Mexico has again shown its commitment to the people of this state.

For field testing the book with their students and for lending credence to its readability and its appropriateness for use with middle school and junior high students, we acknowledge the help of Ms. Ann Hume and Mrs. Gilbertson, Tse' Bit'ai Junior High School at Shiprock, Ms. Helen Maker, Bernalillo Junior

High School, and William D. Varuola, Gadsden Junior High School. Special thanks go to various Albuquerque Public Schools colleagues, including Jean Craven, Social Studies Coordinator, for reading and commenting on parts of the manuscript and Henrietta Loy, former Social Studies Coordinator, for her longstanding interest in New Mexico history textbooks for students throughout our state. David Margolin, an anthropologist and copy editor, skillfully applied his training on our behalf.

For assisting us in locating audio-visual, bibliographical, and other resource material, we acknowledge the aid of Fawziya Blachly and Maryanna Cheney, both librarians with the Albuquerque Public Schools. And for facilitating the process of locating photographs to illustrate the text, we acknowledge the assistance of Frank Anaya at the state's Economic Development and Tourism Department and the work of the photoarchivists at the History Museum of the Museum of New Mexico and at the State Records Center and Archives.

Finally, we would like to thank our children, David Lucien Roberts and Laura Kirsten Roberts, to whom we dedicate this book. Only with their cooperation and understanding could we have completed this project. It was for them and for the other young people of New Mexico that we labored so long.

Illustration Credits

Museum of New Mexico, pp. 36, 65 (from *Harper's New Monthly Magazine,* July 1880), 75, 86, 94, 113, 125, 141, 163, 164, 191, 204, 205, 207, 219, 228 (School of American Research Collection), 236, 241, 242, 263 (top), 266, 273, 275 (right), 276, 291, 317 (top left), 318.

Economic Development and Tourism Department, pp. 6, 23, 25, 26, 34, 37 (left), 37 (right), 42, 45, 48, 95, 98, 116, 135, 149, 156, 160, 173, 209, 210, 212, 218, 220, 222, 224, 232, 237, 261, 274, 278, 301, 305 (bottom), 316, 320, 321, 323, 324.

New Mexico State Records Center and Archives.

Bergere Collection, p. 138.

B. Farrar Collection, pp. 194, 256 (bottom).

CCC File, p. 290.

C. Olsen Collection, pp. 240, 263 (bottom).

Cultural Properties Review Committee, Bureau of Immigration, 1905, Territory of New Mexico, p. 32.

Dale Bullock Collection, p. 319.

Department of Development Collection, pp. 118, 144, 193, 262, 288, 304 (top), 304 (bottom).

E. Boyd Collection, pp. 71, 142.

Ina Sizer Cassidy Collection, p. 69.

K. Shiskin Collection, pp. 167, 170, 172.

L. File Collection, p. 67.

McNitt Collection, pp. 159, 188, 196, 197, 202.

R. Vernon Hunter Collection, p. 296.

SRC Misc. Collection, pp. 84, 243 (top), 244, 254, 256 (top), 258, 260.

State Parks and Recreation Agency, p. 90.

State Planning Office Collection, p. 211.

V. Johnson Collection, p. 38.

Albuquerque Public Library, p. 317 (bottom right).

Ele Baker, pp. 16, 93.

Governor Jerry Apodaca, p. 306.

Fred Harvey, p. 230.

Mrs. Tony Grenko, p. 264.

Neil Jacobs (photographer), p. 199.

Senator Pete V. Domenici, p. 305 (top).

Susan Roberts and Calvin Roberts, pp. 21, 200, 243 (bottom), 265, 275 (top).

Wide World Photos, Inc., p. 287.

New Mexico: A Pictorial History, by Andrew K. Gregg, UNM Press, pp. 8, 9, 70, 88, 139, 151, 168, 227.

Index